Francesca Granata is Director of the Fashion Studies MA and Assistant Professor in the School of Art and Design History and Theory at Parsons School of Design, the New School, New York. She holds a PhD from Central Saint Martins, University of the Arts London and is the editor and founder of the journal Fashion Projects. Her work has appeared in Fashion Theory, Fashion Practice, and The Journal of Design History, as well as in a number of books and exhibition catalogues.

'Experimental Fashion is very well written and rich in illustrations. It is highly engaging and thought provoking. It is a very welcome contribution to the field of fashion studies, not least through its attention to an aspect of fashion - experimental fashion - that has so far been given little attention'.

Agnès Rocamora, Reader in Social and Cultural Studies at London College of Fashion, University of London and author of Fashioning the City (I.B. Tauris, 2009)

Series Editors: Reina Lewis & Elizabeth Wilson

Advisory Board: Christopher Breward, Hazel Clark, Joanne Entwistle, Caroline Evans, Susan Kaiser, Angela McRobbie, Hiroshi Narumi, Peter McNeil, Özlem Sandikci, Simona Segre Reinach

Dress Cultures aims to foster innovative theoretical and methodological frameworks to understand how and why we dress, exploring the connections between clothing, commerce and creativity in global contexts.

Published and forthcoming:

Branding Fashion: Bridging the Self and the Social Consumer
by Anthony Sullivan

Delft Blue to Denim Blue: Contemporary Dutch Fashion
edited by Anneke Smelik

Dressing for Austerity: Aspiration, Leisure and Fashion in Post-War Britain
by Geraldine Biddle-Perry

Experimental Fashion: Performance Art, Carnival and the Grotesque Body
by Francesca Granata

Fashion in European Art: Dress and Identity, Politics and the Body, 1775-1925
edited by Justine De Young

Fashion in Multiple Chinas: Chinese Styles in the Transglobal Landscape
edited by Wessie Ling and Simona Segre Reinach

Fashioning Indie: Popular Fashion, Music and Gender in the Twenty-First Century
by Rachel Lifter

Modest Fashion: Styling Bodies, Mediating Faith
edited by Reina Lewis

Sinophilia: Fashion, Western Modernity and Things Chinese after 1900
by Sarah Cheang

Styling South Asian Youth Cultures: Fashion, Media and Society
edited by Lipi Begum, Rohit K. Dasgupta and Reina Lewis

Thinking Through Fashion: A Guide to Key Theorists
edited by Agnès Rocamora and Anneke Smelik

Veiling in Fashion: Space and the Hijab in Minority Communities
by Anna-Mari Almila

Wearing the Cheongsam: Dress and Culture in a Chinese Diaspora
by Cheryl Sim

Wearing the Niqab: Fashioning Identities among Muslim Women in the UK
by Anna Piela

Reina Lewis: reina.lewis@fashion.arts.ac.uk
Elizabeth Wilson: mail@elizabethwilson.net
At the publisher, Philippa Brewster: philippabrewster@gmail.com

Experimental Fashion

Performance Art, Carnival and the Grotesque Body

Francesca Granata

BLOOMSBURY VISUAL ARTS
LONDON • NEW YORK • OXFORD • NEW DELHI • SYDNEY

BLOOMSBURY VISUAL ARTS
Bloomsbury Publishing Plc, 50 Bedford Square, London, WC1B 3DP, UK
Bloomsbury Publishing Inc, 1359 Broadway, New York, NY 10018, USA
Bloomsbury Publishing Ireland, 29 Earlsfort Terrace, Dublin 2, D02 AY28, Ireland

BLOOMSBURY, BLOOMSBURY VISUAL ARTS and the Diana logo
are trademarks of Bloomsbury Publishing Plc

First published in Great Britain 2017 by I.B.Tauris & Co. Ltd
Reprinted by Bloomsbury Visual Arts 2021, 2022 (twice), 2023, 2024, 2025

Copyright © Francesca Granata, 2017

Francesca Granata has asserted her right under the Copyright,
Designs and Patents Act, 1988, to be identified as Author of this work.

For legal purposes the Acknowledgements on p. xii constitute
an extension of this copyright page.

All rights reserved. No part of this publication may be: i) reproduced or transmitted in any form, electronic or mechanical, including photocopying, recording or by means of any information storage or retrieval system without prior permission in writing from the publishers; or ii) used or reproduced in any way for the training, development or operation of artificial intelligence (AI) technologies, including generative AI technologies. The rights holders expressly reserve this publication from the text and data mining exception as per Article 4(3) of the Digital Single Market Directive (EU) 2019/790.

Bloomsbury Publishing Plc does not have any control over, or responsibility for, any third-party websites referred to or in this book. All internet addresses given in this book were correct at the time of going to press. The author and publisher regret any inconvenience caused if addresses have changed or sites have ceased to exist, but can accept no responsibility for any such changes.

A catalogue record for this book is available from the British Library.

A catalog record for this book is available from the Library of Congress.

ISBN: HB: 978-1-7845-3378-6
PB: 978-1-3502-4800-7
ePDF: 978-1-7867-3029-9
eBook: 978-1-7867-2029-0

Series: Dress Cultures

Typeset by Newgen
Printed and bound in Great Britain

For product safety related questions contact productsafety@bloomsbury.com.

To find out more about our authors and books visit
www.bloomsbury.com and sign up for our newsletters.

To Jay and Corinna, with love

CONTENTS

	List of Illustrations	viii
	Acknowledgements	xii
Introduction		1
1	Against Power Dressing: Georgina Godley	15
2	Fashioning the Maternal Body: Rei Kawakubo	36
3	Performing Pregnancy: Leigh Bowery	54
4	Deconstruction and the Grotesque: Martin Margiela	74
5	Carnivalised Time: Martin Margiela	103
6	Carnival Iconography: Bernhard Willhelm	119
7	The Proliferation of the Grotesque: Lady Gaga	149
Interview with Nicola Bowery		161
Interview with Georgina Godley		169
	Notes	179
	Bibliography	198
	Filmography	211
	Index	212

LIST OF ILLUSTRATIONS

1	Publicity shot from Working Girl, 1988, ©20thCentFox/ courtesy Everett Collection	16
2	Georgina Godley, Muscle Dress, spring/summer 1986, The Face, March 1986, no. 71, photograph by Stevie Hughes	26
3	Elsa Schiaparelli, Skeleton Dress, 1938, courtesy of the Victoria and Albert Museum	27
4	Georgina Godley, padded undergarment 'Bump and Lump' collection, autumn/winter 1986–87, photograph by Cindy Palmano, courtesy of the artist and Georgina Godley	28
5	Georgina Godley, dress, 'Bump and Lump' collection, autumn/winter 1986–87, photograph by Cindy Palmano, courtesy of the artist and Georgina Godley	29
6	Robert Mapplethorpe, Lisa Lyon 1981, courtesy of the Robert Mapplethorpe Foundation	37
7	Rei Kawakubo for Comme des Garçons, padded dress, 'Body Meets Dress' collection, spring/summer 1997, courtesy of Firstview	39
8	Rei Kawakubo for Comme des Garçons, padded top, 'Body Meets Dress' collection, spring/summer 1997, courtesy of Firstview	40
9	Fashion spread juxtaposing Jean Paul Gaultier' and Rei Kawakubo's work, Six, no. 2, 1982	42
10	Cindy Sherman, Untitled 296, created for Comme des Garçons advertising campaign, autumn/winter 1994–95, courtesy of Metro Pictures and the artist	44
11	Cindy Sherman, Untitled 302, created for Comme des Garçons advertising campaign, autumn/winter 1994–95, courtesy of Metro Pictures and the artist	45

LIST OF ILLUSTRATIONS   ix

12	Merce Cunningham, *Scenario*, BAM, Brooklyn, 1997. Photograph by Dan Rest, courtesy of Louie Fleck at the BAM Hamm Archives	49
13	Merce Cunningham, *Scenario*, BAM, Brooklyn, 1997. Photograph by Dan Rest, courtesy of Louie Fleck at the BAM Hamm Archives	50
14	Leigh Bowery designed coat for sale, i-D, no. 57, April 1988	56
15	Leigh Bowery at a club in London, i-D no. 57, April 1988	57
16	Lucian Freud, *Naked Man* (painting of Leigh Bowery), back view, 1991–92. Oil on canvas, 72¼ × 54⅛ in. (183.5 × 137.5 cm). Purchase, Lila Acheson Wallace Gift, 1993 (1993.71). © The Metropolitan Museum of Art, Image source: Art Resource, NY	58
17	Leigh Bowery, Look 9, July 1989, photograph by Fergus Greer, courtesy of the artist	64
18	Leigh Bowery, Look 10, July 1989, photograph by Fergus Greer, courtesy of the artist	65
19	Leigh and Nicola Bowery, Look 37, June 1994, photograph by Fergus Greer, courtesy of the artist	66
20	Leigh and Nicola Bowery, birth performance with Minty, Wigstock, New York, 1993, © *Wigstock: The Movie*	67
21	Martin Margiela, autumn/winter 1989–90, *Details*, September 1989	75
22	Martin Margiela, spring/summer 1990, *Details*, March 1990	76
23	Customised 1930s dress form used as inspiration for Martin Margiela's oversized collections, photograph by the author	83
24	Martin Margiela, enlarged sweater, autumn/winter 2000–01, courtesy of Firstview	85
25	Martin Margiela, enlarged garments, autumn/winter 2000–01, courtesy of Firstview	86
26	Martin Margiela, enlarged doll's jeans, spring/summer 1999, courtesy of Firstview	90
27	Martin Margiela, enlarged GI Joe badge, spring/summer 1999, courtesy of Firstview	93
28	Photographs of 'Nostalgic Barbie' alongside Margiela's 'Doll Collection', ModeMuseum, Antwerp, 2008 © RST	96
29	Martin Margiela, *tabi* shoes, photograph by Ronald Stoops, courtesy of the MoMu, Antwerp	98

30	Martin Margiela, *tabi* gloves in the ModeMuseum collection, courtesy of MoMu, Antwerp	99
31	Martin Margiela, 'Theatre Costumes', spring/summer 1993, photograph by Anders Edstrom, courtesy of the artist	106
32	Martin Margiela, 'Theatre Costumes', spring/summer 1993, photograph by Anders Edstrom, courtesy of the artist	107
33	Martin Margiela, 'Tromp-l'oeil' collection, spring/summer 1996, photograph by Guy Voet, courtesy of MoMu, Antwerp	109
34	Martin Margiela, 'Tromp-l'oeil' collection spring/summer 1996 photograph by Guy Voet, courtesy of MoMu, Antwerp	110
35	Dress forms installed outside the museum's pavilion, Margiela retrospective at the Museum Boijmans Van Beuningen, Rotterdam, 1997, courtesy of Caroline Evans	114
36	Bernhard Willhelm, financial adverts top and leggings, spring/summer 2005, photograph by Shoji Fujii, courtesy of Bernhard Willhelm	122
37	Bernhard Willhelm, financial adverts top and skirt, spring/summer 2005, photograph by Shoji Fujii, courtesy of Bernhard Willhelm	123
38	Bernhard Willhelm, detail of financial adverts prints in the ModeMuseum collection, spring/summer 2005, photograph by the author, courtesy of MoMu, Antwerp	124
39	Bernhard Willhelm, detail of financial adverts prints in the ModeMuseum collection, spring/summer 2005, photograph by the author, courtesy of MoMu, Antwerp	124
40	Bernhard Willhelm, 'Ms Behaviour' dress, spring/summer 2005, photograph by Shoji Fujii, courtesy of Bernhard Willhelm	126
41	Bernhard Willhelm, print detail from 'Ms Behaviour' dress in the ModeMuseum collection, spring/summer 2005, photograph by the author, courtesy of MoMu, Antwerp	127
42	Bernhard Willhelm, Harlequin inspired look, autumn/winter 2002–03, photograph by Shoji Fujii, courtesy of Bernhard Willhelm	129
43	Bernhard Willhelm, image of a hanging man embroidered on a sweater in the ModeMuseum collection, autumn/winter	

LIST OF ILLUSTRATIONS

	2002–03, photograph by the author, courtesy of MoMu, Antwerp	131
44	Bernhard Willhelm, aerial bombing embroidery from a sweatshirt in the ModeMuseum collection, autumn/winter 2002–03, photograph by the author, courtesy of MoMu, Antwerp	132
45	George Grosz as Dada Death, Berlin, 1918, courtesy of VAGA	136
46	Bernhard Willhelm, look inspired by George Grosz, autumn/winter 2007–08, photograph by Shoji Fujii, courtesy of Bernhard Willhelm	137
47	Bernhard Willhelm, embroidered skirt and shirt, spring/summer 2005, photograph by Shoji Fujii, courtesy of Bernhard Willhelm	141
48	Bernhard Willhelm, embroidery of toilet and neo-classical building, detail of shirt from the ModeMuseum collection, spring/summer 2005, photograph by the author, courtesy of MoMu, Antwerp	142
49	Bernhard Willhelm, embroidery of a dung beetle, detail of skirt from the ModeMuseum collection, spring/summer 2005, photograph by the author, courtesy of MoMu, Antwerp	143
50	Bernhard Willhelm, embroidery of person mooning, detail of skirt from the ModeMuseum collection, spring/summer 2005, photograph by the author, courtesy of MoMu, Antwerp	144
51	Bernhard Willhelm, François Sagat clad in Willhelm's gold spandex jumpsuit, men's, spring/summer 2008, photograph by Lukas Wassmann, courtesy of the artist and Bernhard Willhelm	147
52	Lady Gaga in Comme des Garçons outside the Park Hyatt Paris Vendôme Hotel, 22 September 2012, photograph by Marc Piasecki, © Getty Images	154

ACKNOWLEDGEMENTS

Many people and institutions have helped and supported this book from its inception to its final stages. Chiefly, I thank my director of studies Caroline Evans for her invaluable advice and support throughout all aspects of my research and writings. I also thank her for her enthusiasm for the 'discipline' and the greater fields of visual and cultural studies, which is infectious. I would also like to thank my dissertation advisors Alistair O'Neill and Elizabeth Wilson, as well as Joanne Morra. My thanks also go to the staff at the Metropolitan Museum of Art's Costume Institute for allowing me, through a year-long fellowship, access to their collection and library – and, in particular, to Andrew Bolton. I also thank the staff of the ModeMuseum of Antwerp, and in particular Kaat Debo, for allowing me to do extensive research in their collection.

I also would like to thank professors who, in retrospect, led me to this path, in particular the medieval art historian Madeline Caviness, with whom I studied *Imitatio Christi* in late medieval female piety. That study introduced me to the grotesque body, the power of visual images and performative practices. I am additionally grateful to performance art professor Marilyn Arsem, to Valerie Steele for introducing me to the field early in my career, as well as Lourdes Font. My thanks also go to the Administration and Research Offices at the University of Arts London, in particular the Research Office at Central Saint Martins, for having given me great help and support throughout my time at CSM and for awarding me with a research studentship for the completion of my studies. Further thanks go to my colleagues at Parsons the New School for Design and especially the Fashion Studies faculty: Hazel Clark, Heike Jenss and Christina Moon, plus Sarah Lawrence, the Dean of the School of Art and Design History and Theory. Invaluable feedback was provided by graduate and undergraduate students in my seminars, starting from the first class I developed on the topic at Goldsmiths' Visual Arts department under the auspices of Pennina Barnett. Philippa Brewster has been an enthusiastic and knowledgeable editor, as have the editors of the Dress Cultures series, Elizabeth Wilson and Reina Lewis.

Parts of this book were presented at the Metropolitan Museum of Art, as well as the College Art Association Annual Conferences in 2009 and 2014 and the Benaki Museum in Athens, thanks to generous support from the American Embassy in Athens and Atopos. Chapter 4 was previously published in the *Journal of Design History* under the title 'Deconstruction Fashion: Carnival and the Grotesque', while an abridged version of Chapter 6 was published as part of the *Bernhard Willhelm and Jutta Kraus* catalogue to the exhibition of the same name at the Groninger Museum of Modern and Contemporary Art. Part of Chapter 5 was published as 'Fitting Sources – Tailoring methods: A Case-study of Martin Margiela and the Temporalities of Fashion', in *Research Methods, Sites and Practices*, edited by Heike Jenss.

My warmest thanks also go to my mother and father, Elisabetta Pietroluongo and Nini Granata, to Marsha and Barnett Ruttenberg, as well as to Patty Chang and Enrico Granata for their unwavering hospitality. Finally, I would like to thank Jay Ruttenberg, without whose invaluable support this book never could have come to fruition.

INTRODUCTION

> It is interesting to trace the struggle of the grotesque and classical concept in the history of dress and fashion.
>
> Mikhail M. Bakhtin, *Rabelais and His World*[1]

Writing in the 1930s, the Russian scholar Mikhail M. Bakhtin characterises the grotesque as a phenomenon of reversal and of unsettling ruptures of borders, in particular bodily borders. The grotesque body is an open, unfinished body, which is never sealed or fully contained, but it is always in the process of becoming and engendering another body. In *Rabelais and His World* Bakhtin theorises the open-ended, collective body of carnival as the grotesque body par excellence in contrast to the 'sealed' and individualised classical body. He isolates the late Renaissance as the period in which the classical model starts to displace a grotesque understanding of the body, one that, according to the Russian scholar, finds its outmost expression in 'the grotesque realism' of François Rabelais's *Gargantua and Pantagruel*.[2]

This 'struggle' between the classical and grotesque concepts of the body within the West can be observed in a number of different areas starting from the 'canon of behaviour', which Bakhtin sees as an attempt 'to close up and limit the body's confines' to the history of dance and to fashion which, as the Russian scholar suggests, makes for a particularly fertile case. In an endnote, he writes that it would be 'interesting to trace the struggle of the grotesque and classical concept in the history of dress and fashion'.[3]

Taking on this unrealised project (if only in part), I explore how this struggle was played out at the end of the previous century from the 1980s up to the turn of the millennium. The 1980s were the years that planted the seeds for the more forceful break with 'classical' fashion imagery that occurred in the 1990s, a break whose ripples continue to make their effect felt in the new millennium.[4] The book examines the reasons beyond a proliferation of bodies-out-of-bounds in fashion starting in the 1980s; why did fashion from the 1980s onwards see an explosion of grotesque imagery – a kind of imagery that had been lurking just beneath the surface throughout the twentieth century? Why is it that, during this period, the sealed and 'perfect' body of high fashion is forcefully challenged by fashion practitioners?

I argue that the bodies and subjects circulating within fashion at the turn of the millennium are undisciplined ones that upset gender and bodily norms and rules of propriety and beauty. They can be read as provocations and attempts to escape what Michel Foucault referred to as the 'anatomo-politics of the human body':[5] the disciplining and optimal management and self-management of the human body, in part achieved through fashion, beauty and health regimes. I view fashion, in its mainstream variety, on a continuum with a number of technologies of the self at work in neoliberal societies. Fashion can be in line with discourses of health and fitness promoting 'healthy' and normative bodies and subjects – a process that began to intensify in the 1980s, the starting point of my exploration.

However, it is also in the 1980s that we begin to witness a proliferation of grotesque imagery and bodies-out-of-bounds in fashion – something that should be understood as a critique of these normative discourses. I argue that this shift, which was particularly evident within experimental fashion at the turn of the twenty-first century, was, in fact, influenced by feminism's desire to open up and question gender and bodily norms and particularly the normative bodies of fashion. It was also tied to the AIDS epidemic. Experimental fashion often mediated the fears of contagion and the obsessive moral policing of bodily borders that characterised the 1980s and part of the 1990s and cannot be read separately from the powerful discourses of contagion, bodies and health surrounding the AIDS crisis. Starting in the 1980s, a climate of fear and paranoia surrounded bodily borders, and particularly those of urban gay men within the US and much of Europe. AIDS, as Susan Sontag aptly wrote, was constructed through a politically and socially conservative discourse, 'a disease not only of sexual excess but of perversity'.[6] This continued well after the medical establishment determined the dynamics of AIDS transmission.[7] The conservative politics of Thatcher and Reagan in the UK and US were, in fact, intertwined and, in great part, responsible for the slow response to the AIDS crisis and the stigmatisation of AIDS patients. On the one hand, the response was delayed because of the cuts to public health programmes advanced in the name of neoliberal economic policy. On the other hand, due to the disease's initial spread within the gay male population, people affected by AIDS were often seen as morally to blame, in part due to the renewed social conservatism characterising those administrations.[8]

Fashion was central to the visual and material culture of those decades and it played an important role alongside performance, visual arts, dance, film and photography in teasing out the political and social issues that characterised those decades. Throughout the book, I argue that fashion should be interpreted on a par with other aspects of visual and material culture as a constitutive and influential part of culture as opposed to simply reflecting a culture that gets made elsewhere. The designers discussed in this book are tackling feminist issues of how the pregnant body is represented in visual culture of the 1980s and 1990s, as well as challenging anxieties over bodily borders and contagion characterising the period. They are questioning norms and standards of beauty as well as exploring changing ideals of masculinity at the beginning of the millennium. They often do so through collaboration with other practitioners whose work has been amply discussed in relation to these cultural shifts, as perhaps most evident with Rei Kawakubo's (of Comme des Garçons) collaboration with Cindy Sherman.

The designers discussed in the book also moved towards a critique to power and status dressing and its attendant neoliberal enterprising culture. The 1980s were in fact the period associated with the development of neoliberalism, most visibly in the UK and the US, through Thatcherite and Reaganite economic policies that favoured free markets, free trade and small government. This shifted responsibilities from the state to the individual and private enterprise. Since then, the anthropologist David Harvey argues:

> Neoliberalism has […] become hegemonic as a mode of discourse. It has pervasive effects on ways of thought to the point where it has become incorporated into the common-sense way many of us interpret, live in, and understand the world.[9]

Thus it is no surprise that the fashion designers I discuss often mediated these political and social shifts in their work. *Experimental Fashion* provides ample evidence of the centrality of fashion to contemporary culture and should be read in the context of work on visual and material culture at the turn of the millennium.[10]

Throughout the book I examine the kind of fashion that, while circulating fairly widely as an image primarily in independent style magazines throughout the 1980s and 1990s, remains elusive as a product, as it is usually produced in limited runs and deemed challenging. As the term suggests, it is the kind of fashion that experiments with silhouettes, construction, materials and/or mode of presentation. I borrow the term 'experimental' to describe this fashion from film studies, where it is used to describe films that do not follow a narrative strategy. I use 'experimental' over the more common term 'avant-garde' to avoid the latter's association with teleology and progressive notions of history.[11]

At the border of fashion itself, the work I discuss often spills into the realm of performance art. This shares with fashion a deep relation to the body and gender, and constitutes an important cultural trope for exploring the grotesque body and bodily practices. These have been of central importance to performance art, particularly from the 1960s onwards, when the practice became strongly influenced by feminist theory and, later, queer theory.[12] Time-based and process-oriented, performance art has never been defined with a level of consensus but, similarly to the grotesque, it has been discussed through its association with liminality, in-betweenness and border crossings.[13]

The book focuses on those fashion designers and other fashion practitioners whose work circulated transnationally through the system of press, distribution and sales of Paris and London, two cities that remain epicentres of experimentation in fashion. More often than not the practitioners discussed inhabit a number of different cultures and geographical spaces in an increasingly globalised industry, as is the case most exemplarily with the Japanese designer Rei Kawakubo, who created hybrid transcultural designs. However, this could be said to apply to all the practitioners discussed. It has been argued that, particularly within the design realm, 'as the link between territory and culture becomes more tenuous, design becomes an increasingly global language, with practitioners in any given nation drawing upon a range of signifiers from all over the world in their work'.[14] Moreover, I argue that globalisation and the condition of otherness and estrangement developed by living cross-culturally is central to development of grotesque imagery within fashion of this period. Writing about visual arts, Frances Connelly similarly argues that the proliferation of the grotesque in modern 'image culture' is tied to globalisation as well as to contemporary theoretical discourses centring on the concept of otherness.

This relation of the grotesque with what is 'other' to dominant Western culture is also noted by film theorist Robert Stam, who underscores the importance of a culture's self-consciousness, its capacity to see itself as only one among other cultures, as central to its ability to generate a grotesque canon and its attendant carnivalesque humour. Stam views 'decentring' – the inhabiting of more than one culture simultaneously – as one of the reasons behind an exponential escalation of grotesque imagery within film, something, I argue, that is also true for fashion.[15]

The book builds on two important studies of experimental fashion at the end of the last century; Caroline Evans's book *Fashion at the Edge* and Rebecca Arnold's *Fashion, Desire and Anxiety*.[16] Both give insightful readings of the crisis of the fashionable body within late capitalism, a crisis that gave rise (at least among experimental fashion designers and photographers) to a new kind of aesthetic, one that allowed for an exploration of contemporary social anxieties and the instability of the self in lieu of the polished, completed and ultimately reassuring ideal preferred by mainstream fashion.[17] *Fashion at the Edge* examines how fashion at the end of the century stages a return of the repressed.[18] In *The Civilizing Process*, and particularly in its first volume, *The History of Manners*, Norbert Elias discusses the ways in which complex technologies of manners were employed through European history from the Middle Ages onwards towards the creation of a civilised society. Despite discussing in details a series of codes of behaviour pertaining to eating and drinking habits and bodily functions, he does not specifically discuss dress practices and fashion.[19] Following Elias's writings in *The Civilizing Process*, their elaboration in relation to the grotesque body by the cultural theorists Peter Stallybrass and Allon White and their relation to fashion by Evans, I argue that in 'late capitalist' societies these returns occur precisely through disciplinary discourses such as fashion.

Evans's text, however, examining more closely the uncanny and images of 'death, disease and dereliction',[20] is primarily concerned with the 'Romantic' version of the grotesque, one that articulates anguish and terror, as opposed to Bakhtin's sanguine and humorous concept.[21] In her understanding of the inherent ambivalence of much of the fashion imagery she examines, Evans also acknowledges generative potential: '[f]ashion, with its affinity for transformation, can act out instability and loss but it can also, and equally, stake out the terrain of "becoming" – new social and sexual identities, masquerade and performativity'.[22]

Focusing on these possibilities for 'becoming', throughout the book I explore the transformative and subversive import of fashion and its potential for resignification of norms. These discussions are informed by Judith Butler's writings, in particular her two books *Bodies that Matter* and *Gender Trouble*, which argue that gender is performative, thus a socially constructed category, instilled and maintained in the subject, from a very early age, via the repetition of 'appropriate' gender performances.[23] Gender, Butler writes:

is in no way a stable identity or locus of agency from which various acts proceed; rather, it is an identity tenuously constituted in time – an identity instituted through a *stylized repetition of acts*. Further, gender is instituted through the stylization of the body and, hence, must be understood as the mundane way in which bodily gestures, movements, and enactments of various kinds constitute the illusion of an abiding gendered self [...] If the ground of gender identity is stylized repetition of acts through time, and not a seemingly seamless identity, then the possibilities of gender transformation are to be found in the arbitrary relation between such acts, in the possibility of a different sort of repeating, in the breaking or subversive repetition of that style.[24]

Butler's relevance to the fashion I discuss throughout the book can be found in her understanding of gender construction as a *stylisation* of the body, and gender acts as having an affinity with theatrical performances. If we understand gender identity as a performative act repeatedly enacted through time, we clearly see the importance of fashion as a tool for upholding gender norms and, more generally, normative processes of identity formation, yet retaining the potential for subversion. Fashion, as the work of the designers discussed in this book highlights, could allow for the expansion of 'the cultural field bodily through subversive performances of various kinds'.[25]

However, Butler warns us against understanding performative constructions of gender as acts of volition. In *Bodies That Matter* – the work she partially produced in response to misreadings of *Gender Trouble*, which led to an understanding of gender as something that can be 'put on and taken off at will' – she explains that these performative acts are so thoroughly naturalised that they occur for the most part before the formation of the subject. 'Gendering', Butler writes, 'is, among other things, the differentiating relations by which speaking subjects come into being'.[26] They are what enable the subject to be, yet their constant repetition allows for disruptions, misappropriations and re-articulations. Thus, my analysis of the transformative potential of fashion nevertheless takes account of the notion that fashion should not be equated with an act of self-invention free from rules and constraints. To use Butler's terminology, it is important not to confound the term 'performance' with 'performative'. I use the terms 'performative' and 'performativity' throughout the book specifically not to indicate a performance – understood as a self-conscious act of volition by a performer – but rather as something that occurs most often without the consciousness of the subjects, as it precedes and engenders the subject.

Experimental fashion's relation to the modernist body of mainstream fashion is also discussed in Rebecca Arnold's *Fashion, Desire and Anxiety: Image and Morality in the Twentieth Century*. In her book Arnold gives a feminist reading of a number of works produced within late twentieth-century fashion that 'brutalise' the female body. She argues that in many cases this brutalisation is a compensatory strategy that can be best understood as a mediation of anxieties surrounding changes in gender roles, as well as more general anxieties regarding the shifting borders of the 'natural' body in the late twentieth century.[27] However, Arnold also points out that certain 1990s fashion imagery (almost always female) that shows the body as imperfect and fatigued can, in fact, be read as a challenge to the polished façade promoted by mainstream fashion.[28] Her book, like Evans's, does not explicitly draw on Bakhtinian constructs, but it nevertheless makes a number of important references pertinent to my reading of this period's fashion through the lens of the grotesque. In particular, her discussion of the resistance to representation of the maternal within twentieth-century fashion has informed my own analysis.[29]

Rather than being a survey of experimental fashion within the period from the 1980s to the 2000s, a task which, given the sheer number of designers, would be impossible in scope, *Experimental Fashion* focuses on those practitioners whose work most noticeably taps into a Bakhtinian understanding of the grotesque. An important theme that surfaces in an application of Bakhtin's theories to fashion design of this period is its relation to the maternal body — something I discuss in the first three chapters.

These three chapters focus on the work of Rei Kawakubo, Georgina Godley and Leigh Bowery, all of whom, from the mid-1980s to the late 1990s, presented a seemingly pregnant silhouette. They constructed garments suggesting the maternal body — a model of a body-in-process — that contrasted sharply with the twentieth-century fashion silhouette in general and with the masculinised, broad-shouldered silhouette of 1980s fashion in particular. This silhouette, which was epitomised by the so-called 'power suit', was deeply implicated with neoliberal ideals of the 'enterprising self'.

Employing Bakhtin's theories of the grotesque and Kristeva's notion of the subject-in process, alongside medical anthropology and science studies, these chapters examine how late twentieth-century experimental fashion problematises demarcations between bodily boundaries and questions the integrity of the subject via references to the pregnant body and birth processes. It examines the different ways in which Godley, Bowery and Kawakubo re-appropriated the relation between the grotesque, the feminine and the maternal to create work which challenged the sealed and 'contained' body characteristic of much twentieth-century fashion. This model, which conforms to Bakhtin's definition of the classical body, can be read not only in relation to a latent gynophobia in 'dominant' Western thought and representational tradition, but also in relation to neoliberal models of selfhood that developed during this period.

Chapter 1 discusses the 1980s power suit and its relation to enterprising models of the self and sartorial engineering promoted during the period through a range of media including dress manuals such as John T. Molloy's *The Woman's Dress for Success Book* and films such as *Working Girl*. It focuses on the work of the British designer Georgina Godley and in particular her 'Bump and Lump' and 'Corporate Coding' collections. Godley's work created a body that referred to the pregnant body, and brought to mind the sprouts and bulges of the Bakhtinian grotesque. This body, as the designer made explicit in an interview I conducted with her, was a conscious critique of not only the 1980s masculine silhouette and attendant models of dress and self-care intrinsic to neoliberal economic models, but also of the extreme body consciousness promoted by fashion of the period.

Chapter 2 unpacks the relation between the maternal and the grotesque as it is articulated in the work of the Japanese designer Rei Kawakubo, and in particular her spring/summer 1997 collection 'Body Meets Dress' for Comme des Garçons, and her subsequent collaboration with Merce Cunningham for the dance *Scenario*, which premiered at the Brooklyn Academy of Music (BAM) in 1997. It explores how Kawakubo subverts the masculine silhouette and über-healthy toned body introduced in the previous decade through the very means used to created such silhouette. She uses padding, which had been traditionally used to build up the shoulder to create oddly-shaped bodies with protruding regions on the back, hips and belly. Kawakubo's work allows for a remapping and reformulation of the body that invokes the maternal as a model for a subject that is tolerant of alterity, in the deep awareness of his or her own difference.

In Chapter 3, I discuss the work of the Australian-born and British- based fashion designer, club figure and performance artist Leigh Bowery, and in particular his birth performances. An in-between figure, whose work could not be easily assimilated in fashion or art, Bowery constituted a modern day incarnation of 'the carnival spirit', whose practice questioned strict divisions between art and life. He employed humour to disrupt gender and bodily boundaries, and through his elaborate costumes, which were at the basis of his performances, he created 'a wholly artificial self'. Some of his most iconic looks from the late 1980s refer to the maternal body. These culminated in his birth performances with his band Minty. In its graphic and threatening quality, his birthing performance externalised and rendered visible the problematic Western understanding of the maternal body (and by extension the female body) with its unstable borders and generative potential as 'grotesque' and in some way monstrous. This chapter discusses how Bowery's performances, in their references to birth processes and exchanges of bodily fluids, placed on a continuum the bodies of pregnant women and gay men as grotesque and immunologically problematic, particularly considering their contemporary context and Bowery's untimely death from complications of AIDS in 1994.

Chapters 4 and 5 examine the work known as 'deconstruction' fashion and/or 'deconstructivist' fashion and revisit its journalistic and academic reception. These chapters constitute the first study to recover the carnivalesque and grotesque element of the fashion that has been identified under this rubric, and to read it in relation to humour. This discussion does so with a particular focus on the work of Martin Margiela, the designer for whom the term was coined and who is arguably its most visible exponent. Chapter 4 begins by teasing out deconstruction fashion's journalistic and academic reception from the early 1990s onwards and untangling the various theoretical notions that have been used to describe the work in question. It then moves to a close analysis of individual pieces and specific presentations by Margiela and discusses his work's grotesque and carnivalesque strategies of alterations of scale, garments' inversions and play with functionality as well as his play with and inversion of linear temporalities. The chapters build on and bring further evidence to the argument that fashion of this period is aligned with a Bakhtinian understanding of the grotesque. As is the case with Kawakubo, Godley and Bowery, Margiela, in a number of his collections and presentations, explores a grotesque non-normative body, which stands in contrast to the classical body of fashion in general, while rejecting 1980s aesthetic language through the use of recycling, the ready-made and seemingly unfinished and torn garments. His clothes' disregard for symmetry and proportionality up-end and question Western ideals of beauty and classical aesthetics, while his presentations and exhibitions make reference to processes of birth and growth.

Chapter 4 focuses on deconstruction fashion's journalistic and academic reception from the early 1990s onwards. Through research in museum collections and libraries, this chapter identifies how the term began to be used in relation to fashion within the English language and traces its initial reception within the press to journalist Bill Cunningham. It untangles the various theoretical notions that have been used to describe the work in question. The chapter brings evidence of the connection between deconstruction fashion and the grotesque through a close object-analysis of a range of Margiela's garments and accessories, with a particular focus on his oversized and enlarged collections. These collections refer to the gigantic and the miniature by scaling garments to non-existent sizes and enlarging Barbie and Ken doll clothes to human size. Through these alterations of scale, coupled with garments' inversions and play with functionality, these collections are not only reminiscent of Surrealist strategies but are also aligned with a Bakhtinian understanding of the grotesque as the ultimate expression of the carnival spirit.

Chapter 5 is a study of a number of collections by Martin Margiela from the 1990s as well as the designer's retrospective exhibition from 1999 in Rotterdam. The chapter examines how the Belgian designer carnivalises time by ageing garments overnight and by layering different 'histories' onto a single garment, most notably by reworking vintage theatre costumes into contemporary dress. Margiela's work not only highlights fashion's non-linear cyclical time but, through his experiments with bacteria cultures in his Rotterdam retrospective, he creates 'living' garments, pointing to fashion's generative potential.

Chapter 6 brings us to the new millennium as it examines the work of the German-born and Belgian-trained fashion designer Bernhard Willhelm. The designer's work is reminiscent of Kenneth Clark's discussion of 'the alternative canon', as it employs grotesque imagery, frequently rooted in the northern European representational tradition, while making direct references to carnival iconography through the *commedia dell'arte*. His work also explores an important site – according to Freud's theories – for the articulation of the grotesque as a return of the repressed in its constant melding of humour and horror, often within the same collection, garment or fashion show. Willhelm's work defies conventions of symmetry and proportionality that could be understood as classical and neoclassical, not only by making references to northern European representational traditions of the late Middle Ages, which have been defined in opposition to the classical model of the Italian Renaissance, but also through references to southern German tailoring traditions. He also evokes the grotesque via references to the bodies of contemporary pornography and low-horror, which, following Bakhtin's definitions, defy borders as they couple with other bodies and become unsealed. Like Godley's and Bowery's work, Willhelm's fashion, which was generated in the booming early 2000s, parodies 1980s status dressing and concomitant neoliberal ideals of selfhood. Finally, not only through its elaborate staging of fashion shows, but also through its interest in liminality, in-betweenness and transgression, the German designer's work brings to the fore the narrowing of boundaries between fashion and performance.

In the book's concluding chapter, I discuss how this proliferation of grotesque imagery in fashion reached the mainstream with the pop phenomenon Lady Gaga. Here, I read Lady Gaga's grotesqueries as a symptom of the cultural shifts that my book has analysed. I focus on her performances of 'fat' drag through her use of one of the experimental fashion designers discussed – Rei Kawakubo of Comme des Garçons. This discussion brings us back to the shifting grounds of identity, and particularly gender identity, and makes the argument that the weakening of fixed identities and borders is central to the proliferation of the grotesque within fashion of the period.

METHODOLOGY

My research started from a close study of objects understood both as garments and accessories, as well as a close study of images, primarily moving images in the form of fashion show recordings, plus videos and films produced by designers in lieu of or in addition to fashion shows.

Object-based research is central to my project and is employed as a way to build and test theories against examples of actual garments and accessories. A close examination of the work I discuss is, in fact, necessary to 'unveil' the garments' construction techniques, which are often impossible to ascertain from photographs. For instance, a close study of the pieces from Rei Kawakubo's spring/summer 1997 collection allows one to understand fully the ways in which the pieces articulated a 'different' understanding of the silhouette, and the extent to which individual pieces did (or did not) reinforce a maternal body-shape. Object-based research is also indispensable to establish, with a level of certainty, the textiles and alternative materials used in a number of experimental garments produced within the period, as with the work of Martin Margiela, and the effects these materials might have ultimately produced. As a result, through the course of my research, I have closely examined, photographed, measured and, whenever possible, handled surviving garments in museums and private collections, chiefly through repeated visits to the collections of the ModeMuseum in Antwerp, the Metropolitan Museum of Art's Costume Institute in New York, and the Victoria and Albert Museum in London. I also visited Nicola Bowery's private collection of Leigh Bowery's work in Brighton in the south of England. As far as methods to approach the study of garments is concerned, I partially rely on Valerie Steele's article in the 'Methodology' issue of *Fashion Theory*, which is based on research methods developed by Jules Prown and is thus deeply indebted to a material culture approach.[30]

Additionally, a close study of moving images – which starts with the techniques of video and film-making (i.e. camera angle, image and sound editing techniques) as well as the *mise en scène*[31] – is central to my research methods, as I analyse videos and films produced concomitantly with the garments in question. In fact, as fashion shows became more prominent in the 1990s, some designers not only staged increasingly elaborate shows, but also often produced short videos and films in lieu of or in addition to the shows. Moreover, fashion shows were staged to circulate as short videos as well as functioning as extemporaneous performances, an intention that is corroborated by the careful image and sound editing of the fashion show recordings. Consequently, the recordings of the shows often function as works in their own right, as opposed to mere documentations of a performance, and for my purposes therefore constitute a primary source of a similar order to the garments themselves.

The importance of stylistic analysis and the way techniques and *mise en scène* generate meaning alongside the narrative has been amply discussed in film and media studies. (The film scholars David Bordwell and Kristen Thompson provide particularly thorough guidelines to the formal analysis of film in their *Film Art: An Introduction*.)[32] This is particularly important to the analysis of fashion show films and videos, which are generally 'non-narrative', and where the *mise en scène* (which includes garments and make-up) undoubtedly takes centre stage.

The style press was also central in reconstructing the fashion of the period. It often played a central role in validating and promoting it. In the case of Leigh Bowery and Georgina Godley, the independent British style press – particularly i-D and later *The Face* – were most useful in tracking the development of their work in print. One could argue, in fact, that these two titles were indispensable to defining British independent fashion throughout the 1980s and 1990s.[33] Rei Kawakubo's and Martin Margiela's work was mainly written about or included in editorials within avant-garde publications, such as *Purple* and *Visionaire*. The latter published an entire issue in collaboration with Rei Kawakubo in 1997. Comme des Garçons also published its own magazine called *Six* throughout most of the 1980s, which featured Kawakubo's work alongside that of other designers and gives an important insight into the way the company envisioned itself.[34] For runway photos of Margiela's and Kawakubo's collections, I relied on trade publications such as *Officiel* and *Gap*, which did not begin documenting Margiela's collection until the late 1990s, at which point his fashion presentations started to become available online. Margiela's work was also extensively discussed in a number of newspapers – a fact that attests to his critical acclaim and intellectual aura.[35] The New York-based independent magazine *Details* also featured extensive coverage of Margiela's first few collections, which were otherwise not as thoroughly commented upon and photographed as the Belgian designer's later work. (During those years, *Details* was strikingly different from its later Condé Nast incarnation as a men's style magazine. It was a fashion magazine featuring extensive coverage of the Paris shows, often exceeding 30 pages, which were both written and photographed by Bill Cunningham.) In the case of Margiela, videos of his early collections were also available at the archives of the ModeMuseum in Antwerp, and photographs of some of his more obscure collections were made available to me by his Paris-based press office and the British photographer Niall McInerney. In the case of Bernhard Willhelm, his work was thoroughly catalogued by the ModeMuseum, which acquired his entire archive and fashion show recordings. Informative interviews with the designers and articles about his work were published in a range of publications, including the zine *Butt Magazine* (for which Willhelm was the first cover subject), the New York-based web publication *Hint Magazine* and the London-based style magazine *Dazed and Confused*.[36]

My methodology also involves oral history, albeit to a lesser extent. Whenever possible and when there was scant documentation, I conducted interviews with practitioners and/or their surviving collaborators. This proved helpful and, at times, necessary in providing additional contextual information about the production of the work which, despite – or perhaps because of – the fact that it dates to the recent past, is often insufficiently catalogued and/or documented. Moreover, this method allows for a 'dialogical encounter' between practitioners and interviewers, in which new meanings and interpretations can potentially develop, as is evident in my interview with Georgina Godley.[37] However, as discussed by a number of oral historians, there are obvious limitations to and common pitfalls with this approach. Of particular relevance to my research is the 'intentional fallacy', the misreading of the practitioners' intentions as the work's primary meaning. Instead, it has been suggested that interviews with practitioners provide not a direct and/ or more authentic reading of the work, but rather an instance of the author's 'self-reception'.[38] In addition, oral history foregrounds self-reflexivity in the research process, since it makes evident the extent to which the researcher frames the interview questions.

Experimental Fashion draws on a number of theoretical approaches to the subject. It employs a psychoanalytical approach, as it discusses grotesque fashion using Freudian concepts of the repressed and of the unconscious and its relation to the comic. It draws on feminist theory, science studies and gender studies when it discusses the grotesque in fashion in relation to constructs of feminine subjectivity and the maternal. It borrows from anthropology, and in particular cultural anthropology, in its reading of the fashion in question in relation to inversions and the view of the world-upside-down.[39] Partially as a result of cultural anthropology having deeply influenced the humanities, my encounter with anthropological approaches has been mediated and integrated (more often than not) through works of cultural history and critical theory, in particular through Bakhtin and Stallybrass and White.[40] Chiefly concerned 'with the symbolic and its interpretation', cultural history understands carnival and festivities as central to a culture, and thus provides an important framework for understanding works that borrow from these cultural modes.[41] I also employ oral history as well as methods of 'formal' analysis from material culture and film studies.

This combination of approaches and methods is needed to examine an inter-media phenomenon such as contemporary fashion. My book, however, does not do away with earlier approaches to the study of fashion; rather it attempts to integrate the empirical work that characterised early dress studies with a more theorised and multidisciplinary approach.[42] As fashion historian Christopher Breward suggests, and many have put into practice, close object analysis is helpful, and in the case of my particular case studies, essential in providing a base onto which more critical methods can be applied.[43] I employ a number of different methodologies to the study of experimental fashion at the turn of the past century as I integrate theories and methods from cultural history and critical theory, psychoanalysis and material and visual culture. My book, in fact, views fashion on a continuum with visual and material culture and integral to discourses developed simultaneously within photography performance visual arts, film and advertising, while placing itself within the emerging field of fashion studies.

1
AGAINST POWER DRESSING
Georgina Godley

The 1980s saw an aesthetic emerge in Western fashion in which a recuperation of past styles cobbled together into a pastiche came to the fore, and with it came a silhouette which, although partially quoting earlier periods, particularly the 1940s and 1950s, altered the female body in novel ways. This recuperation of sartorial styles from earlier decades, albeit not limited to this period, could be argued to have reached a certain frenzy in 1980s fashion in particular, and late twentieth-century fashion more generally.[1]

The female fashionable body that is most closely associated with the 1980s, particularly within women's work wear across Europe and North America, was characterised by exaggerated overly padded shoulders matched by oversized clothes. This coexisted with the bodycon look, characterised by form-fitting garments and in part developed in response to the growing focus on health and fitness, but also more simply as a result of technical improvements in stretch materials. Women's work wear in the 1980s was epitomised by the so-called 'power suit', which, through its attendant rhetoric about the importance of self-presentation in the increasingly corporatised work environment of the 1980s, has since become inextricably tied to the rise of the enterprising self and the neoliberal politics of Margaret Thatcher-era Britain and Ronald Reagan-era United States.[2] It was immortalised by the 1988 Mike Nichols film *Working Girl* (Fig. 1). The film recounted the way in which Melanie Griffith's character is able to scale the career ladder specifically by undergoing the kind of sartorial engineering widely promoted by the popular literature and visual culture of the period, and perhaps most successfully by the John T. Molloy dress manual *The Woman's Dress for Success Book*.[3]

Fig. 1 Publicity shot from *Working Girl*, 1988, ©20thCentFox/courtesy Everett Collection

The power suit, which soon became a work uniform in its own right, was an obvious approximation of men's career wear, one which seemed specifically based on the ideal fit male body of the 1980, while retaining a level of 'appropriate' femininity by being, in most cases, a skirt suit. This somewhat literal imitation of male dress as a requirement of entry in certain positions of power is of course problematic, as it falls within an understanding of women as an imperfect version of men. The shortcomings and false progressiveness of 1980s power dressing and its attendant feminine ideals are further highlighted by the fact that it persisted alongside a wholesome and traditional version of femininity which is best encapsulated in the period's fashion reference to the 1950s. Significantly, the decade staged various returns to the 1950s through its popular culture as well, perhaps most explicitly in the Robert Zemeckis's film *Back to the Future* (1985).

While 1980s fashion created a masculine broad-shouldered silhouette, the so-called 'fashion avant-garde' and figures who operated at the margin of fashion appeared to be subverting this silhouette, both within the same decade and, perhaps more overtly, in the next. Among the designers who explored new shapes and ideals of female bodies in the twentieth century are some of the most seminal figures of the 1980s, and to some extent 1990s, fashion: the Japanese Paris-based designer Rei Kawakubo of Comme des Garçons, the British designer Georgina Godley and the British designer, artist and club figure Leigh Bowery. In keeping with the 1980s, Kawakubo, Godley and Bowery resorted to excessive padding and oversized clothes, yet they subverted these signs and produced a silhouette that is antithetical to the mainstream 1980s silhouette and to the history of fashion more generally. They produced, instead, a pregnant body shape. In spite of their different positions and relations to the fashion markets, all three created a silhouette implying the maternal body, which had been palpably avoided by fashion design in the twentieth century.

Vivienne Westwood also challenged the fashionable silhouette of the period through her use of non-fashion models and by reclaiming undergarments from prior centuries, such as the bustle, the cage crinoline and the pannier, to create a silhouette that accentuated parts of the bodies, particularly the hips and the buttocks, which were generally 'contained' by twentieth-century high fashion. She never, however, created what could be construed as a pregnant silhouette, perhaps as a result of her work's indebtedness to Western fashion in the eighteenth and nineteenth centuries, a period that did not accentuate an oversized abdomen but, rather, its opposite. Thus, even though Westwood's work is often in line with the grotesque canon, she does not take on the reproductive female body and its attendant pregnant body shape as a number of designers of this period do, which is the focus of the first part of this book.[4]

The maternal body appears in utmost contrast with the high fashion silhouette of the greater part of the past century. The twentieth-century fashion body remains one of the most articulate attempts at the creation of a 'perfect' and perfectly contained body restrained and sealed, which greatly contrasts with the pregnant one. The reason for this exclusion can be attributed to the long and entrenched history in Western thought of assigning negative connotations to the generative female body and reading the maternal as threatening and *grotesque*, and can be ultimately read as evidence of a pervasive gynophobia within twentieth-century Western fashion. (I use the term gynophobia, as opposed to the more commonly used term misogyny, because it more aptly describes the fear of the maternal, the prefix 'gyno' from the Greek *gyne*, woman, being often associated in the English language with female reproduction. It is also a more pliable term. It has been theorised as allowing for a greater agency on the part of women, and as implying a fear of femininity and of the maternal, which can be experienced regardless of gender or sexual orientation.)[5]

THE MATERNAL AND THE GROTESQUE

Tracing the fear of the pregnant body within the history of Western thought goes well beyond the scope of this work. However, it is important to note how this revulsion towards the generative body shaped the history of the grotesque across disciplines, and how it has been read as one of the principal reasons why the grotesque has been marginalised within the Western aesthetic canon.[6] Alternatively, it can be argued that the maternal body has been, in great part, excluded from the Western representational tradition as a result of its association with the grotesque canon.[7] As Mary Russo points out in her book *The Female Grotesque*, references to the pregnant body are somewhat implicit in the term's etymology. "The word itself [...] evokes the cave" – the grotto-esque … As a bodily metaphor, the grotesque cave tends to look like (and in the most gross metaphorical sense be identified with) the cavernous anatomical female body.'[8]

The relation between the pregnant body and the grotesque was perhaps most clearly articulated during the Enlightenment, particularly within the arguments on the nature of conception. A number of Enlightenment thinkers attempted to purify and dematerialise birth processes by aligning them with creation and the mind, which, according to the Cartesian model, was inextricably male. That this realignment could never be fully completed was used to explain the persistence of the grotesque: 'Natural imperfections and corporeal defects were caused when that fleeting spark mixed with matter (which, according to eighteenth century thought was inextricably female), giving rise to distortions, passions, and disease.'[9] And since ultimately 'nature was permitted to take the substance for the reproduction of man only from his mother … [this] became the source of many accidents'.[10]

Gynophobic discourses surrounding birth processes and the maternal body, particularly as articulated within medical discourses in the West, have, however, persisted into the present. A thorough discussion of the way the birth process and the maternal body have been pathologised in the medical discourse, particularly in their relation to dirt, can be found in *Exploring the Dirty Side of Women's Health*.[11] Employing Mary Douglas's definition of dirt as 'matter out of place' representing a dangerous mixing of categories,[12] the book explores the ways in which the maternal body and birth processes are categorised in the medical establishment and placed at the bottom of hierarchies of power due to their association with dirt: 'The pregnant woman is a paradigm case of boundary transgression as well as the forbidding mixing of kinds', a condition which, explains the pathologisation of birth processes.[13] The current fascination with the pregnant bodies of celebrities underscores its relation to the abject, as opposed to reading as an acceptance of pregnancy, by substituting a relation of revulsion to one of almost morbid attraction. It is also important to note how part of the interest in the bodies of pregnant celebrities consists in their sudden return to a 'normal' and fit pre-pregnant body. It is dependent on representing pregnancy as a fashion to be worn, as the perfect bump becomes a commodified object of fashion through celebrity culture and the media, as opposed to an embodied experience.[14]

It is partially in opposition to Enlightenment thought that Bakhtin reclaims the grotesque, the attributes of which he celebrates as a much-needed corrective to 'abstract rationalism', which could not accommodate 'the contradictory, perpetually becoming and unfinished being'.[15] And if one understands the grotesque in Bakhtinian terms, its references to the maternal become particularly explicit. According to Bakhtin's theories, the grotesque is a phenomenon of reversal, of unsettling ruptures of borders, in particular bodily borders. The grotesque body is an open, unfinished one that is never sealed or fully contained, but it is always in the process of becoming and engendering another body. He writes in *Rabelais and his World* that the grotesque body 'is a body in the act of becoming … it is continually built, created, and builds and creates another body'. In contrast, the twentieth-century fashion body conforms to Bakhtin's notion of the classical body of official culture:

> a strictly completed, finished product. Furthermore, it was isolated, alone, fenced off from all other bodies. All signs of its unfinished character, of its growth and proliferation were eliminated; its protuberances and offshoots were removed, its convexities (signs of new sprouts and buds) smoothed out, its apertures closed. The ever unfinished nature of the body was hidden, kept secret; conception, pregnancy, childbirth, death throes, were almost never shown. The age represented was as far removed from the mother's womb as from the grave … The accent was

placed on the completed, self-sufficient individuality of the given body ... It is quite obvious that from the point of view of these canons [meaning the classical canons] the body of grotesque realism was hideous and formless. It did not fit the framework of the 'aesthetics of the beautiful' as conceived by the Renaissance.[16]

Confirming Bakhtin's assessment, Kenneth Clark, in his seminal – albeit by now controversial – study on the history of the nude, places the phenomena of growth and what appear to be pregnant enlarged female bellies in the so-called alternative convention. These were conventions of bodily representation alternative to the principles of symmetry and harmony characteristic of the classical model. Clark traces the origin of the alternative conventions to the northern Gothic, but regards it as having survived into twentieth-century painting and sculpture through artists such as Paul Cézanne and Georges Rouault. Significantly, he also traces an analogy between the alternative convention and the non-Western cultures of India and Mexico, which unsurprisingly he does not place in any kind of chronology. Unlike Bakhtin, Clark places these canons at the bottom of the representational hierarchy in a series of descriptions that read as undoubtedly gynophobic:

> This is what distinguishes the Gothic ideal of the female body: that whereas in the antique nude the dominating rhythm is the curve of the hip, in the alternative convention it is the curve of the stomach. This change argues a fundamental difference of attitude to the body. The curve of the hip is created by an upward thrust. Beneath it are bone and muscle, supporting the body's weight. However sensuous or geometric it may become, it remains in the end an image of energy and control. The curve of the stomach is created by gravity and relaxation. It is a heavy, unstructural curve, soft and slow, yet with a kind of vegetable persistence. It does not take its shape from the will but from the unconscious biological process that gives shape to all hidden organisms.[17]

In descriptions that very much bring to mind the way Kawakubo's and Godley's pregnant body shapes were described and, at times, ridiculed by their contemporary press, Clark describes the female body of the alternative convention as a 'bulb-like' body, where 'the sense of healthy structure, the clear geometric shapes and their harmonious disposition, has been rejected in favour of lumps of matter, swollen and inert'.[18] Clark's assessment has been subsequently criticised by a number of feminist art historians, and in particular Linda Nead in her book-length study of the female nude.

Bakhtin, on the other hand, despite celebrating as opposed to denigrating the generative body of the alternative convention, does not sufficiently explore how the maternal body came to be firmly placed within the grotesque tradition. In his protracted discussions of the associations between the grotesque and the female body, he never stops to take into account the gynophobic genealogy of such associations. This becomes particularly evident in the section of his discussion that is meant to absolve *Rabelais* from potential attacks of misogyny, but which ultimately ends up essentialising the connection between woman, the maternal and the grotesque:

> The popular tradition is in no way hostile to woman and does not approach her negatively. In this tradition woman is essentially related to the material bodily lower stratum; she is the incarnation of this stratum that degrades and regenerates simultaneously. She is ambivalent. She debases, brings down to earth, lends a bodily substance to things, and destroys; but, first of all, she is the principle that gives birth.[19]

As a result, he argues, she is deeply connected to the grotesque canon. And even though Bakhtin understands the grotesque image in a positive light, he does not unveil the gynophobic implications in understanding the female biological organs as grotesque par excellence but, rather, by leaving them under-analysed he ends up naturalising these connections. Thus, even though he ennobles and romanticises images of pregnancy, he remains, to some extent, complicit in a gynophobic discourse. As pointed out by Mary Russo:

> Bakhtin, like many other social theorists of the nineteenth and twentieth centuries, fails to acknowledge or incorporate the social relations of gender in his semiotic model of the body politic, and thus his notion of the Female Grotesque remains in all directions, repressed and undeveloped.[20]

As Russo, like Stallybrass and White, points out, there are particular risks for women in aligning themselves with the grotesque body, insofar as the female body is already *marked* by grotesque associations. In fact, if one understands the grotesque as that which transgresses and deviates from the norm, the female body as understood vis-à-vis the model of the male body is *always* grotesque.[21] However, like Connelly, Russo points out the possibility for feminist re-appropriation of the grotesque category, and the ways in which the grotesque can become a particularly important tool for negotiating ideals of norms and deviations. And it is a site of exploration of norms and deviations, and as a critique and an intervention into what constitutes the ideal body of fashion that Godley, Kawakubo and Bowery re-appropriate the maternal body and re-inscribe it into the fashion vocabulary.

GEORGINA GODLEY'S BACKGROUND

As early as the mid-1980s, the British designer Georgina Godley, to whose work Kawakubo's seems to be much indebted, radically altered the female silhouette by adding padding on the hips, thighs and the belly. Interestingly, the relation between Kawakubo's and Godley's collections is not unpacked in any of the existing literature on the designers. Although it is impossible to ascertain whether Kawakubo was aware of Godley's work when developing her 1997 'Body Meets Dress' collection, the Japanese designer tried to disavow the connection, as Godley pointed out in my interview with her. For instance, for a 1999 exhibition at the Hayward Gallery, she refused to allow pieces from her spring/summer 1999 collection to be hung in the same room as Godley's 'Bump and Lump' collection despite their aesthetic and thematic connections.[22]

As the art critic Mariuccia Casadio writes: '[Georgina Godley's] clothes altered and emphasised the form and volume of the female belly, and buttocks with the aid of spectacular padding.' Her autumn/winter 1986–87 collection, titled 'Bump and Lump', drew inspiration

> from medical, scientific, orthopaedic and gynaecological circles, with a series of fabrics and forms reinforced to support specific parts of the body. This 'clinical' aesthetic provided her starting point for her new concept of the silhouette. Her clothes formalised unprecedented possibilities of mutation.[23]

This point is echoed by the fashion historian Richard Martin who, discussing the designer's work in relation to Surrealism, referred to her garments as 'biomorphic'.[24]

Despite the aesthetic relation to Kawakubo's spring/summer 1997 collection, Georgina Godley is, however, much closer to Leigh Bowery in terms of production scale and cultural milieu, as she herself admits. In an interview the designer recounts having participated with Bowery and other fledgling British designers in a fashion show called 'London Goes to Tokyo', organised in 1984 to showcase young British designers in Japan.[25] Godley also discussed how she was acquainted with Bowery through Rachel Auburn, with whom she lived in the mid-1980s. Auburn was, at the time, a fledgling fashion designer who had opened a stand at Kensington Market in the early 1980s, together with Bowery. Later she became increasingly involved in the club scene, eventually becoming a DJ. Recounting her early years as a designer, Godley points out how her community was made up of people spanning a variety of artistic disciplines. In an interview I conducted with Godley, she explained:

> I had a studio on All Saints Road and a whole gang – Leigh Bowery, Rachel Auburn, Tom Dixon – who I was very close to at this time. I didn't necessarily exchange ideas mainly with fashion designers – my best friends were furniture designers and painters. We did belong to a community – there was actually a community.[26]

Another influential member of Godley's creative community was Scott Crolla, a fellow art-school trained designer with whom Godley started a company prior to striking out on her own. The company, called Crolla, was founded in 1981 and was both critically and commercially successful, with a self-standing store in London's Dover Street. Godley credits her experience at Crolla as being her first foray into the exploration of gender norms and dress:

> [Crolla] is the collaboration that started in 1981 and it's significant, in a way, to put things in context. Crolla was as much a journey into sexuality as my solo collections, which showed my interest in feminism. It was the birth of the 1980s dandy.[27]

By expanding the vocabulary of acceptable menswear, Crolla's work constituted an exploration of Anglo-Saxon masculinity, one that was partially achieved by borrowing patterns and fabric from non-Western traditions: 'And also there was huge cross cultural interest, particularly in London we had a big Arab presence. There was a mix of cultures. Everyone was using ethnic fabric.'[28] Crolla was best known for extremely colourful and heavily patterned men's suits and shirts, which combined ethnic fabric with traditional British fabric such as chintz, an interior-decorating fabric with clear associations to domesticity. In addition to its association with an idyllic notion of Englishness, chintz also shares a colonial lineage as 'a printed fabric inscribed and modified by the commercial trade between Indian and Britain'.[29]

BODY-ALTERING GARMENTS

Ultimately, it was precisely their success that induced Godley to leave Crolla and start her own brand, which allowed her to experiment more freely: 'Crolla itself was very successful. Many artists, when they are successful, get recognized for one thing and the commercial demand is to produce the same thing'.[30] Godley started out in her own name by doing a mini-collection in autumn/winter 1985–86 that introduced themes that are recurrent in her work, such as the exploration of gender and the body. Revolving around the theme of 'Transgender and the Body', it included a piece that was 'male from the front and female from the back', by resembling a skirt at the front and a pair of trousers at the back.[31] It is, however, another dress in this collection, made of the medical rubber sheeting used under bedsheets that protect against incontinence, that provides the first instance of Godley's subversion of 1980s fashion vocabulary. In this case, this subversion was articulated in her use of a quintessential 1980s material against the grain. Rubber and rubberised materials, most often latex, were used by fashion designers in the 1980s to create a perfectly sealed and contained model of the female body that exposed the form-fitted ideal silhouette, as is most evident in the work of Thierry Mugler. Mugler's use of rubber was influenced by fetish wear, which had been originally incorporated into fashion by Vivienne Westwood and Malcolm McLaren in the 1970s. The copious use of latex in the 1980s was also theorised in relation to the AIDS epidemic as representing skin-tight armour.[32] Godley instead used rubber to make a reference to the porous and leaking body. By employing a material that is most often used in hospitals, she made rubber refer not to the plastic and surgically enhanced bodies of the 1980s but to the hospitalised sick body in all its vulnerability and fragility. In its reference to the body's vulnerabilities, its leakages and what remains embarrassing about the human body, Godley's work is once again aligned with Bowery's, where an interest in physical boundaries and the anxieties created by bodily fluid, particularly during the 1980s AIDS epidemic, took centre stage.

Following this first mini-collection, Godley produced a complete collection titled 'Body and Soul' for spring/summer 1986, which furthered her exploration of a body that did not conform to ideals of the time. For this collection, Godley created garments that alternately followed and veered away from the body through a system of boning inserted in a stretch silk-jersey fabric that clung to the figure. Many of the garments played with body shapes, often singling out particular anatomical parts, such as the collarbones and the pectoral muscles, which Godley recreated in crinkled velvet as an exoskeleton for a piece aptly titled 'muscle dress' (Fig. 2). Although not mentioned as an influence by the designer, the collection makes a reference to Schiaparelli's skeleton dress from 1938 (Fig. 3), a fact that suggests a connection between the work I am discussing and earlier iterations of the grotesque in fashion, which were most evident in Surrealism. In an in i-D magazine interview with the designer, the collection was described as a rebuke to the 'emphasis placed on the 'body beautiful' and 'a reply to Alaïa', thus introducing the ideas that were further developed in the winter collection of the same year, 'Bump and Lump'.[33]

This collection comprised padded undergarments worn underneath dresses made of see-through stretch fabric; the undergarments exaggerated and hence emphasised areas of the female body, particularly the buttocks, hips and belly, that were generally suppressed within fashion at the time. They were designed to be worn underneath sheath dresses, which came in both short and long versions (Figs 4 and 5). Other pieces in the collection – which, unfortunately, are mostly undocumented – were padded 'overgarments' that achieved a similar effect to the undergarments, that of enhancing the belly, hips and buttocks, but were meant to be worn on top, as opposed to underneath, the sheath dresses. The only 'overgarment' I was able to see was a belt that was padded in front, thus suggesting a pregnant silhouette. Godley described this piece as 'an abstracted farthingale' that exaggerated the female form:

> It idealised it in a way, but in a way that people hadn't addressed it because it was all about a masculine silhouette; so [by wearing the pieces] you would achieve a beautiful hip or you would have a wonderful rear.[34]

The collection was read by both the press and museum curators as a critique of fashion's promotion of a lean and 'contained' female form. Godley's work has been hailed as 'a challenge to the fashion world's preoccupation with the slender female body'[35] and to 'conventional notions of femininity'.[36] British

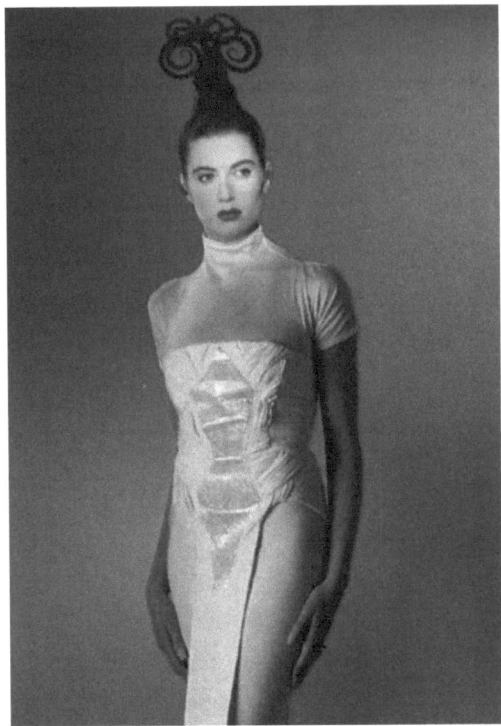

Fig. 2 Georgina Godley, *Muscle Dress*, spring/summer 1986, *The Face*, March 1986, no. 71, photograph by Stevie Hughes

Vogue praised Godley for 'designing from a social premise, often parodying the climate of the time', and pointed out how her work provided a commentary on the period's 'body-consciousness'.³⁷ The designer herself backs such claims, stating that her garments are 'wrapped up in the role of woman in society and the way that we are perceived'. Describing the overgarments, she discusses her collection as a response to the 1980s masculine silhouette in particular, and more generally to the demands the decade had made on women and their bodies:

> But the interest, the obsession if you like was: a very hard and aggressive generation of women had evolved through the early '80s period and in America there was a big trend to aerobic Jane Fonda body toning. Everybody had the perfect body. And then there was Azzedine Alaïa. All those clothes angered me, because I found them very hostile to women, I didn't see it as celebrating women at all ... My work was all about changing the perspective of what could be beautiful. It was all the things we learned to consider ugly. I was challenging that.³⁸

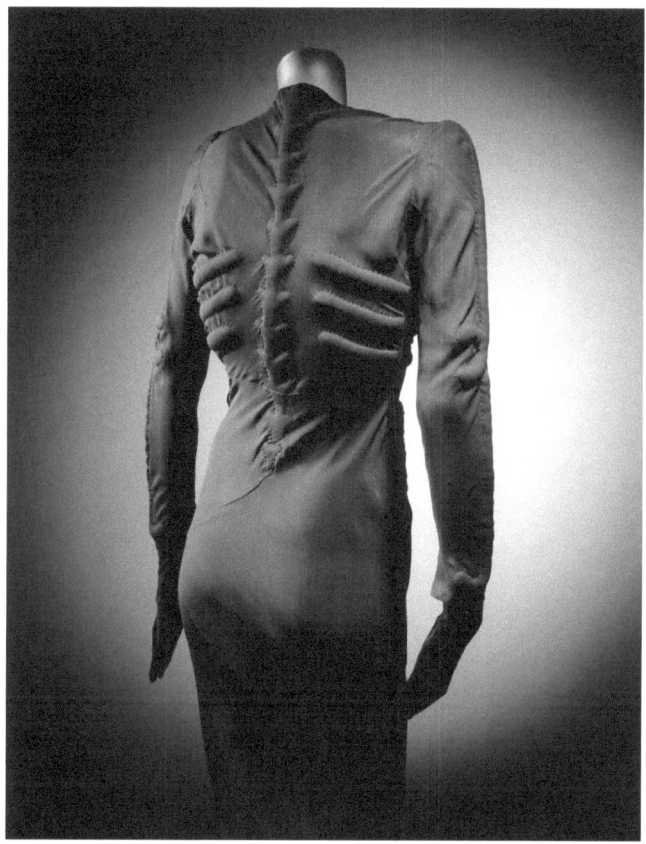

Fig. 3 Elsa Schiaparelli, *Skeleton Dress*, 1938, courtesy of the Victoria and Albert Museum

The collection evolved from research into contemporary dolls, particularly Barbie dolls, as well as prehistoric 'fertility dolls'. Using clay, she re-formed the shape of the Barbie dolls to resemble those of the fertility ones:

> That was how the whole idea came about, because Barbie is the definition of extreme, almost pervy, femininity. Again there was this obsession with a boyish figure. So I got a whole line up of Barbie dolls and played around with body and clay and built them out in different places. At the time I was studying fertility dolls, which informed this exercise. It was from them that I worked on a selection of padded underwear.[39]

Fig. 4 Georgina Godley, padded undergarment 'Bump and Lump' collection, autumn/winter 1986–87, photograph by Cindy Palmano, courtesy of the artist and Georgina Godley

Thus Godley's work is making amends and re-inscribing the maternal body within Western fashion. Significantly, she starts the process by transforming the sealed and contained body of the Barbie doll, which is perhaps the ultimate representation of normative femininity and unattainable bodily ideals.[40] Godley's exploration resembles theoretical work, such as Linda Nead's The Female Nude, which it shortly preceded. Like Nead's writings, Godley's designs are part of the 1980s feminist debates. Her work constitutes a feminist intervention and critique to prevailing fashion discourse that are articulated, for instance, through Alaïa's body-hugging silhouettes, as Godley herself noted. Speaking of the commercial viability of her designs, Godley admitted that the sheath dresses from the collections sold much better than the padded undergarments. Notably, Godley's collections, despite their experimental nature, were sold in Harrods and Whistles in London and specific collections

Fig. 5 Georgina Godley, dress, 'Bump and Lump' collection, autumn/winter 1986–87, photograph by Cindy Palmano, courtesy of the artist and Georgina Godley

in Bloomingdales in New York. However, her primary and more lucrative market was the Japanese one, so much so that shortly after the start of the Japanese economic crisis of the early 1990s, Godley stopped production.

Nead's feminist revision of the history of the nude also set out to reinscribe the maternal body, in her case, to the history of Western art. Like Godley, Nead starts with a reclamation of early representations of fertility, best known through the example of the Willendorf Venus, which had been amply disparaged and excluded from the canonical history of the Western nude, solidified in Kenneth Clark's work. Similarly to the comparison set up by Godley between Barbie and prehistoric fertility images, Nead, repudiating Clark's arguments, compares a more contained and 'orderly' representation of femininity, the Cycladic doll, with the Willendorf Venus to interrogate the reasons behind the latter's exclusion from Western ideals of the nude:

> He [Clark] compares two early examples of the female nude: A prehistoric figure of a woman and Cycladic doll which he designates respectively Vegetable and Crystalline Venus. In the first example, the body is lumpy and protruding, but in the second image 'the unruly human body has undergone a geometrical discipline'. This is the important point – the female body has undergone a process of containment, of holding in and keeping out. It is commonly recognized that prehistoric statuettes such as the Willendorf Venus were images of fertility: they represented the maternal body, the female body in parturition. Clark alludes to this image of the female body as undisciplined, out of control; it is excluded from the proper concerns of art in favour of the smooth uninterrupted lines of the Cycladic figure … The female body has become art by containing and controlling the limits of form – precisely by framing it.[41]

One can easily see how Nead's argument has a bearing on the history of dress, where the female body is arguably entering the realm of fashion through containment, similarly to the way it entered the realm of art in the codified form of the female nude:

> If the female body is defined as lacking containment and issuing filth and pollution from its faltering outlines and broken surface, then the classical forms of art perform a kind of magical regulation of the female body, containing it and momentarily repairing the orifices and tears.[42]

However, in its constant quest for change and shifting identities fashion often problematises this containment model and can also give way, at times unwittingly, to unbounded subjects. Godley's exploration of the subject and body out of bounds is instead clearly thought out, and her work is aligned with feminist theory, which developed contemporaneously.

At times, however, just as is true of a certain strand of feminist theory, Godley's argument falls into a problematic essentialism, as her invocation of a stable, cross-cultural idea of a female natural form makes evident:

> I did a lot of research into much more primitive cultures and what fecundity meant and what fertility dolls looked like, into African fertility dolls, Egyptian, different shapes of body, different cultures as opposed to what we evolved, which was this rather Masculine [form]. Partially I felt angered that we so - called achieved women's liberty, but in fact we were not allowing ourselves to be true to our natural form.[43]

In another revealing interview, she adds:

> I suppose at the time when I was most aggressively doing this kind of work it was because it was a very informative time, the beginning of the '80s. It was all power-dressing and *Dynasty* shoulders and I hated what was going on. It was like women were denying their main strength by trying to be more like men … I find this obsession with women and flat tummies bizarre and unnatural. The whole nature of fecundity and fertility, again it's like denying one's essential.[44]

Here, Godley, perhaps unwittingly, invokes biological essentialism – an understanding of women as a universal category on the basis of biological characteristics. Prior to the second wave of feminism, and to a certain extent throughout it, this belief was commonly held both within and outside of the feminist movement.[45] Starting from the 1970s onwards, it came under attack by proponents of social constructionism, who argued that the category of woman, like that of femininity, is in fact always socially and culturally constructed.[46] Subsequently, Judith Butler developed this view to argue that the body itself could not be read as stable and outside of culture, but was in fact equally socially and culturally constructed, thus rendering biological essentialism a further impossibility.[47] The response to this work was often that of a strategic essentialism, one that would still allow for a cohesive feminist cultural critique and activism without believing in universals and essentials common to all women.[48] This would be attained by the balancing act of strategically invoking a universal category of woman within certain social and political contexts in order to promote collective action, while in fact admitting that such a category does not exist.[49] Another, perhaps more convincing solution, was brought forth by Alison Stone, who, after Judith Butler, argues that femininity and women themselves share a 'genealogy' and are thus historically constructed in complex and often diverging ways: 'women always acquire femininity by appropriating and reworking existing cultural interpretations of femininity, so that all women become situated within a history of overlapping chains of interpretation'.[50]

Returning to the specifics of Godley's work, it should be noted that her designs are not necessarily aligned with her arguments, in what is perhaps a clear instance of the intentional fallacy. If one looks beyond the problematic essentialism of some of her statements, one finds in the British designer's work an exploration of the human body that, while invoking the maternal through a pregnant silhouette, goes beyond a simple celebration of an allegedly 'natural' female body and creates body formations that, in their asymmetry and strangeness, are in utmost contrast to the ideals of the classical body (the ideal against which the grotesque is articulated) and fully embrace a condition of alterity.[51] In a description of one of her padded undergarments from 1986, Godley mentions how departing from 'the idea of the bustle, [her garment] was taken over padded from behind and then brought onto one thigh so that she had a very enlarged one tight and bottom'.[52] This placement, which is visible in a piece reconstructed by Godley for the Brighton Museum in which the bustle-like structure is lopsidedly placed on the buttock, enlarging the left hip and the right thigh in the process, adds an asymmetrical element to the already strange shape created by the bustle.

Thus, ultimately, the padded undergarments created hybrid shapes. In the process, they referred to prehistoric statuettes, non-Western cultures and the ways they articulated erogenous zones, and nineteenth-century Western fashion via the bustle.[53] Godley's interest in the *displaced* bustle is further explored in pieces which place this padded structure onto the belly, creating the illusion of pregnancy, while more generally invoking a sense of instability and otherness:

> It wasn't just a replica of pregnancy. It came in and then it had dipped on the side. I could almost model it again. It went down and came out. It was a very organic and rather magical shape – a very lyrical look at the body.[54]

CORPORATE CODING

Godley's refusal to perpetrate a mode of dress that was in fact an imitation of menswear, and particularly of men's career wear, has not only a gender implication but also a socio-economic one. Her critical stance towards power dressing cannot be dissociated from a critical stance towards the 1980s political and economic climate. As the fashion theorist and sociologist Joanne Entwistle notes, the power suit is inextricably intertwined with, and, in fact, instrumental to, the new modes of self which were promoted during this period (especially within the US and the UK), and particularly the so-called 'enterprising self'. This term was coined and has been subsequently discussed in relation to the development of advanced late capitalist societies and the erosion of systems of welfare.[55] The 'enterprising self' was understood as a direct correlate to the New Right (Thatcherite and Reaganite) 'enterprise culture'. This mode of self, however, developed and survived well past the 1980s.

As it is theorised in relation to post-Fordism and neoliberalism, this model of culture gives greater and greater importance to the individual and the principles of self-reliance and self-construction:

> Enterprise here designates an array of rules for the conduct of one's everyday existence: energy, initiative, ambition, calculation and personal responsibility. The enterprising self will make a venture of its life, project itself a future and seek to shape itself in order to become that which it wishes to be. The enterprising self is thus a calculating self, a self that calculates *about* itself and that works *upon* itself in order to better itself.[56]

Thus power dressing, epitomised by the power suit, can be understood as a dress practice that is aligned with these new modes of self, as it allowed for 'an embodiment' of the new culture at the level of daily practice:

> What is significant then about 'power dressing' as it develops in the 1980s is the degree of fit between this discourse on the presentation of self in the workplace and the emergence of an enterprising self. The rallying call to 'dress for success' or 'power dress' is a call to think about every aspect of one's self, including one's appearance, as part of a 'project of the self'. The mode of self advocated by the rallying phrase 'dress for success' is an enterprising one; the career woman is told she must be calculating and cunning in her self-presentation.[57]

Godley's critique of these new modes of self, which developed in response to the political and economic realities of the 1980s, remained implicit in her refusal to create anything akin to power dressing, and became explicit in two of her last collections 'School Colours', (autumn/winter 1987–88) and the subsequent spring/summer collection titled 'Corporate Coding'. 'School Colours' was presented in a lecture hall at the Victoria and Albert Museum, where each look was carefully described and the inspiration of the collection thoroughly discussed, to the dismay of most of the editors, who criticised the event as pretentious and didactic.[58] Most notably, the collection included an ironic version of the power suit made of tea towels and yellow dusters sewn together with waffle towels. Making reference to the sphere of domesticity, the piece constitutes an obvious critique of the alleged gender equality claimed for the power suit. It also serves as a reminder of the 1980s references to 1950s models of traditional femininity through both its prevailing fashions and culture at large.

However, a more explicit engagement with the late-capitalist notion of the engineering of the self (promoted throughout the decade) was articulated in some of the prints Godley used for the collection. Of particular relevance is a photographic print that combined the image of the English rose – chosen for its historic association with traditional ideals of femininity – with images of slimming pills, low-fat milk cartoons, and deodorant labels.[59] These constituted important and, in some instances, relatively novel tools for the engineering of the self, which were employed for the achievement of contemporary ideals of femininity. This notion of an engineered and calculating self, as both Entwistle and the sociologist Nikolas Rose point out, is, clearly indebted to Foucault's writings on the 'technologies of the self', practices

> which permit individuals to effect by their own means or with the help of others a certain number of operations on their own bodies and souls, thoughts, conduct, and way of being, so as to transform themselves in order to attain a certain state of happiness, purity, wisdom, perfection, or immortality.[60]

Following this collection, Godley created 'Corporate Coding' for spring/summer 1988, which constituted an attempt to ironise the corporate culture of the 1980s and the alleged progress it had brought forth. Describing the collection, Godley stressed how it was conceived as a direct response to the economic and political climate of the late 1980s: 'One must imagine the climate at the time. London was so incredibly affluent, and the City boom and all the yuppies. Margaret Thatcher and the whole corporate culture were overwhelming.'[61] The collection was partially composed of dresses with padded hips, empire waists and ballooning backs made of pinstriped suiting and shirting materials, a clear reference to the workers in the City and thus a feminisation of traditionally masculine symbols. The centrepieces of the collection were a number of cap-sleeved dresses made of a cotton fabric in the high contrast colours typical of corporate logos. The fabric sported prints created specifically for the collection by the British artist Tim Head. Head was commissioned by Godley to create textile designs reminiscent of logos. This resulted in four bold prints: 'Deep Freeze' (the three dots generally found on home freezers), 'TV Dinner' (represented by knives and forks on a tray), 'Home Security' (the stylised silhouette of an oversized lock) and 'Test Tube' (the print of a test tube). Rather than suggesting power suits, these dresses, in their primness and colour schemes, are reminiscent of uniforms, and in particular those that used to be worn by airline stewardesses. Yet, as with the ironic power suit of the previous collection, they make explicit reference to the domestic realm and the private sphere and perhaps to the way new 'technologies of the self' had fully colonised them.

Ultimately, Godley's 'Corporate Coding' collection critiques power dressing and its attendant corporate models of femininity that developed in the 1980s. The collection also takes on the return of 1950s ideals of wholesome traditional femininity that was pervasive through the 1980s.

2

FASHIONING THE MATERNAL BODY
Rei Kawakubo

Rei Kawakubo created a pregnant silhouette in her spring/summer 1997 collection 'Body Meets Dress' for Comme des Garçons. This collection, like much 1990s experimental fashion, can be understood as a response to the 1980s and particularly to the image of the über-healthy, wholesome and powerful body that was promoted with particular force throughout the period. As Evans and Arnold have argued in relation to fashion, and Linda Sandino has argued in relation to design more generally, 1990s experimental fashion developed partially as a critique and renegation of 1980s fashion language.[1] Kawakubo was able to fully explore this critique of the sealed classical bodies thanks in great part to her collaboration with visual artists of the period, chiefly Cindy Sherman, as well as the choreographer Merce Cunningham, for the 1997 dance *Scenario*. As Godley's work makes evident, the 1980s saw ever-increasing attention paid to the toned and exercised version of women's bodies. The bodies of female bodybuilders, for instance, became the site of increased fascination and scrutiny, as Helmut Newton's and Robert Mapplethorpe's photographs of the 1979 female bodybuilding champion Lisa Lyon attest (Fig. 6).

According to Lynda Nead, Lyon, by perfectly framing and hardening her own body through exercise, actually exemplified the classical ideal and the perfectly contained version of the female body. Despite the apparent feminist discourse of bodybuilding, Nead writes that 'her body [referring to Lisa Lyon] reached the highest or utmost degree of contained form'.[2] Bodybuilding, much like the masculinised fashionable female silhouette of the 1980s, occupied an ambiguous position. It could be understood as a kind of armour, apparently promoting an image of strength, but ultimately,

Fig. 6 Robert Mapplethorpe, *Lisa Lyon* 1981, courtesy of the Robert Mapplethorpe Foundation

as Nead points out in relation to Lisa Lyon's sculpted body, it simply replaced one form of containment with another.³ In line with the solidification of enterprising model of the self, which positions the body as an ongoing betterment project, the 1980s also saw the popularisation of other techniques of body manipulations, chiefly plastic surgery, which was heavily employed towards the attainment of the 1980s ideal silhouette.[4] But what puts Kawakubo's collection in a more direct and, perhaps, more effective dialogue with the preceding decade is its ample use of padding. Although the shoulder pads were a less advanced or permanent technology of bodily modification than cosmetic surgery or muscle building, it was nonetheless a pervasive one throughout the 1980s, used to achieve a wholly 'distorted' silhouette. In the 1980s, in fact, the oversized shoulder pads were famously central to the achievement of the period's desired body shape. As the very first paragraph of *Excess: Fashion and the Underground in the 80s* emphasised, the decade introduced 'clothes that construct and model the body ... Padding builds up the shoulders and lends an imposing and authoritative touch to the female figure'.[5]

Kawakubo uses the same means to very different, almost diametrically opposite end, in a classic instance of subversion. While throughout the 1980s padding produced a strong, masculinised female body, in her 1997 collection Kawakubo's padding (feather down pads, to be precise) create a vulnerable and oddly shaped body with protruding regions on the back, the hips and belly.

The collection was comprised of a number of sleeveless and cup-sleeved dresses, as well as shirts and skirts, in stretchable nylon fabric. Much of the fabric was printed with a gingham pattern, which is traditionally used for casual daywear and carries an association with domesticity, as it is often employed for tablecloths and aprons. Other pieces were rendered in a lightweight translucent and colourfully patterned fabric more suggestive of nightwear. All of the pieces whose internal structure I have been able to study were accompanied by see-through nylon slips, their colour matching that of the dresses with which they were paired. The down pads were sewn to the slips yet were easily removable in order to simplify cleaning processes. Two kidney-shaped pads approximately 24 centimetres in length and 15 centimetres at their widest point were placed at shoulder level, while two others placed at the waist were considerably bigger and of a rounder shape vaguely reminiscent of a womb (Figs 7 and 8).

Kawakubo's use of padding gives a vulnerable and softened aspect to the female body rather than invoking the masculine careerist bodies of the previous decade. In its abundance of organic shapes, the Japanese designer's collection can be read as overtly female, particularly in its reference to the maternal body. This reference was noted by Hilton Als in *Artforum* of December 1996: 'Yet another girl sports a pod placed directly on her

FASHIONING THE MATERNAL BODY: REI KAWAKUBO

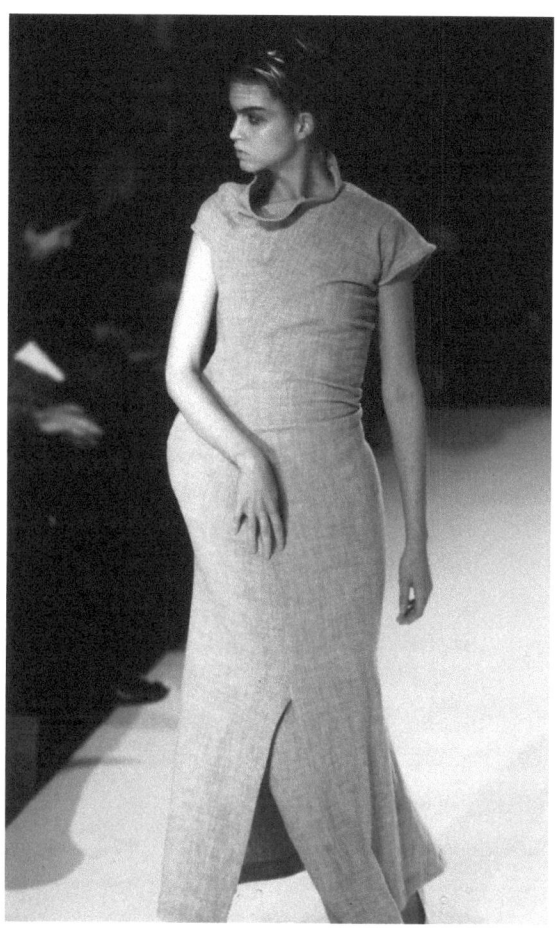

Fig. 7 Rei Kawakubo for Comme des Garçons, padded dress, 'Body Meets Dress' collection, spring/summer 1997, courtesy of Firstview

stomach; when she stood in profile, she looked as if she had been *defeated* by pregnancy, or was simply disinterested in the effect her cosmetic pregnancy had on us.'[6] This quote is particularly telling because not only does it spell out the maternal references but it also unveils, perhaps inadvertently, the gynophobic discourse surrounding much of Western fashion, and Western society at large, as is apparent from Als's choice of wording. The model is not simply pregnant; rather she is *defeated* by pregnancy. Conversely, it is implied that the audience is made uneasy by being presented with a pregnant female body, albeit cosmetically achieved, within a bastion of high fashion such as the Paris runways.

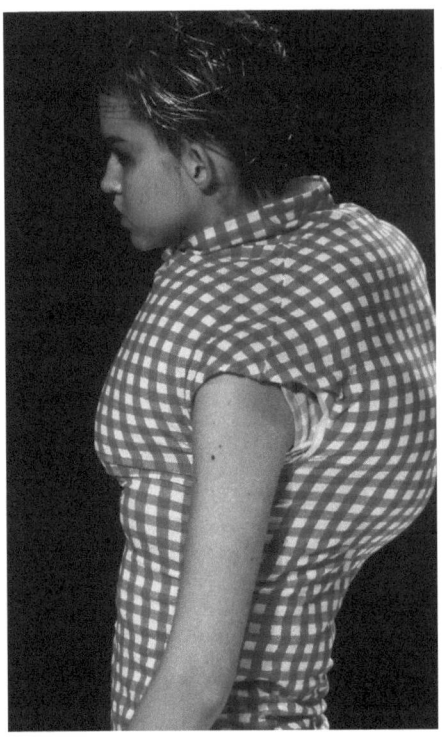

Fig. 8 Rei Kawakubo for Comme des Garçons, padded top, 'Body Meets Dress' collection, spring/summer 1997, courtesy of Firstview

The spring/summer 1997 collection of Comme des Garçons set out to explore and question assumptions about female beauty and notions of what is sexually alluring and what is grotesque within the Western vocabulary.[7] This exploration was, however, not always well received or easily digested by the fashion establishment. While some of the press praised Kawakubo's collection (particularly the art press and newspaper-based journalists), the collection was not unconditionally embraced by the fashion glossies. Both *Vogue* and *Elle* made an indirect critique to the Japanese designer's work by photographing the collection with the pads removed, a practice that was embraced by a number of otherwise adventurous Comme des Garçons customers. Despite Kawakubo's insistence on shipping her collection as it was shown on the runway – with the slips and pads attached to dresses, shirts and skirts – store clerks reported some of the customers taking the pads out.[8] It is important to note that by the late 1990s, Comme des Garçons was already fairly widely distributed for the standards of experimental fashion brands, thanks primarily to its self-standing boutiques across the US, Europe and Japan, as well as in fashion-forward multi-brand stores such as Barneys.

This resistance brings further proof to the fact that the designer had tapped into what was, perhaps, one of few remaining taboos in fashion design of the period. Pregnant bodies did not, in fact, become glamorised in contemporary visual culture until the new millennium – and even then primarily through celebrity culture and Hollywood as opposed to high fashion. A notable precedent is the by-now tame, but then controversial, photograph of a nude, eight-months pregnant Demi Moore on the cover of *Vanity Fair* in 1991.[9] The issue was banned in many mass market stores in North America or circulated under a black plastic wrap – akin to those used to cover pornographic magazines.[10]

This kind of investigation was far from novel for Kawakubo, whose inclination to present unorthodox relations of clothes to the bodies, which imply novel understandings of female sexuality and beauty, had characterised the great part of her career and her ascent to international fame in the 1980s. Deyan Sudjic, writing about Comme des Garçons in the early 1990s, points out:

> Another theme in Kawakubo's work that initially caused some consternation was the challenge her unfamiliar silhouettes present to the body-shaping tradition of Western female fashion – indeed some of her clothes in her first Paris collection were interpreted as a direct attack on Western ideas of female beauty.[11]

Kawakubo's different articulations of sexuality and beauty ideals is epitomised by a fashion editorial in the second issue of *Six*, a Comme des Garçons publication, from 1988, which juxtaposes Rei Kawakubo's and Jean Paul Gaultier's work throughout the 1980s (Fig. 9). The juxtaposition with Gaultier's fashion, which represented one of the most vivid examples of the hyper-sexualised female silhouettes of the 1980s – often achieved through body-hugging garments – provides a perfect foil to observe the extent to which Kawakubo's work diverged from this model. The first spread, for instance, juxtaposes a model smiling directly out of the frame, in Kawakubo's ample black hole sweater, lace-up flats and opaque tights, with a Gaultier look from the same year in which the model Cindy Crawford, in pronounced eye make-up, her full lips seductively parted, wears a tight-fitting short grey dress and heels.

Moreover, through object-based research of works by Rei Kawakubo in museum collections I found a precedent for the pregnant silhouette explored in her spring/summer 1997 collection in one of her previous collections.

Fig. 9 Fashion spread juxtaposing Jean Paul Gaultier' and Rei Kawakubo's work, *Six*, no. 2, 1982

For spring/summer 1996, she created a number of striped dresses cut so that the striped fabric took a sharp turn at two darts at the height of the waist, so much so that when worn, the stripes would go from vertical to horizontal. This could be styled to leave an abundant amount of fabric in front of the belly in the guise of a pouch, thus creating the suggestion of pregnancy, this time achieved exclusively by ingenious pattern-cutting. The theme of asymmetry was introduced in some of Kawakubo's earliest work, as is the case with a 1976 shirt whose width is in excess of its length; the neck is placed at the side as opposed to the centre of the shirt. Later on, a number of jackets from her autumn/winter collections for both 1982–83 and 1983–84 were rendered asymmetrical and given the impression of being misbuttoned through complex pattern-cutting techniques. In this period, the theme of asymmetry and mismatching was also being explored by Vivienne Westwood in London, particularly in her Pirate collection from 1981.

Kawakubo's interest in the grotesque, her explorations of different standards of beauty and her rejection of fashion conventions is perhaps most evident in her entrusting the American artist Cindy Sherman to create images accompanying her spring/summer 1994 and autumn/winter 1994–95 collections at a time when the artist was explicitly exploring grotesque imagery. As curator Eva Respini points out, 'Sherman's early fashion work marks the beginning of her exploration of the ugly, macabre and grotesque and a trajectory of the physical disintegration of the body'.[12] Thus, Sherman's work appears an obvious match for the experimental fashion of the period and its exploration of fashion's polished façade. It has been argued that the artist's work was precipitated by feminism and the AIDS crisis;[13] the same can be said of the period's experimental fashion.

The majority of Sherman's photographs for the Comme campaigns were, like the rest of her work, self-portraits or, more accurately, disguises for the self. They employed the use of masks and/or prosthetic make-up to visibly age Sherman's face and render the artist unrecognisable (Fig. 10). In one of the portraits, Sherman wears a striped coat and a small ruffled collar which, together with a gold ribbon tied around her flowing long hair, are reminiscent of Renaissance fair attire. However, the character depicted contradicts the associations of the attire: she is partially balding, her remaining hair is grey and her wrinkled face is frozen in a disturbing grin, which renders her closer to a character in a horror film than a young woman in a Renaissance re-enactment or a fashion model. Another image, the most gruesome of those Sherman produced for the campaign, is a clearly grotesque photograph where the bodily borders are open and porous. It shows a mannequin whose gender is left ambiguous and whose chest is open, containing the head of a doll. The mannequin's lipstick is smeared and reminiscent of blood, thus referring to cannibalism. Incongruously, the mannequin is wearing a pristine Comme des Garçons silk skirt and trousers (Fig. 11).

The Japanese designer's exploration of gender conventions, which characterised her 1997 'Body Meets Dress' collection, had been present throughout her work since the 1980s and was very explicit in her spring/summer 1995 collection titled 'Transcending Gender'. The image accompanying this collection was a portrayal of Claude Cahun, a controversial early twentieth-century artist and writer whose work constituted an early exploration and rebuff of gender norms. A series of self-portraits depicting an androgynous Cahun in formal menswear attire was displayed at the Commes Aoyama store in Tokyo alongside the collection, which they had obviously inspired. 'Transcending Gender' comprised classic menswear staples combined with clearly feminine elements. An apron was paired with a man's suit, organza was paired with pinstripes, while ruffles were added to an otherwise austere suit jacket.

Fig. 10 Cindy Sherman, *Untitled 296*, created for Comme des Garçons advertising campaign, autumn/winter 1994–95, courtesy of Metro Pictures and the artist

Thus, the 'Body Meets Dress' collection was very much in keeping with Kawakubo's oeuvre and with the work she produced throughout the 1980s and 1990s. Still, it is ironic (and certainly hard to imagine as not at all deliberate) that, when padding reigned sovereign in the 1980s, Kawakubo's

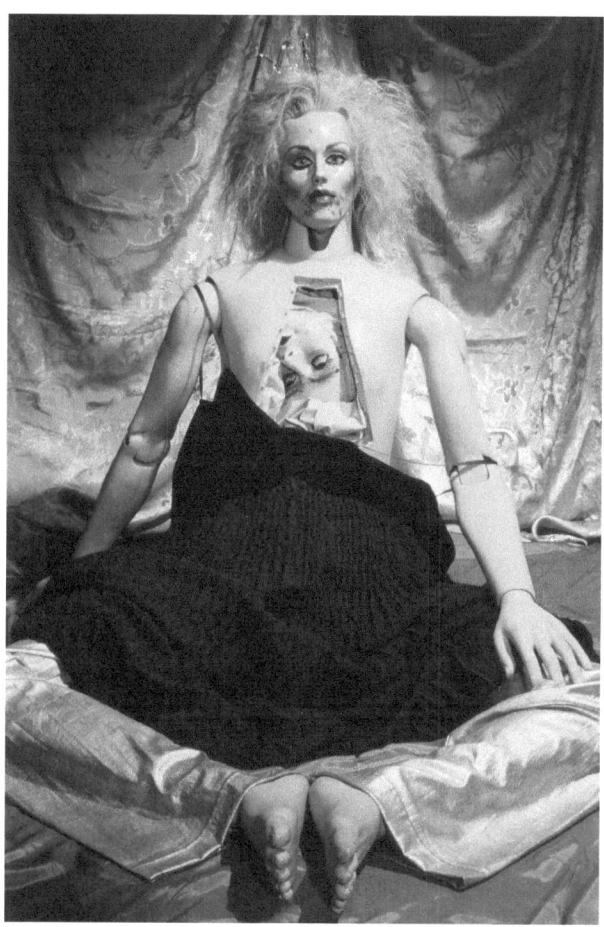

Fig. 11 Cindy Sherman, *Untitled 302*, created for Comme des Garçons advertising campaign, autumn/winter 1994–95, courtesy of Metro Pictures and the artist

work was very much characterised by a sparse and subtle use of it – yet she made padding a centrepiece of her iconic 1990s collection.[14] It is in light of Kawakubo's resistance in the 1980s to the use of padding for the creation of a masculinised female silhouette that her 1997 collection, with its unorthodox use of pads, can be read as an ironic revisiting and a subversion of 1980s fashion language. Ultimately, as Rebecca Arnold writes, Kawakubo 'want[s] to explode the arguments surrounding the size of the flesh'. Along with a number of visual artists, she

> attempt[s] to use plastic surgery's message that the limits of our bodies are no longer fixed in a liberating way, and use[s] their work to push out into negative space, to embrace diversity rather than the homogeneity of the flesh.[15]

This comment is particularly significant, as it starts to address a certain 'ethical' viewpoint that can be seen as intrinsic to the work of Kawakubo. In fact, if one understands the pod-like bodies of her 'Dress Becomes Body' collection as grotesque in the Bakhtinian sense, insofar as they represent and make visible the spaces where the bodies exceed their borders and meet other bodies, then one can easily see how these garments offer novel concepts of subjectivities that ultimately are very much in line with Julia Kristeva's notion of the 'subject-in-process'. Kristeva originally theorised her notion of the subject-in-process/on trial in *Revolution in Poetic Language*, which she defines in opposition to the Cartesian unified and stable model of subjectivity as heterogeneous, always becoming and in question.[16] This description is, of course, much in line with Bakhtin's understanding of the grotesque body, as well as his work on dialogism, which he developed in *The Problems of Dostoevsky's Poetics* and *The Dialogical Imagination*. A concept similar to intertextuality, dialogism focuses on the dialogical nature of the utterance and particularly the literary text (above all the novel) as open-ended and deriving its constantly fluctuating meaning from interactions with other utterances and other texts.[17] Dialogism makes indispensable an open-ended and ever-evolving model of subjectivity, which was later developed by Kristeva. The subject in process has, in fact, been read as a synthesis of Lacanian theories of the subject and Bakhtin's writing on the classical and the grotesque body, a synthesis that overcomes the dyad of subject and object.[18] This model of the subject allows for a remapping and reassessment of the self and the relation between self and other: for 'a reconception of identity and difference, without a collapse of processes of signification'.[19] This stands in contrast to Lacan's alienated subject position formed through the mirror stage, which creates an irremediable distance between self and other plagued by misrecognitions.[20]

Particularly as they refer more or less explicitly to the maternal body, Kawakubo's garments allow for a remapping and reassessment of the self and the relation between self and other: for 'a reconception of identity and difference'. According to Kristeva, in fact, the maternal can point to a new ethic, one in which alterity is tolerated and embraced by the subject without a complete collapse of meaning. The philosopher Kelly Oliver argues that for Kristeva, maternity, together with psychoanalysis and poetry, is 'one model for a new ethics, in which relation to the others are founded on the relations to the other within oneself'. Maternity, in fact, poses a model of a subject-in-process, a subject whose boundaries are not sealed (as it indeed contains another within), and thus ultimately represents 'a model of discourse' that, together with psychoanalysis and poetic language, 'admit[s], even embrace[s], the alterity within them'. It allows 'the redrawing of the boundaries of the social' and allows for an embracement of alterity within the self and within society.[21]

Kristeva's understanding of the maternal subject as a model for a subject-in-process that opposes Cartesian models of a sealed and atomised subject has parallels with later scientific writings. The anthropologist of science Emily Martin comes to a similar conclusion as she explores the way in which pregnancy, as a case of boundary transgression, does not fit current immunological models based on the concept of the pure self. By tolerating another within, pregnancy constitutes an immunological 'problem' as it contains both '"self" and the immunologically "other"'.[22] It problematises the immunological metaphors of warfare in which foreign entities are to be expunged for the body and are most often understood as tumorous enemies: 'From an immunological point of view, the foetus is credibly described as a "tumour", that the woman's body should try furiously to attack.'[23] According to Martin, this often translates to the pathologisation of birth processes, a fact that was eerily reflected in the disparaging descriptions of the protuberances of Kawakubo's garments as 'tumours'. Thus, her collection manifests the relation between the pregnant body, the female body and the disabled body – three types of body that deviate from the norm – a construct which, as shown by a number of theorists, is deeply gendered and raced.[24]

Like Martin, I do not equate the potentialities of new models of the subject and self suggested by pregnancy with the overall experience of actual individual pregnant women – an experience that is singular and specific to each situation.[25]

In some ways, fashion itself is complicit with Kristeva's theorisation of a subject-in-process; in its emphasis on constant renewal and flux it underlines the instability of the self and of fixed identities, and corroborates the notion of a subject in a continual state of change, who is always in the process of 'becoming', rather than simply in a state of unadulterated 'being'. As discussions of dress in relation to constructions of gender have highlighted, fashion is central to an understanding of identity as inherently performative and artificial, yet it is ironically just as often enlisted in the attempts to maintain the illusion of a sealed and fully atomised and individualised self.[26]

KAWAKUBO AND MERCE CUNNINGHAM'S *SCENARIO* 1997

Kawakubo, however, clearly aligns herself with fashion's ability to problematise the subject's boundaries, as can perhaps best be observed in the context of the Japanese designer's collaboration with the New York-based choreographer Merce Cunningham, which occurred shortly after the presentation of her spring/summer 1997 collection and allowed the designer to create even more extremely padded costumes and to submit them to a much greater range of motions. The dancers' costumes came with prominently 'enhanced' protruding areas on both the front and back of the torso, particularly the hips and buttocks, which quite literally brought to mind 'the sprouts' and 'bulges' of Bakhtin's grotesque body (Fig. 12).

The performance, titled *Scenario*, premiered in October 1997 at the Brooklyn Academy of Music, where the dancers' movements took place against a stark all-white stage, lit with fluorescent lighting, to the contemplative repetitive music of Takehisa Kosugi, the company's musical director.[27] The dance is roughly made up of three movements punctuated by the change of the pattern and colour of the outer garments from gingham and striped blue and green, to all black and finally all red, while the padding understructure remains the same throughout. The way Kawakubo's garments became activated by the dancers' bodies in motion allowed for the creation of novel and unexpected bodily formations, which at times do refer to the pregnant body. Yet this reference to maternity is more often enacted on the body of male dancers, in a dance that often frustrates an immediate establishment of the performers' sex. This is underscored by the poster for *Scenario*, a close-up of Cunningham wearing one of the costumes protruding in the front, thus giving the impression of pregnancy, while his identity and gender are made ambiguous by cropping his face and most other identifying features while leaving his advanced age visible through his wrinkled feet. Yet the dance also leads into uncharted formations and articulations of body shapes, as

Fig. 12 Merce Cunningham, *Scenario*, BAM, Brooklyn, 1997. Photograph by Dan Rest, courtesy of Louie Fleck at the BAM Hamm Archives

Kawakubo herself notes: 'I was excited by the prospect of the shapes being broken down by movements and new forms being created. When I saw the rehearsal for the first time, I was fascinated by how the shapes changed and came alive.'[28] The alteration of proportions, and of one's relation to one's body and to the body of the other dancers and the subsequent sense of estrangement it creates,[29] was summed up by dancers in Cunningham's company, who described the experience as alternately liberating and unsettling: 'If I were to be asked about it as a dancer, I would say it was more of a liberation when I came onto this incredibly wide stage in the costume.' 'It's bizarre to roll on the floor. Or when you touch someone, you're a foot away from them.'[30] There is, in fact, an element of absurdist humour in Cunningham's dance. This is especially evident in the first movement of the piece, where the dancers are wearing the costumes with oversized gingham and striped patterns, which are not altogether unlike the heavily patterned costumes characteristic of the *commedia dell'arte*, and Harlequin, in particular (Fig. 13).

In the duets, the strength of *Scenario* and of Kawakubo's and Cunningham's exploration of bodily boundaries is at its most evident. In the final section,

Fig. 13 Merce Cunningham, *Scenario*, BAM, Brooklyn, 1997. Photograph by Dan Rest, courtesy of Louie Fleck at the BAM Hamm Archives

immediately after the dancers change from black costumes into red ones, one of the dancers gives a puzzled and curious look at another dancer in the midst of a solo. At times observing, at times following her movements, his reactions seem to suggest a refamiliarisation and a remapping of his own body and of the body of the other. It reaches its climax as the two start dancing together and the male dancer lifts the female dancer into the air, creating unexpected shapes, where a viewer cannot quite tell where one body ends and the other begins. This *pas de deux* reverberates as other dancers enter the stage and dance in couple 'formations'.[31] Another pivotal moment within the 45-minute piece occurs roughly half-way through, when a female dancer enters the stage upheld by other dancers and fully enwrapped in a cocoon-like red dress, from which only her legs and her head surface. As she is moved about by the other dancers, while she herself remains completely immobile, the processes of birth and bodily transformations are suggested. She resembles a chrysalis about to unravel, an apt metaphor for the notion of a subject that is always in the act of 'becoming'.[32]

KAWAKUBO, CUNNINGHAM AND THE 'UNCANNY MATERNAL'

As the dance progresses, it takes on an increasingly ethereal, ghostly aspect, as the repetitive droning music estranges one from the passage of time. The unfamiliarity of the dancers' movements, further enhanced by Kawakubo's costumes, renders the viewing experience progressively more entrancing, as well as disorienting. Cunningham was, in fact, famous for exploring the range of possibility of human movements. Together with his lifelong collaborator John Cage, he built his pieces based on chance, developing the dancers' movements and their sequences according to a system of 'chance operations'. Cage did the same for the music component of the pieces. Starting in the 1990s, Cunningham began to experiment with the computer software Life Forms, a 3D character animation program, to choreograph his dances. Both methods (the chance system and Life Forms) allowed Cunningham to develop physical movements that did not belong to either the modern or the classical vocabulary, and read as utterly alien and unfamiliar, as they often explore the limits of what the body is able to do. The dancers' movements in Cunningham's work thus appear uncanny and 'grotesque' in their own right, especially when combined with the fact that the music and the choreography for the pieces were developed separately and did not come together until the dress rehearsal. This practice enhances the sense of estrangement and disorientation conveyed by the pieces.[33]

These unfamiliar movements, combined with the stark white stage and the white fluorescent lights, limiting the sense of depth, bring to mind a number of horror and science-fiction films, most significantly Ridley Scott's *Alien* (1979), a film in which births and maternal functions propel the narrative. The dance at times becomes particularly reminiscent of the film's closing scene, which replays in reverse the opening scene (where the characters are awoken): a medium shot of the Sigourney Weaver character asleep in a pod-like structure, wrapped in white sheets and enveloped in a suffused white light.

Scenario, similarly to *Alien*, particularly in its opening and closing shots, communicates a sense of estrangement and of the uncanny that can be read as an articulation of a sense of loss and longing.[34] The way in which the dancers reach for one another, often ineffectually, suggests Freud's relation between the experience of longing, the sense of the uncanny and the maternal body. According to Freud, the uncanny is something that was once familiar 'which has undergone repression and then returned from it'. The maternal body 'fulfils this condition':

> It often happens that neurotic men declare that they feel there is something uncanny about the female genital organs. This *unheimlich* [unfamiliar, uncanny] place, however, is the entrance to the former *Heim* [home] of all human beings, to the place where each one of us lived once upon a time and in the beginning. There is a joking saying 'Love is home-sickness'; and whenever a man dreams of a place or a country and says to himself while he is still dreaming: 'this place is familiar to me, I've been there before', we may interpret the place as being the mother's genitals or her body. In this case too then, the *unheimlich* is what was once *heimisch*, familiar; the prefix 'un' ['un-'] is the token of repression'.[35]

And it is this repressed maternal body that Kawakubo's work in part reclaims for late twentieth-century fashion – this once familiar place – that makes us aware of 'that uncanny strangeness', 'the foreignness within ourselves', a precondition, according to Kristeva, for the acceptance of the 'foreignness' in others.

In *Strangers to Ourselves*, Kristeva reads Freud's writing on the uncanny, and the project of psychoanalysis more generally, as a means to arrive at a new politics and a new ethics, and writes an ode to the discipline stressing its relevance to the society to her contemporary.

> The foreigner is within us. And when we flee from, or struggle against the foreigner, we are fighting our unconscious – that 'improper' facet of our impossible 'own and proper' … Freud brings us the courage to call ourselves disintegrated in order not to integrate foreigners and even less

so to hunt them down, but rather to welcome them to that *uncanny strangeness*, which is as much theirs as it is ours.[36]

In the case of Kawakubo, this foreignness is actual as opposed to exclusively symbolic, a fact that allowed her to more readily access the grotesque canon. The condition of foreignness is not only, as Kristeva points out, a preferential vantage point into an understanding of the integrated subject as illusory but also into the perception of cultural codes as relative and, to some extent, arbitrary. This has been discussed as a prerequisite for the exploration of the grotesque and carnivalesque canon. According to Stam, the film theorist, belonging to two or more cultures translates into a cultural decentring, which allows for the carnivalisation and re-ordering of cultural codes. Discussing the grotesque in the context of Latin American culture, he writes: 'As necessarily bicultural and often tricultural people, Latin American artists and intellectuals inhabit a peculiar realm of irony where words and images are seldom taken at face value, whence the paradigmatic importance of parody and carnivalisation.'[37]

Coming as she did from a drastically different culture to Paris relatively late in life, and working in Japan but showing in France, one can safely argue that Kawakubo is a hybrid subject who acquired a cultural self-consciousness in relation to both her native and adoptive culture, particularly in relation to codes of dress, and the way they relate to bodily ideals and gender conventions. This vantage point translated into her unorthodox combination and carnivalisation of Western and Japanese fashion codes and bodily conventions. It led to the creation of a hybrid transcultural fashion, which fully explored a grotesque canon.[38]

3

PERFORMING PREGNANCY
Leigh Bowery

LEIGH BOWERY'S BACKGROUND

> The grotesque tends to operate as a critique of a dominant ideology which has already set the term, designating what is high and low. It is indeed one of the most powerful ruses of the dominant to pretend that critique can only exist in the language of 'reason', 'pure knowledge' and 'seriousness'. Against this ruse Bakhtin rightly emphasized the logic of the grotesque, of excess, of the lower bodily stratum, of the fair.
> Peter Stallybrass and Allon White, *The Politics and Poetics of Transgression*.[1]

While Kawakubo's 'Body meets Dress' and Godley's 'Bump and Lump' collections and their distorted silhouettes are characterised by a subtle irony, the work of Leigh Bowery, which Kawakubo's and Godley's padded bodies undoubtedly bring to mind, is characterised by an exaggeratedly carnivalesque character.[2] This is partially the outcome of Bowery's different relation to the fashion market: he was predominantly a club figure who inhabited a space at the margin of both fashion and art markets, and who could not be easily assimilated within either, at least in his lifetime.

Leigh Bowery originally trained in fashion design at the Royal Melbourne Institute of Technology in Australia, which he left because he was frustrated by the lack of creative freedom. He moved to London in 1980 and soon started attending various clubs and, under the encouragement of British designer Rachel Auburn, designing clothes and selling them at a stall in Kensington Market. He was an expert pattern-cutter and eventually sold his designs at a few 'avant-garde' fashion boutiques, such as Charivari in New York, and was included by the fashion promoter Susanne Bartsch in presentations of fledging British designers in Tokyo and New York alongside Crolla, Bodymap and Rachel Auburn. At the same time he was creating various looks for his flatmate Trojan to wear outside, as Bowery claims to have been initially embarrassed to don his extravagant looks himself.[3] It was not until 1982 and the creation of his first 'total look', which was also presented as a collection at Camden Palace for London Fashion Week, that he started wearing his own creations more systematically. In 1984 he began designing for the stage, making costumes for the Michael Clark dance company on a regular basis. He eventually won a Bessie (New York Dance and Performance Award) in 1988 for his design. By 1984, he had also become the host of the club night Taboo, for which he designed progressively more extravagant costumes and became the primary wearer and performer of his designs, a fact precipitated by Trojan's sudden death in 1986.[4] It is around this time that he started phasing out producing clothes for stores, partially due to their lack of commercial success.[5] It is also in 1986, as 'his creations become increasingly bound to his physical self', that Bowery started performing in the dancer and choreographer Michael Clark's modern ballet company, wearing his own costumes.[6]

Thus his varied career ranged from fledgling fashion designer to notorious club figure to performance artist – three strands of his practice that remain inextricably intertwined. Their co-existence is punctuated by the fact that Bowery and his clothes were often separately featured in style magazines of the period, at times within the same issue. The 'Surreal' issue of i-D from 1988, for instance, includes Bowery's design worn by a model as part of a fashion spread, while also featuring Bowery himself in connection with his 'costumed' club appearances in the front of the book (Figs. 14 and 15).[7] Throughout his lifetime his work was not, for the most part, circulated within the art market and its institutions, but in 1988 he was asked to install himself as a living spectacle in a week-long show at Anthony d'Offay's Dering Street Gallery in London's West End, and attended a number of Lucian Freud's openings instead of the painter, for whom he famously modelled (Fig. 16).

After Bowery's premature death in 1994, however, the perception of his status changed. Thanks in great part to his surviving collaborators, Bowery is thought of more and more as primarily a performance artist, whose work is routinely included in prominent international shows and whose image remains consecrated in the art-world pantheon via Lucian Freud's famous

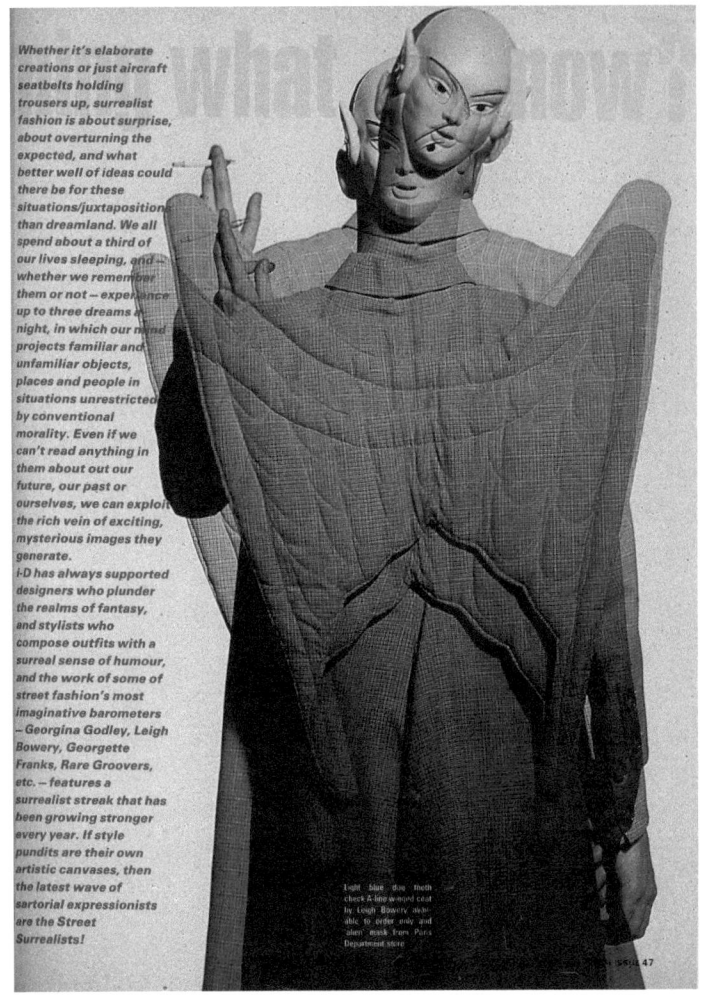

Fig 14 Leigh Bowery designed coat for sale, i.D no. 57, April 1988

portraits. The intent to 'institutionalise' Bowery became obvious in my interview with his widow Nicola Bowery, and from Charles Atlas's filmed documentary about him, The Legend of Leigh Bowery.[8] Both stress his status as a performance artist over his involvement with fashion and club culture.

Partially as a result of his ambiguous position in relation to established disciplines-at least during his lifetime-Bowery was free to unleash the repressed in fashion in carnivalesque, over-the-top self-fashioning within

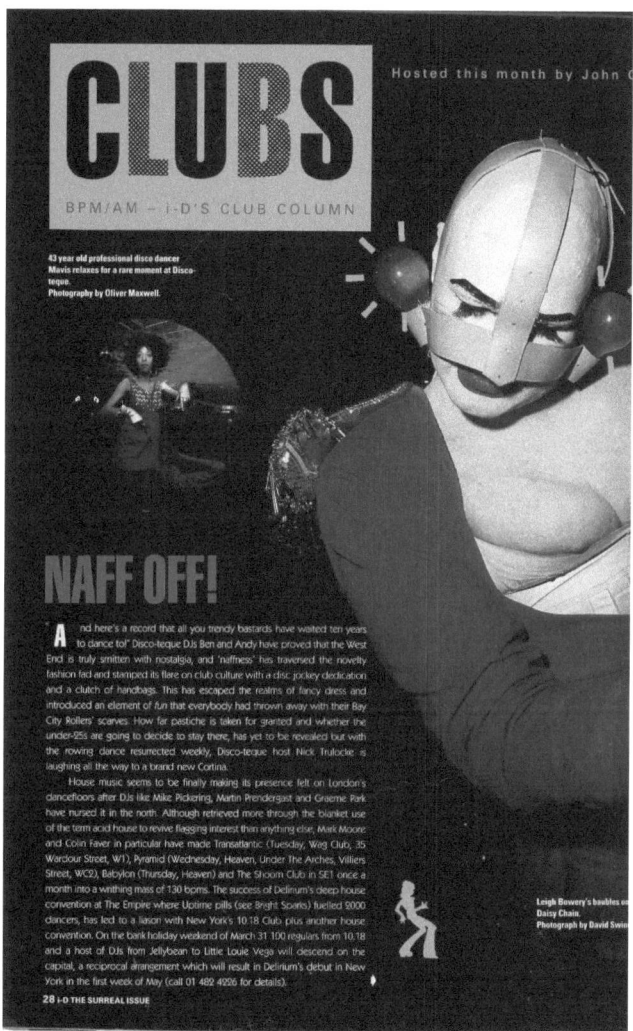

Fig 15 Leigh Bowery at a club in London, *i-D* no. 57, April 1988

the London club and art scenes, and by the 1990s in more scripted performances with his band Minty. Thus he presented his ensembles, which were often worn exclusively by him, in a more humorous and flamboyant way (especially when compared to the gravitas of Kawakubo's 1997 presentation, which took place in the Paris Musée national des Arts d'Afrique et d'Océanie

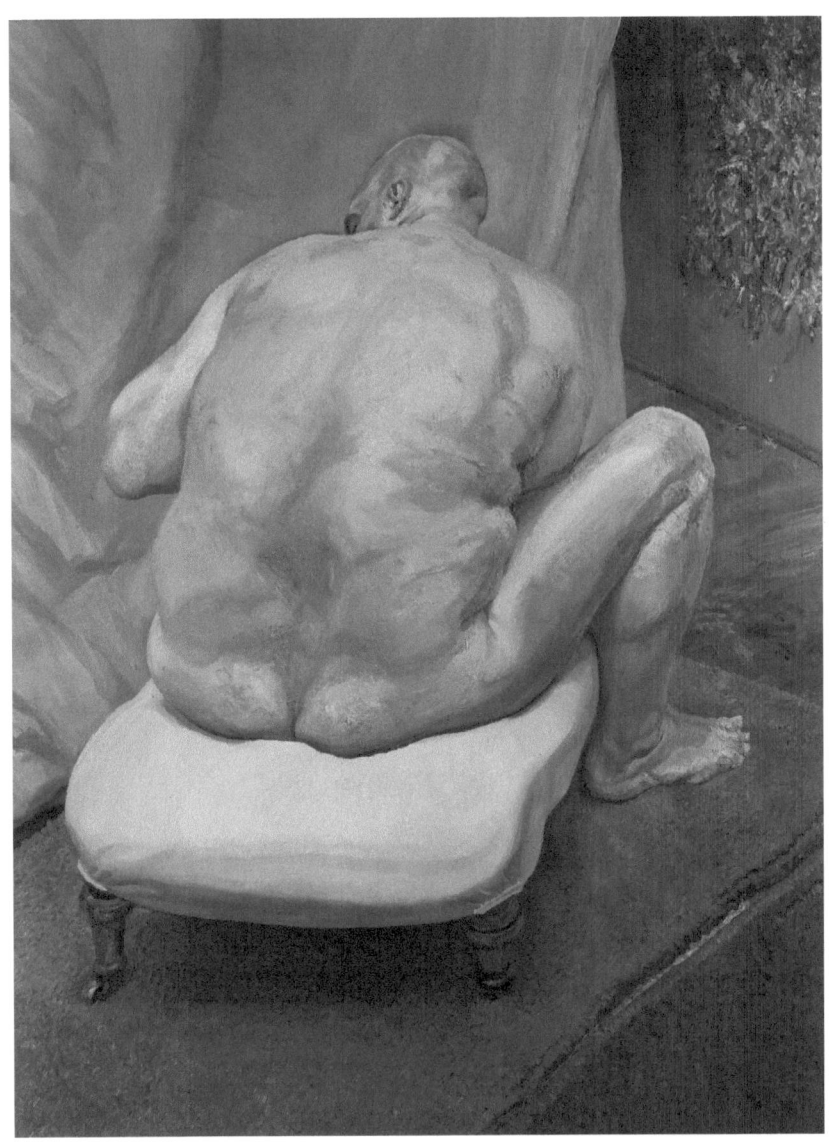

Fig. 16 Lucian Freud, *Naked Man* (painting of Leigh Bowery), back view, 1991–92. Oil on canvas, 72¼ × 54⅛ in. (183.5 × 137.5 cm). Purchase, Lila Acheson Wallace Gift, 1993 (1993.71). © The Metropolitan Museum of Art, Image source: Art Resource, NY

in complete silence). Bowery's 'costumes' and performances, in their excessive and carnivalesque character, are even more in line with a Bakhtinian grotesque, and fully exploit its liberating and subversive potential. In their penchant for humorous and irreverent critiques of social conventions, they conform to Bakhtin's understanding of carnival as the act of bringing down the high to the low domain and ridiculing the existing social order, thus ultimately suggesting a reading of Bowery as a modern-day medieval clown or fool. Upon being asked to mention one ridiculous thing he did, Bowery himself concluded: 'Just my life is a bit of a joke, you know, coming to London, putting on wacky clothes and dressing about.'[9] This statement falls very much in line with Bakhtin's description of clowns and fools as

> the constant accredited representatives of the carnival spirit in everyday life out of carnival season. [...] [T]hey were not actors playing their parts on stage [...], but remained fools and clowns always and wherever they made their appearance. As such they represented a certain form of life, which was real and ideal at the same time. They stood on the borderline between life and art, in a peculiar midzone as it were.[10]

PREGNANT LOOKS

One of these clowns' and fools' main functions, according to Bakhtin, was 'to degrade' meaning 'to concern oneself with the lower stratum of the body, the life of the belly and the reproductive organs; it therefore relates to acts of defecation, and copulation, conception, pregnancy and birth'.[11] Consequently, it is not surprising that Bowery's extreme fashions provide a more explicit and confrontational instance of the pregnant body than Kawakubo's and Godley's. These references to the maternal body were of course all the more 'grotesque' as they were enacted on Bowery's male body. Throughout his career, his clothes overemphasised the belly, frequently rendering it extremely pronounced through the use of padding. In an interview included in Charles Atlas's film *The Legend of Leigh Bowery*, Bowery stated that 'the only modern [part] left to exaggerate is the belly'.[12] This prescription counteracted the common understanding of the belly as a region to be suppressed.

According to his wife, Nicola Bowery, he was initially ashamed of his size, which did not conform to the rather well toned and fit look popular at the time. This look was best epitomised by the Calvin Klein underwear advertisements photographed first by Bruce Weber and later by Herb Ritts.

The chiselled body of the Olympian pole vaulter Tom Hintnaus, immortalised by Bruce Weber in the 1982 campaign, embodied the healthy, beautiful and powerful male body and could be seen as a male counterpart to female body builder Lisa Lyon. In its wholesome classical beauty, it presented an antidote to the threat represented by AIDS and its porous and sick bodies. As Rebecca Arnold argues about 1980s fashion more generally, Weber's portrayals of male beauty were 'a protective shield a perfected exterior, which acted as a fetish to ward off anxieties surrounding death and disease'.[13] This portrayal of fit, sealed male bodies was further explored by Herb Ritts, who photographed Calvin Klein campaigns in the early 1990s, and later died of complications from AIDS.

'When he first came to London, he was quite conscious of his weight and he dieted at some point as well', she said, but he eventually started to embrace his body and use it strategically as a tool for his costumes:

> It started with his bum. In the very early 1980s he made a lot of jackets which exposed the bottom with knickers or frilly knickers. And then he started creating breasts of a kind by squeezing his belly up to create bosoms. He wasn't like every other drag queen – he didn't want to be like a woman. He just liked to emphasize certain parts of his body and he was a big bloke and he did have a belly. So as to some of the things he wore later on ... well that was the shape of his belly, and he would emphasize it even more through his costumes.

Nicola added that Bowery reached a full appreciation of his body through posing for Lucian Freud:

> I think it was probably after he started sitting for Lucian Freud and Lucian was so into his body and thought it was so fantastic. They had this mutual thing going on: they both loved his body and so Leigh started to use more of it in his costumes.[14]

Indeed, Lucian Freud's monumental nudes, which remain the best known representations of Bowery's body, are also the ones which best convey his 'extra-ordinary' size. Freud's paintings point to the fact that Bowery was already grotesque in his size, especially if one understands the relationship between the prescribed body type ('the body beautiful', among whose central attributes is leanness) and the body that deviates from those prescriptions as 'social relationships of norms and deviations, and therefore political relationships aimed at naturalising in the body the norms of those with the most power in social formation'. Within these relations 'being defiantly fat can, therefore, be an offensive and resisting statement, a bodily blasphemy'.[15] A similar interest in 'defiant' flesh is, of course, explored by Kawakubo's and Godley's collection, albeit through clothes which can ultimately be put on and taken off at will and, in the case of Kawakubo's, first shown on conventional fashion models.

Bowery's efforts to further increase his already notable size through padding, building up the body and elevating his shoes to add to his height, further characterise him as a figure out of bounds through his assimilation to the category of the gigantic. As the theorist Susan Stewart discusses, the gigantic, in its defiance of the classical properties of proportions, symmetry and containment, has been historically aligned with the grotesque: 'The giant, from Leviathan to the sideshow freak, is a mixed category; a violator of boundary and rule; an overabundance of the natural and hence an affront to cultural systems.'[16]

Bowery's interest in questioning categories of normalcy dovetails with his interest in exploring the boundaries and limits of the body and the embarrassment produced by bodily functions. In an interview with Richard Torry and Donald Urquhart, he explained how he seeks out embarrassment:

> I also like doing things that embarrass people. The other things that I find that I keep coming back again and again are the things that I really like because they are hard for me; they are painful but they are really rewarding as well. I suppose I figured that out when I was living with my parents and the things from that time that really stayed with me were the difficult things, the embarrassing things, the cruel things and all. So they are the things I like. But I am not saying that I am a masochist or anything ... obviously there is pain and pleasure in all of the things I do. In the work that I do there is a tension between a really light-hearted side and also a very dark sort of side and maybe something glamorous, but maybe also something horrifyingly twisted so there is sort of a tension between the two things.[17]

Because of the intensely physical nature of Bowery's work, this sense of embarrassment, often coupled with an exploration of the boundaries of the body and its vulnerability, is somatically transferred from the performer to the audience. A number of his costumes and performances are highly uncomfortable both to watch and to execute. The sensations they evoke in the viewer veer between the unsettling and the comic, between cringing and laughter. Many of his looks involved taping up part of his body, a technique that provoked varying levels of pain and discomfort. For a number of his looks from 1990, he gaffer-taped his genitalia back and glued a wig onto them to give the impression of female genitalia, while some of the aforementioned looks involved pushing and taping up his belly to create the impression of bosoms. Additionally, a number of his performances involved the spillage of bodily fluid, which underscored the fluid boundaries of the body and its vulnerabilities. In one of his earlier performances he took part in a catwalk show right after giving himself an enema, so as to be able to spurt liquid from his anus onto the audience; in a later performance in a Tokyo's department store, he self-induced vomit, to the consternation of the audience.[18] In a 1994 performance in Fort Asperen in the Netherlands – perhaps the most difficult of Bowery's performances to watch – he is seen hanging upside down wearing only black platform shoes and black stockings, with clothes pegs clipped to his genitals, and he is pushed towards a glass pane which shattered on impact, resulting in copious bleeding.

Among Bowery's most explicit references to the pregnant body is one of his most iconic looks, which Fergus Greer, Bowery's 'official' photographer, identifies as Look 9 (July 1989). Bowery is dressed in what could be regarded as feminine clothes, though his ensembles are often hard to reduce to either gender (Fig. 17). He is, in fact, wearing a skirt, though his face is invisible, replaced by an organza pouffe. And he sports a very sizable protuberance in the front of his costume (achieved by a sculpted piece of foam), whose reference to a pregnant body is hard to miss.[19] This costume was originally inspired by a book on Transformer robots – the toy robots known for their potential to *shapeshift* – a point that corroborates his interest in the possible mutations and transformations of the human body. In this spirit of transformation, he later used this same costume to create two new looks: he employed it as an understructure for two garments of stretchy material – one made of white Lycra and the other of green velour – which covered his entire body, suggesting a sort of pregnant Gumby look (Look 32/33, 1992).[20] This allusion to the pregnant body is, perhaps, even more explicit in Look 10 (July 1989), where Bowery is clothed in a white stretchy Lycra fabric, which tightly envelopes his monumental body (Fig. 18). The ensemble is completed by a white top that stops right below the breast area and is characterised by puffed oversized shoulders and padded breasts. The high-waisted jacket, combined with the stretchiness of the material and with Bowery's prominent belly, creates the illusion of pregnancy, which is accentuated by his posturing, as it is most evident in the second of Greer's Look

10 photos, where he is in profile, his body slouching forward and with a hand on his sizable belly, a common pose in the iconography of pregnancy.[21]

BIRTH PERFORMANCES

These references to the pregnant body culminated in his performances with Minty, the most prominent one being the band's 1993 performance at Wigstock, New York's annual dragfest in Tompkins Square Park, for which Bowery devised a complex costume allowing him to conceal a body (that of his wife, Nicola Bowery) as an oversized belly, through the use of a system of harnesses and tights (Fig. 19) The costume was completed by a huge fake foam bosom to counteract the size of the 'enhanced' belly, a proper velvet skirt suit, and a face mask made out of a stocking with exaggerated painted-on facial features.[22]

The hidden body of Nicola was unveiled when, in the middle of the performance, Bowery staged a 'bona fide' birthing scene, which was followed by Bowery introducing her as 'the first Wigstock baby', a pun on the more 'conventional' births which took place at Woodstock in 1969. In a profile he wrote for the *New Yorker*, Hilton Als describes the scene in vivid detail: 'Facing the audience, he lay back on the table, screaming and moaning, as if he were going into labour. He then parted his legs, and a human figure began to emerge from between them – a nude women, slathered in "blood".'[23] (Fig. 20). Thus Bowery's birthing performance, in its graphic and threatening quality, externalises and renders visible the problematic Western understanding of the maternal body and, by extension, the female body – with its unstable borders, and generative potential – as 'grotesque' and in some way monstrous. That Bowery was unveiling a side of womanhood that is most often suppressed is further emphasised by Als's insightful comment that it was certainly not the side of womanhood that drag cultures explores: 'This was not the aspect of womanhood that the Wigstock audience was seeking to emulate.'[24]

Prior to the Wigstock performance, Bowery had staged a number of 'birth-scenes' in clubs around Britain, the first of which took place at the popular monthly nightclub event Kinky Gerlinky and was closely based on a scene in John Waters' *Female Trouble*, where Divine's character, Dawn Davenport (who, in her rollers, reads like a caricature of a distressed 1950s housewife) gives birth to her daughter Taffy. Bowery recreated Divine's costume piece by piece from the striped dress, whose pattern recalls the stripes and the gingham motif of Kawakubo's 1997 collection, down to the sunglasses and headscarf,

Fig. 17 Leigh Bowery, Look 9, July 1989, photograph by Fergus Greer, courtesy of the artist

and re-enacted scenes from the film.[25] Divine, who exercised a great fascination for Bowery, represents another 'grotesque' take on femininity, which could be seen in its disturbing elements as a challenge to the more traditional and conventionally feminine beauty often enacted within drag culture. Moreover, Divine's performance represented another instance of a man giving birth, a common trope within the carnival tradition. The *commedia dell' arte* is rife with examples of men, and particularly fat men, giving birth. One clear instance, which is brought up by Roger Malbert in his discussion

Fig. 18 Leigh Bowery, Look 10, July 1989, photograph by Fergus Greer, courtesy of the artist

of Bowery and grotesque humour in contemporary art,[26] is the eighteenth-century play *The Marvellous Malady of Harlequin*, in which Harlequin gives birth to three boys.

Another element linking Bowery and Divine is their relation to 'deliberate' camp.[27] If one understands camp according to Susan Sontag's definition of the concept as being characterised by 'its love for the unnatural: of artifice and exaggeration' then one can see how both Divine and Bowery undoubtedly partake of its power. Sontag adds:

Fig. 19 Leigh and Nicola Bowery, Look 37, June 1994, photograph by Fergus Greer, courtesy of the artist

camp sees everything in quotation marks ... It's not a lamp, but a 'lamp'; not a woman, but a 'woman'. To perceive camp in objects and persons is to understand Being-as-Playing-a-Role. It is the farthest extension in sensibility, of the metaphor of life as theatre.[28]

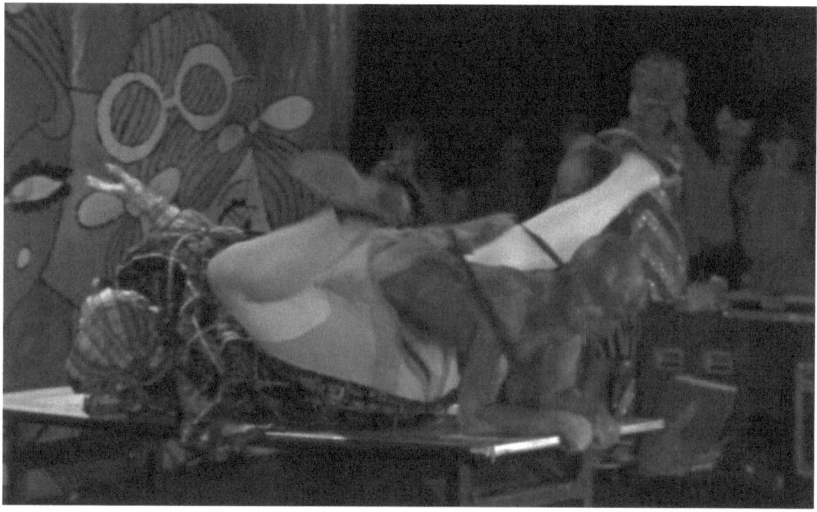

Fig. 20 Leigh and Nicola Bowery, birth performance with Minty, Wigstock, New York, 1993, © *Wigstock: The Movie*

Much like the Bakhtinian carnivalesque, camp is shaped by its opposition to seriousness: 'The whole point of camp is to dethrone the serious. Camp is playful, anti-serious. More precisely, camp involves a new more complex relation to 'the serious'. One can be serious about the frivolous, frivolous about the serious.'[29] Bowery's often hyperbolic artificiality, combined with his questioning the dividing line between life and art, as well as an opposition to a 'common sense' understanding of what constitutes the serious aspect of life, places him squarely within its realm.

This notion of camp, particularly in its relation to drag, dovetails with an understanding of gender, and identity more generally, as inherently performative. This relation is made evident in the extensive discussion of camp in gender studies and queer theory.[30] As the film scholar Caryl Flinn spells out:

> camp troubles prevailing assumptions about body and gender identity. For what body camp does is to take the signs of human identity and place them into a performative situation, distancing them from their 'original' sites or indeed the notion of an original or natural condition at all, in much the same way that Butler ... and others have argued about drag and

gender identity ... Body camp exaggerates gender codes, making them obvious, grotesque.[31]

However, much like drag, camp occupies a similar ambiguous position because it retains the potential to denaturalise and/or reinforce gender roles, particularly in relation to constructions of femininity.[32] Yet not all camp is created equal and I would argue that Bowery, by going beyond drag, successfully exploits camp's subversive potential.

Bowery problematises traditional understandings of womanhood, and challenges 'the masquerade of femininity' epitomised by drag culture which, as Judith Butler points out, in the context of her discussion of Jennie Livingston's 1990 documentary *Paris Is Burning*, can actually reinvest 'the gender ideals' as opposed to displacing them. 'It reidealizes them – reconsolidates their hegemonic status.'[33] However, one can also argue (as Fiske does and Butler herself has done) that

> making norms spectacular rather than naturalizing them is a potentially subversive semiotic practice: it is the naturalized and thus invisible norms that perform their ideological and disciplinary work most effectively. By making itself invisible and natural, discourse makes itself believable: its credibility is weakened to the extent that its discursivity is foregrounded.[34]

In addition, Bowery explodes the gynophobic discourse surrounding women and the maternal function. His work can be read as probing and disrupting the equivalence between a certain traditional understanding of femininity, womanhood and maternity (a problematisation which is also emphasised in Divine's character in *Female Trouble*). Returning to Kristeva's writing on the maternal function, particularly as it relates to the abject, Bowery's work can be seen as proposing, through the lens of grotesque humour, novel relations among gender, maternity and femininity. It can be read as questioning the unproblematic equivalence of women and the maternal and supporting the notion that 'the maternal operates as a function that, in principle, can be performed by both men and women'.[35] This is a necessary understanding, according to Kristeva, in order to go 'beyond categories that have traditionally been used to limit us'.[36] As Kelly Oliver explains, Kristeva, particularly in her later writing, started to unpack this equivalence between women and the maternal, and saw the lack of distinction between the two as one of the main problems at the basis of women's oppression. According to her theories, the child must 'abject' the mother in order to become a fully formed subject, but if a culture were to be successful in making a distinction between the maternal function and womanhood, it would ultimately become apparent that the child needs only abject 'the maternal container'. Whereas in a culture which does not distinguish between motherhood and the feminine, 'women themselves become abjected within society'.[37]

Bowery ultimately complicated gender binaries even further. His performances conflate markers of differences as his large pregnant body is further queered through the birthing of a fully-grown woman, his wife. His birth performances reflected his own gender instability, which rendered him *a priori* a grotesque figure. As previously discussed in relation to his club attire, in his endless body formations and transformations he would hide his genitals and cover the area with a wig, thus giving the illusion of female genitals, as well as squeezing his belly to function like breasts. This instability would carry over into his more 'private' life. His daywear, which usually consisted of a wig, various suits and, at times, stiletto shoes worn inside men's boots (a fact that rendered his instability rather literal) was, in some ways, more unsettling than the flamboyant get-up he wore in clubs, as it conveyed a relatively unintentional 'ambiguity' and a quiet, and perhaps melancholic, alterity. Moreover, despite being openly gay, he was married to and cohabited with a woman, his assistant Nicola Bowery, an aspect of his life that seems, despite the extremity of his performances, to be the one to attract the greater puzzlement and questioning. Thus, both his life and art, in their repetitions of various subversions of gender norms, seem to take aim at the notion of naturalised gender identity.

The fact that he referred to his wedding as a 'performance', further shows how his theatricalisation of gender norms was a conscious attempt at denaturalising them. However, perhaps ironically, the marriage also placed Nicola Bowery in a rather traditional position after Leigh Bowery's death. It entrusted her with a privileged legal position vis-à-vis his legacy and estate, a fact that does not seem fully to account for the range and scope of Bowery's network of collaborators. This shows the potential for co-option of an act that was intended as subversive or, as Butler discusses, its potential to change in time as the context changes. In discussing the difficulty in 'delivering judgments' on what constitutes a subversive act, she writes:

> Not only do I believe that such judgments cannot be made out of context, but that they cannot be made in ways that endure through time

('contexts' are themselves posited unities that undergo temporal change and expose their essential disunity).[38]

Ultimately, if one agrees with Butler that 'gender is what is put on, invariably, under constraint, daily and incessantly, with anxiety and pleasure',[39] then Bowery 'dramatises' these repeated acts of gender constructions. However, instead of naturalising them, he not only highlights their artificiality, like a drag queen would, but constantly plays with and up-ends them. As a result, he follows Butler's invitation 'to expand the cultural field bodily through subversive performances of various kinds'.[40]

Bowery precipitates a blurring between performance and the performative, between art and life, as he remained in character — albeit a rather different and often evolving character — during both his stage performance and club appearances, as well as within his highly artificial 'daywear self', whose constant ambiguity and alterity put on in repeated daily acts of both dress, speech and mannerism (he mimicked Lucian Freud's Queen's English and upper-class mannerism) falls more closely, in its repetitive quotidian nature, under Butler's definition of the performative. Bowery up-ends and interjects into the daily 'punitive' and 'normative' act of gender repetition, by continuously underlining the performative aspect of daily life and denaturalising it, as well as by creating over-the-top performances in a range of more or less obviously theatrical settings.

Elizabeth Wilson writes of Bowery, whom she considers in the context of the New Romantics and defines as 'the culture's high priest', and his contemporaries:

> [they] costumed their (then) poverty in costumes that defied nature and biology to create a wholly artificial self. Bowery, a massive Australian, went far beyond gender, let alone mere drag, to transform his being into a parody of glamour that astonished with its effrontery.[41]

This effrontery ultimately became intolerable even within the relatively permissive environment of London nightlife. His last birth performance, which took place on 24 November 1994 at the Freedom Cafe in Soho, shortly before he died of complications from AIDS, unexpectedly caused the club to be shut down by Westminster Council on the basis of a rather arcane and seldom enacted law that prohibited the display of nudity in clubs. This last performance was perhaps among the most graphic, as during the performance Bowery disrobed to change his costume; in line with previous performances, he fed his 'newborn' wife what appears to be his own urine, although Nicola Bowery has since explained that it was not.[42] Thus, Bowery's interest in the grotesque and the abject can be read not only as a potential challenge to drag-representation of femininity and to gynophobic discourses surrounding maternity but, in its insistence on the 'improper exchange' of bodily fluids such as blood, urine and faeces, it also points to the lingering anxiety surrounding bodily borders, particularly those of gay men, that characterised the period. Bowery's birth performances actualises the continuum between discourses of the maternal body – characterised by 'mixing of kinds' and leakages – as an immunological problem, and the way the AIDS crisis reinforced immunological theories promoting the need for a pure and uncontaminated self. This model, which, to use Martin's terms, is both 'gendered and raced', is not only inimical to the maternal body and the female body more generally, but also to the body of gay man, who were initially closely bound to the immunological deficiencies of HIV.[43]

Ultimately, if one understands the body in Foucauldian terms as the place 'where power-bearing definitions of social and sexual normality are, literally, embodied',[44] then the prohibition on continuing his residency at the Freedom Café can be read as an attempt to discipline and punish a body – that of Bowery and, to some extent, of his consort – which deviated from the accepted social and cultural norms. It is an instance that perfectly illustrates the workings of the body politic; the way in which the body, as the place 'where the social is most convincingly represented as the individual and where politics can best disguise itself as human nature', becomes the site of an intense power struggle.[45] As Foucault writes and Bowery's practice makes evident:

> Mastery and awareness of one's own body can be acquired only through the effect of an investment of power in the body: gymnastics, exercises, muscle-building, nudism, glorification of the body beautiful. All of this belongs to the pathway leading to the desire of one's own body by way of the insistent, persistent, meticulous work of power on the bodies of children or soldiers, the healthy bodies. But once power produces this effect, there inevitably emerge the responding claims and affirmations, those of one's own body against power, of health against the economic system, of pleasure against the moral norms of sexuality, marriage, decency … Power, after investing itself in the body, finds itself exposed to a counter-attack in the same body.[46]

BOWERY AND 1980S FASHION

What can be easily missed in the midst of Bowery's extreme fashion is that his ensembles are very much aware of fashion trends – even if at a first look they appear different from what constitutes fashionable garments – and are undoubtedly much in debt to 1980s fashion. Bowery, not constrained to create clothes that appealed to anyone other than himself (at least from a point of view of wanting to wear them), renders an even more extreme and parodic version of 1980s fashion. (His lack of concern for the wearability of his pieces is what might have ultimately caused his inability to sustain sufficient sales at the beginning of his career.) Through exaggeration, his work estranges elements of that period's fashion to unveil their absurdity. His use of textiles, for example, is certainly indebted to the 1980s. Look 10, like much of his other costumes, uses Lycra, a quintessential 1980s material, and the majority of his outfits are characterised by vivid colours and extremely patterned textiles. This was the case even with his relatively more toned-down daytime attire. Asked to explain what he was wearing during an interview, he declared it to be 'casual daywear' and added how 'it's slightly mocking the fashions that are around at the moment'.[47] The extreme make-up of his looks, which became progressively heavier and more outlandish, is unmistakably of that period, and so is his generous use of padding, first in his early 1980s pieces to enhance the shoulders, and then other parts of the body. As Als writes: 'Bowery [in the early 1980s] wore his own version of the 'power suit': jackets with ultra-padded shoulders and with pockets that went past the hem of the jacket, parodying excess.' Thus, much like Godley (whose career trajectory overlapped with him) and Kawakubo (whose did not) Bowery's work interjects into the cultural politics of the period, as articulated through fashion, particularly feminist readings of the body, the increasing yet problematic visibility of queer bodies and the economic excesses of the 1980s.[48] From then on, if one were to trace Bowery looks, one would find the clear trajectory of an artist/designer who worked with the signs and conventions of 1980s fashion yet subverted and re-interpreted them, oftentimes bringing them to their outmost limit – no small feat considering the inherent excessiveness of the decade's fashions.

The work of Georgina Godley, Rei Kawakubo and Leigh Bowery was permeated by references to the maternal body in all of its potential for growth and ruptures. The maternal body, however marginally, resurfaced during the 1980s and 1990s, in what can be read as a textbook instance of a return to the repressed. The work of Leigh Bowery, Georgina Godley and Rei Kawakubo not only turns the semiotics of 1980s fashion on its head, but sets out to unleash what is repressed within Western fashion: the maternal body, which, within modern Western thought, is inextricably bound with the monstrous and the grotesque. Thus, if one agrees with Norbert Elias's understanding of fashion as 'part of the civilizing process'[49] enlisted in the promotion of a disciplined, controlled or (to use Bakhtinian words) 'contained self', then in the late twentieth century, the regulatory system themselves (as Kawakubo, Godley and Bowery's work makes evident) spilled over into the grotesque and revealed those aspects of contemporary life that they are supposed to help control. The repressed, once again, returned through the very systems that were meant to regulate it.

4

DECONSTRUCTION AND THE GROTESQUE
Martin Margiela

A less obvious expression of the grotesque and carnivalesque in experimental fashion is 'deconstruction' fashion, and particularly the work of Martin Margiela, the designer for whom the term was coined. Through a rereading of 'deconstruction' fashion's early journalistic reception, as well as through a close study of garments and accessories, this chapter recovers the grotesque element of the fashion that has been identified under this rubric, and reads it in relation to humour, particularly the work that Martin Margiela produced in his first decade in business, which roughly overlaps with the 1990s. During this period, Margiela's work, while critically well regarded and sold internationally through a number of specialised stores, was not as widely distributed as in later years. After Diesel's holding company OTB acquired a majority stake in Margiela in 2002, followed by the retirement of its founding designer in 2008, the Margiela brand become much more widely distributed and more accessible in terms of its designs. In line with multinational acquisition, a diffusion brand MM6 was launched, self-standing stores carrying the brand were opened globally and eventually eyewear, fragrances and even hotels were opened under the brand name, thus fully refashioning Margiela into a lifestyle company.[1]

However, at the height of its experimental drive, the Belgian designer Margiela, in a number of his collections and presentations – as is the case with Kawakubo, Godley and Bowery – explores a grotesque, non-normative body that stands in contrast to the classical body of fashion. His clothes diverge from 'normal' sizing and explore asymmetry and unorthodox shapes and proportions, while his presentations refer to the maternal and

DECONSTRUCTION AND THE GROTESQUE: MARTIN MARGIELA

Fig. 21 Martin Margiela, autumn/winter 1989–90, *Details*, September 1989

suggest an understanding of subjectivity as 'in process', both by referring to processes of births and growths and, more explicitly, by incorporating a visibly pregnant woman.

JOURNALISTIC RECEPTION

Against commonly held beliefs that tie the term 'deconstruction' in fashion to Japanese designs from the early 1980s, the term was first used in the English language by Bill Cunningham to refer to fashion, in an article he published in *Details* of September 1989 to describe Martin Margiela's

At his Paris show, Martin Margiela's arsenal of rebellious imagination exploded amidst the rubble and graffiti-marked walls of a demolition site in a third-world district. Enthusiastic neighborhood children, fascinated by the invasion and the exotic models in various states of deconstructivist style, became part of the show.

Fig. 22 Martin Margiela, spring/summer 1990, *Details*, March 1990

autumn/winter 1989–90 collection, which was shown in Paris in March 1989 (Fig. 22). Only retrospectively was the word used to refer to Japanese designers of the 1980s. Cunningham uses the term in its literal sense of undoing, taking apart a garment at times in a rather violent fashion:

> Martin Margiela, formerly a Gaultier assistant, in this, his second collection on his own, provided quite a different vision of fashion for the 1990s: a beatnik, Existentialist revival ... The construction of the clothes suggests a deconstructivist movement, where the structure of the design appears under attack, displacing seams, tormenting the surface with incisions. All suggest a fashion of elegant decay.[2]

DECONSTRUCTION AND THE GROTESQUE: MARTIN MARGIELA

The term, as Cunningham remarked, 'stuck' and became increasingly used within fashion journalism from the early 1990s onwards, chiefly to describe the work of the Belgian Paris-based designer Martin Margiela, for which it was coined, and to a lesser extent that of some of his contemporaries. These included other Belgian designers, particularly Ann Demeulemeester and Dries Van Noten and (also retroactively) the Japanese designers Rei Kawakubo and Yohji Yamamoto.[3] In the early journalistic reception, the term came to signify a certain rejection of luxury: 'a backlash against established 1980s excess ... an asbestos suit against the bonfire of the vanities'.[4] In their description of 1990s 'deconstruction' fashion, critics detected anger and a *tout-court* rejection of the fashion of the previous decade. They also read it as, to some extent, mediating the new economic conditions resulting from the recession of the early 1990s.[5]

However, it is important to note that the pared down aesthetic dependent on muted colours and 'poor' materials, which in the case of Margiela meant recycled fabric, had precedents in fashion from the 1980s and particularly in Japanese designers such as Rei Kawakubo, whose work borrowed from the Zen aesthetic of poverty known as *wabi-sabi*.[6] This aesthetic – which the writer Angela Carter, in 1983, compared to 'Franciscan habits' – was partially understood by the contemporary press as a refutation of the ostentatiousness of mainstream 1980s fashion.[7] Similar to this interpretation of Kawakubo's fashion design of the 1980s, the fashion journalist Sally Brampton remarked in the *Guardian* in 1993 that 'the movement [meaning deconstruction fashion] formed at the turn of this decade, was born out of an anger with and distaste for the label mania and excess of the eighties'.[8] This reading resurfaces almost verbatim in the *New York Times*, where Amy Spindler (later to become the paper's first fashion critic) wrote: 'In his anger against what too much money and too little imagination had done to his art form, Mr Margiela recycled thrown-away clothes, disembowelled his perfectly cut jackets and wrapped bright blue garbage bags around the clothes he made.'[9] The common elements of deconstruction fashion were crystallised by Brampton as 'fabric edges left unfinished, seams stitched on the outside of cloth and even those materials traditionally used in the construction of garments – tailoring, felt, lining, interlining, bonding and stiffening nylon net – as fabrics in their own right'.[10]

These descriptions seem to ascribe a certain puritanical rigour to 'deconstruction' fashion and Margiela's work in particular alongside a certain revolutionary spirit and an aggressive edge. If one traces an analogy with music, one could read deconstruction fashion interpreted by fashion criticism as a late-punk meets straight-edge aesthetic.[11] Yet unlike punk, to which it was compared on the basis of its aesthetic strategies of rips and unfinished edges, deconstruction fashion was never discussed in relation to humour, either by the contemporary press or in successive scholarly assessments. On the contrary, some of the fashion critics of the time accused deconstruction fashion of excessive seriousness. They suggested that, in Brampton's words, 'deconstructionists', in their attempts to do away with the excess of the 1980s, are at risk of becoming moralistic, or at least 'lamentably humourless'.[12]

These readings, however, clash with Margiela's 'self-reception'.[13] For instance, Margiela's official account of his spring/summer 1990 collection, which is described by Spindler and other journalists as the pivotal moment in the advent of deconstruction fashion, underlines the collection's humorous and festive element. In the catalogue, which the design house published on the occasion of his ten-year retrospective at the Rotterdam Museum, the collection and the presentation are described respectively:

> All is either white, flesh colored or grey. Women's slips twice their normal size are worn as long skirts belted at the waist or draped under fitted T-Shirts. Fitted jackets with their sleeves cut-off, left frayed and closed with snappers. A series of garments made from metal, paper of transparent plastic and plastic shopping bags worn as T-shirts. Most garments are tied around the hips, torsos are almost bare or with undersized tops. Silver glitter decorates the neckline. For the finale the women wear white 'Haute Couture' workcoats and scatter white confetti. Eighteenth century harpsichord music plays on loud speakers [....].
>
> In an area of wasteland in Paris 20th arrondissement. Invitations are handpainted by local children. The women walk along the ground. Rock music plays. Hair is undone chignons with long hair pieces. Eyes are surrounded with white paint, lips are glossed. Children from the area, invited to come and see, join the model in their procession.[14]

The scene it illustrates takes on an increasingly implausible and absurdist tone, as it refers to a number of performances and rituals other than the fashion show. Margiela's presentation quoted a wedding ceremony via the throwing of confetti at the end of the show, a reference that is rendered all the more puzzling as the confetti is thrown in the air by models wearing the white laboratory coat attire typical of haute couture workers as well as medical practitioners. This festive tone is further underscored by the kids joining in the show or, according to Margiela's ironic terminology, 'the procession', and piggyback riding on the model's back (Fig. 22). The festive aspect of this scene is also emphasised in Bill Cunningham's account of the event, which points out how 'the neighbourhood youngsters' became part of the show to which they gave an uninhibited response, often 'prancing along mimicking the walk of the models'.[15]

Through the unlikely mixing of different symbols, the presentation reads as disorienting and humorous in its absurdity, as it referred to, and poked fun at, a range of 'ritual spectacles', from weddings to religious processions to medical practices. The parodying of the language of authority embodied by religion and medicine was a constant in the *Rabelaisian* carnival that Bakhtin describes. Thus, these multilayered references not only bestow a grotesque and carnivalesque quality on the presentation, but they exemplify how the format of the fashion show, understood as 'ritual spectacle' and in its relation to performance, favours carnivalesque appropriations. The grotesque and carnivalesque element of Margiela's show is also mirrored in the clothes presented. The collection introduced carnivalesque techniques of altering scale and changing an item's function, techniques that recur in his work. It presented the first of a series of oversized garments of clownlike proportions, the XXXXL T-shirt, while it played with expectations and disrupted objects' traditional functions by tailoring supermarket plastic bags into tops.

References to the grotesque and carnivalesque have also been left out of academic writings on this topic. However, a thorough account of deconstruction in fashion in relation to Jacques Derrida's work can be found in Alison Gill's essay in *Fashion Theory*, where the author employs Derrida's theories to interrogate deconstruction fashion, and in particular the work of Margiela.[16] This encounter opens up interesting possibilities for the analysis of the work in question. In the first instance, Gill traces the history of deconstruction in literary analysis and philosophy and then traces the way it spread to art and design disciplines such as architecture, pointing out how deconstruction has been identified in opposition to modernism.

In common with analyses of deconstruction in other fields, which are by now numerous, Gill argues that deconstruction in fashion challenges and questions the very mode of operation of a discipline. In this context, she points out how Margiela's work, much like Derrida's, resists closure by addressing the process rather than the finished product of fashion. Gill argues that Margiela, following deconstruction, is questioning 'the seamlessness of fashion', in a similar way to how Derrida questions the seamlessness of philosophical discourse, opening up its ambiguities, contradictions and instabilities.

Building on Gill's extensive analysis and a range of other academic writings on Margiela, I argue that a close analysis of garments and accessories shows that the Belgian designer's play with the function of clothes and accessories, their unfinished nature and denial of seamlessness, not only dovetails with Derrida's refusal of closure and stable meaning, but also with Bakhtin's ideas of the carnivalesque and the ever-becoming unfinished nature of the grotesque.

FASHION OF INVERSION

Margiela's work is, in great part, aligned with a grotesque aesthetic, which can be observed in its disrespect for Western ideals of beauty and classical aesthetics articulated through his clothes' disregard for symmetry and proportion. These characteristics, as previous discussions in relation to Kawakubo's, Bowery's and Godley's work made evident, constituted the pillars of the classical canon in opposition to which the grotesque came to be defined. In addition, Margiela's experimental construction techniques, particularly the use of garments meant for one part of the body to clothe another or unveiling the inside of a garment, retain a close affinity with carnivalesque techniques of inversions, travesties and upset proportions that were central to carnival humour and were often articulated through the participants' apparel:

> This is why in carnivalesque images there is so much turnabout, so many opposite faces and intentionally upset proportions. We see this first of all in the participants' apparel. Men are transvested as women and vice versa, costumes are turned inside out, and outer garments replace underwear. The description of a charivari of the early fourteenth century, in *Roman du Fauvel*, says of its participants, 'They donned all their garments backward'.[17]

These humorous inversions were inherent in the spirit of renewal and the temporary disruptions of hierarchies staged throughout 'the varied popular festive life of the Middle Ages and the Renaissance', which Bakhtin groups under the name of carnival.[18] In its theorisation of inversions and the world upside down, Bakhtin's work anticipated cultural anthropologists' and, in particular, the strand of cultural anthropology known as 'symbolic anthropology', whose work, like Bakhtin's, shared an interest in cultural negations and symbolic inversions. And, as Stallybrass and White point out, cultural anthropology is instrumental in bringing Bakhtin's theories from the realm of the actual historical carnival to bear on a wide range of artistic and cultural expressions.[19] As the cultural anthropologist Barbara Babcock explains in *The Reversible World: Symbolic Inversion on Art and Society*, '"symbolic inversion" may be broadly defined as any act of expressive behaviour which inverts, contradicts, abrogates, or in some fashion presents an alternative to commonly held cultural codes, values, and norms be they linguistic, literary or artistic, religious, or social and political'.[20] This definition of symbolic inversion is reflected in common parlance, where the term is used to mean 'a turning upside down', 'a reversal of position, order, sequence, or relation'.[21]

Thus, inversion, as Bakhtin also points out, is central to various expressions of the comic, which could be understood as practices of cultural negation.[22] In their denial of systems and orders and their play and disruption of category and classificatory systems, they can be read as a critique of closed symbolic systems and fixed categories: 'The essence of such laughter-producing "topsyturvydom" is an attack on control, on closed systems, on, that is, 'the irreversibility of the order of phenomena, the perfect individuality of a perfectly self-contained series.'[23] Echoing Bakhtin's theory, cultural anthropology reinforces an understanding of the liberating function of techniques of inversion – or, to use Bakhtin's term, 'carnivalesque' practices – and the attendant 'laughter' they generate. 'Festive laughter', according to Bakhtin, allowed for a dialectical understanding of the world, which could be used as a tool to unmask prevailing truth and orthodoxy. It was through the relativising lens of humour that (albeit temporarily) a different understanding of the world became possible, one according to which the existing hierarchies were relative and the contemplation of a different social order possible. And it is through these theories that one can understand Margiela's experiments in fashion as a moment (however circumscribed) of disruption through humour.

PLAYING WITH SCALE: GIANTS AND DOLLS

Among Margiela's collections that bring these themes more clearly to the fore are some of the ones the Belgian designer produced at the cusp of the new millennium. Extreme alterations of scale had characterised Margiela's work from its very inception, as his XXXXL T-shirt from spring/summer 1990 makes evident. He developed the theme further in a series of oversized collections (spring/summer 2000, autumn/winter 2000–01 and spring/summer 2001), and in collections based on enlarged Barbie clothes (spring/summer 1999, autumn/winter 1994–95 and spring/summer 1995). All of these collections explore clownish proportions alongside the designer's more common tropes of inside-out and seemingly unfinished garments.

Giants: the oversized collections

The oversized collections enlarge individual garments from an Italian 42 to sizes ranging from Italian men 76/74 to 80 – extremely large sizes that are not actually produced.[24] With his usual meticulousness, Margiela enlarges each aspect of the garment down to its details (buttons, zippers) and to the accessories that complete the collection (i.e., earrings and sunglasses). A customised 1930s dressmaker's form whose proportions had been altered to render a form of Botero-like proportions served as an inspiration for Margiela's first enlarged collections (Fig. 23). This altered form, as well as Margiela's altered clothes, questions the normative body of fashion. From the perspective of dress history, sizing is itself a normative strategy. Its development started in the eighteenth century in the context of military wear, particularly for the Royal Navy, with the intent to standardise and render uniform what was perceived as a motley crew so that they could properly represent the British Empire.[25] It is not, of course, by chance that this normative sizing strategy articulated through dress occurred alongside new regulatory techniques and forms of power. As Foucault has argued, throughout the eighteenth century new forms of power, which remain at work today, took hold. This period saw the development of 'bio-power': 'a power that has to qualify, measure, appraise and hierarchise … it effects distributions around the norm'.[26]

This relation of the dress form to the normative body and the classical canon is fully explored in Margiela's collections from spring/summer and autumn/winter 1997, in which the models appeared to be actually wearing the dress forms. This conflation renders manifest the way in which norms can become inscribed and naturalised onto the body through dress together with a host of other regulatory techniques. The fashion theorist Barbara Vinken, writing on the relevance of the mannequin to Margiela's *oeuvre*, draws a parallel between 'the standardisation of the female form, accomplished by the mannequin' and the 'norms of classical proportion as canonically transmitted through Greek sculpture'. According to Vinken, by bringing the mannequin more directly to the fore, Margiela shows the artifice of the ideal feminine body:

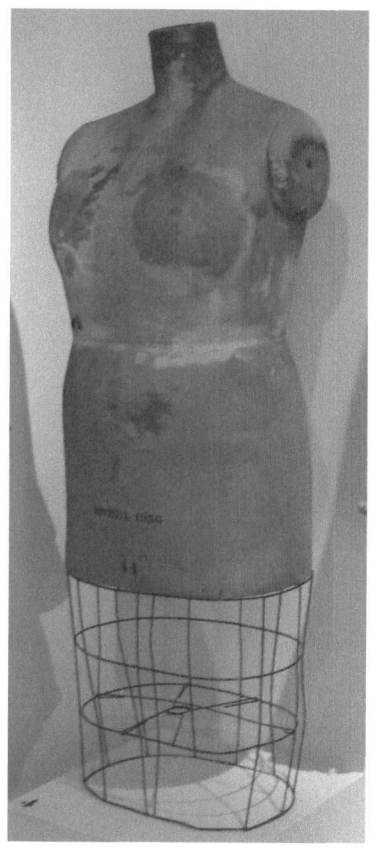

Fig. 23 Customised 1930s dress form used as inspiration for Martin Margiela's oversized collections; photograph by the author

how the uniform, ideal body of the woman is produced by the art of the dressmaker, rather than being an incarnation of nature. The body is artificial, and the art of the dressmaker consists in making this artifice appear as natural, just as the model embodies the doll's body with her own living body.[27]

Margiela's enlarged garments and his interest in the non-normative body share with Kawakubo, Godley and Bowery an interest in moving away from prescribed body types, which in their case was articulated primarily through the pregnant body. It also shares with Bowery a fascination with the gigantic: a quintessential grotesque category. As Bakhtin points out, 'the giant image has … a strong grotesque bodily character'.[28] Its exaggerated size is in fact an apt articulation of the 'exaggeration, hyperbolism, excessiveness'[29] characteristic of the grotesque. It is not accidental that Rabelais's Gargantua and Pantagruel were both giants; the gigantic was central to the folk tradition and to carnival practice, and the literary critic Susan Stewart argues that 'the giant continued to be associated with the inversion of orthodoxy and allegiance to the vernacular, decentralised, local political culture'.[30]

Margiela's enlarged garments appear all the more grotesque and ultimately are read as comical and incongruous when juxtaposed with the diminutive body of the female models. This comical incongruity is furthered by the clothes' presentation, as with the enlarged trousers and jeans folded at the waist to prevent them from falling down, a technique reminiscent of a Chaplinesque tramp or a clown, as well as by the fact that much of the clothes are obviously men's garments worn by female models. On the occasion of the autumn/winter 2000–01 presentation, the models' eyes were entirely covered by bangs, a look which is hard not to read as comical, particularly when paired with the awkwardly big clothes and set against the overly maudlin *Twin Peaks*' soundtrack (figs. 24 and 25).

In line with much of Margiela's work, some of the garments from these collections are literally inverted, as they appear to be worn inside out, as with a black jacket from the autumn/winter 2000–01 collection with label and lining placed on the outside, now in the collection of the ModeMuseum in Antwerp. The label constitutes a further pun, as it refers to high-end tailoring tradition. It reads 'Exclusive Model. Made in Italy', while being placed where a monogram would be. The jacket could also be worn right side out, yet it would still retain the same label on the outside, thus further confounding the matter and in the process playing with and disrupting codified systems and rules. These disruptions of the syntax of fashion resurface throughout Margiela's enlarged collections, and his oeuvre as a whole. For instance, the spring/summer 2000–01 collection includes 'trousers with two fronts'.

A close examination of various garments from these collections reveals the extent to which Margiela's manipulation of scale often transforms a garment's function, as is the case with what would have been a short jacket that, through enlargement, becomes a 'gigantic' pea coat measuring 172 centimetres across the chest and 105 centimetres in length. In another, perhaps more obvious, transformation, a white shirt that measures 146 centimetres across the chest, 51 centimetres across the neck and 91 centimetres in length functions like a dress due to its enlarged size. A short cardigan measuring 114 centimetres across the chest and 81 centimetres in length becomes, in turn, an all-enveloping cocoon, as it was scaled up equally in both length and width, in accordance with Margiela's techniques, whereas an actual garment

DECONSTRUCTION AND THE GROTESQUE: MARTIN MARGIELA 85

Fig. 24 Martin Margiela, enlarged sweater, autumn/winter 2000–01, courtesy of Firstview

of that size would not have been. It is important to note that these measurements are very unusual and suggest gigantic proportions, since within traditional sizing (derived from pattern grading), increments in a garment's width are not met with the same increments in length. This is particularly the case for very large sizes.[31]

Many of the knits I observed and measured in museum collections, all of which are from the autumn/winter 2000–01 collection, are rather stiff, as they have undergone a moulding process. They were moulded to an Italian

Fig. 25 Martin Margiela, enlarged garments, autumn/winter 2000–01, courtesy of Firstview

size 78, thus retaining an extremely large form around the wearer regardless of the wearer's size (Figs 25). In addition, they appear ragged, with frayed hems, holes and loose threads, thus furthering the suggestion of decay or, as Caroline Evans argues, referring to the nineteenth-century figure of the ragpicker. According to Evans, these strategies in Margiela's work are partially a response to anxieties over contemporary modes of accelerated consumption and production.[32] As discussed in the previous chapter and in relation to the work of Godley and Kawakubo, this aesthetic was often read as a rejection of the 1980s culture of excess. And, in fact, a shift in design aesthetic towards recycling and humbler material can be observed across design disciplines. The design historian Linda Sandino points out how the overly-saturated palette characteristic of the 1980s was systematically avoided by young designers in the following decade: 'The shift to recycling and the ready-made', she writes, 'must therefore be seen in the context of cultural and material anxieties arising from the economic excesses of consumer culture and expressed … through the use of material means'.[33] In the case of Margiela, this different relation to materials accompanied by an interest in transience and decay, however evident in this collection, can be best observed in a 'retrospective' exhibition of his work in an art and design museum in 1997, during which his clothes actually disintegrated over the course of the exhibition.

Ultimately, the pieces in Margiela's autumn/winter 2000–01 collection are not only grotesque in their size, but also through their reference to dirt, decay and incompleteness – central characteristics of the grotesque body, which diverge from and challenge the seamless, polished and pristine classical model of official culture. As Norbert Elias argued, cleanliness and hygiene were, in fact, central to processes of civilisation in Western societies and went hand-in-hand with notions of progress. The civilised body is, or rather aims to be, a body without dirt. This becomes clear in Elias's discussion of the refinement of table manners and the shifting meanings of spitting at the table from the Middle Ages onwards.[34] John Fiske makes Elias's theory more directly relevant to Margiela's work, and fashion more generally, as he describes the relation between the aestheticised body, which could be compared to the body of mainstream fashion, and 'the body, that refuses to be aestheticised'. 'The aestheticized body', he writes, 'is a body without dirt that offers no categorical challenges to social control and disciplined "cleanliness"',[35] 'for aesthetics is merely class disciplinary power displaced into metaphors of beauty, symmetry and perfection'.[36] 'Cleanliness', he adds, 'is order – social, semiotic, and moral (it is, after all, next to godliness) – so dirt is disorder, is threatening and undisciplined'.[37] Yet he points out the impossibility for the body, in all of its processes and orifices, to be completely aligned with cleanliness. Thus, the body once again becomes this unstable entity that cannot quite be fully controlled and/or contained:

> The body is inherently 'dirty': all its orifices produce dirt – that is matter that transgresses its categorical boundary, that contaminates the separateness of the body and therefore its purity as a category. In threatening the category of the body, dirt threatens also the category of the individual for

which the body stands as a naturalising metaphor. No wonder than that so many bodily functions and physical pleasures have to be disciplined by the designation 'dirty'.[38]

In the case of Margiela's collection, these references are rendered more explicit as the garments forcefully point to an absent body. Thanks to the moulding process they have undergone, the clothes retain their *gargantuan* shape when unworn. The sweaters are, in fact, reminiscent of fat suits – albeit ill-fitting ones – a further reference to bodies-out-of-bounds.[39]

The gigantic nature of the garments was further underscored by their weight, as it is hard to imagine a person of 'regular' size being able to sustain the weight of the garments over a protracted period. The enlarged cardigans in the archives of the ModeMuseum in Antwerp, for instance, require two people to move them comfortably and cannot be kept on hangers, unlike most of the garments in the museum's collection, a fact that further suggests their alignment with the gigantically grotesque. That Margiela is playing with categories of normality is further emphasised by the fact that white cotton versions of garments in the prescribed size of 42 (which Margiela refers to as stereotypes) were included in the spring/summer 2000 collection as understructures to their enlarged counterparts. His experiments with scale could thus be read as an attempt to destabilise the normative body and metonymically a range of social systems, since the body constitutes 'the ultimate order of things' against which categories of what constitutes norm and deviation are articulated and ultimately naturalised. As Susan Stewart points out:

> Traditionally, the body has served as a primary mode of understanding and perceiving scale ... The world in English is measured by the body – spans of hands and feet, a yard the length from nose to fingers at the end of an outstretched arm.[40]

Dolls: the magnified collections

Margiela's exploration of the normative body becomes even more evident in his doll garments, which were included in his autumn/winter 1994–95 and spring/summer 1995 collections, as well as in the spring/summer 1999 collection. All three collections included 'masculine' and 'feminine' doll clothes enlarged to human scale. The feminine garments were enlarged versions of Barbie clothes, while the masculine ones were enlarged GI Joe clothes. Museum archives have tended to collect the enlarged Barbie clothes. The only enlarged Margiela item from a GI Joe doll for which I was able to find documentation was the action figure's badge. As the Maison Martin Margiela press release points out, the clothes have been 'magnified 5.2 times to human size', down to the garment's every detail, including 'snap fasteners and stitching securing them, knit gauge, etc.'.[41] And as the label, itself comically enlarged to 16.5 cm × 9.5 cm, reads: 'details and disproportions are reproduced in the enlargement'.

As a result, once enlarged, the clothes appear utterly disproportionate, as is most evident in the garments' details. A pair of jeans from the spring/summer 1999 collection, an example of which is in the Costume Institute collection, brings this to the fore. Here, the zipper pull encompasses a quarter of the length of the rise, measuring seven centimetres in length; while the brand of the zipper – the ubiquitous *Lampo* – becomes gigantic and readable from a distance. The stitches, once enlarged to the same scale as the rest of the garment, appear disproportionately big. The loose threads from the knot securing the stitch/seams also become magnified and give the garment an unfinished and hastily made quality, which would have been imperceptible in the original (Fig. 26).

The unfinished quality of the enlarged Barbie clothes points to a lack of 'seamlessness'[42] in her fashion and highlights the relation to strategies of deconstruction in Margiela's work. Because the seams are made visible, the garments not only refer to the process rather than the finished product of fashion, they also expose the illusion of perfection and closure through what could be defined as analytic methods. The designer systematically employs processes of magnification to lay bare the 'ambiguities' and imperfection of the doll. As Gill argues in her discussion of deconstruction fashion, even though it can be interpreted as a critique of fashion, Margiela's work in no way constitutes a form of nihilistic rejection, a criticism that further aligns it with Derrida's theories but, rather, as Harold Koda and Richard Martin have also argued, it should be understood as a process of 'analytical creation'.[43] Perhaps one could theorise that the unfinished nature of hems and edges in some of Margiela's pieces refer to processes of draping that involve slashing the edges of the fabric, as opposed to a declaration of anger against fashion, as some journalists understood it.[44] The painstaking magnification of the doll clothes makes clear that the designer is intent on problematising their seamlessness through an engagement with the processes of garment-construction:

> Margiela's garments indicate an implicit care for the material object and sartorial techniques, and therefore, they would suggest the impossibility

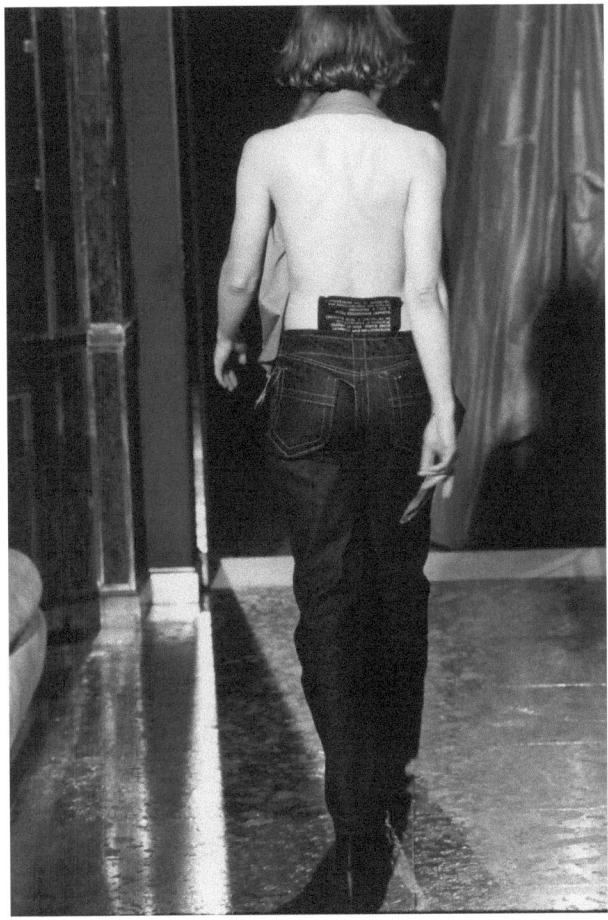

Fig. 26 Martin Margiela, enlarged doll jeans, spring/summer 1999, courtesy of Firstview

of a simple destruction or anarchy; for instance, the look of distressed or unfinished tacking around an arm hole is executed by the tailor's hand with, paradoxically, a quality 'finish'. In Margiela's guiding of the tailor's hand one can see a desire to leave a, trace in an albeit reconceived, fashion tradition of techniques, patterns, and details. His 'trace' will always carry with it its past eras of fashion that cannot simply be eradicated just as for Derrida, Western philosophy cannot be discarded.[45]

The Belgian designer's work is very much in line with Derrida's understanding that deconstruction comes from within, in his case within philosophical texts. Thus, it can be understood as a process of 'auto-construction', something that is already present within the text, just as processes of 'deconstruction' were already there in the Barbie clothes. Writing about his reading and 'deconstruction' of philosophical writings, such as those of Plato, Derrida clearly remarks on and describes these processes:

> The way I tried to read Plato, Aristotle, and others, is not a way of commanding, preserving, or conserving this heritage. It is an analysis which tries to find out how their thinking works or does not work, to find the tensions, the contradictions, the heterogeneity within their own corpus ... What is the law of this self-deconstruction, this auto-deconstruction? Deconstruction is not a method or some tool that you apply to something from the outside ... Deconstruction is something which happens and which happens inside; there is a deconstruction at work within Plato's texts, for instance. As my colleagues know, each time I study Plato I try to find some heterogeneity in his own corpus and to see how, for instance, within the *Timaeus* the theme of the *khora* is incompatible with this supposed system of Plato. So, to be true to Plato and this a sign of love and respect for Plato, I have to analyse the functioning and disfunctioning of his work.[46]

In Margiela's work, the attention to the details of a garment not only highlights the lack of proportions and hastily-finished stitches that remain imperceptible in the diminutive version of the doll clothes, but also introduces the designer's interest in what is 'invisible' to the human eye. In his almost obsessive interest in minute details, Margiela shares an interest in the 'invisible' life of objects, which characterised the nineteenth and early twentieth century and was fuelled by the development of optical devices, many of which were thought to be able to observe the secret life of the inanimate world and show it to be, in actuality, animate:

> That the world of things can open itself to reveal a secret life – indeed to reveal a set of actions and hence a narrativity and history outside the given field of perception – is a constant daydream that the miniature presents. This is the daydream of the microscope: the daydream of life inside life, if significance multiplied infinitely within significance.[47]

These discussions were particularly prevalent in early film theory, which discussed the camera as imbuing the inanimate world with life, as well as revealing the seemingly inert life of the world surrounding us, through the observation of its smallest particles, such as bacteria.[48] This point can perhaps be best observed in the designer's retrospective in Rotterdam, which is discussed at greater length in the next chapter. On that occasion Margiela did in fact employ an optical device – the microscope – and quite literally brought the garments to life by applying a range of bacteria to it.

Further disproportions can be found by closely examining a series of knits the Belgian designer produced for spring/summer 1999, examples of which can be found both in the Costume Institute and the MoMu collections. The weave of the knits becomes oversized, taking on the appearance of rope, and the seams become gigantic, rendering the garments extremely heavy and ungainly and ultimately comical. This is particularly true if one is aware of their relation to the ideal body of fashion represented by the Barbie doll. (That Barbie looms large within the contemporary fashion imaginary is corroborated by the range of established designers who have designed clothes for the doll, such as Marc Jacobs, Calvin Klein, Hèrmes, Prada and Claude Montana, to name a few.)[49]

The decorative elements and 'accessories' are perhaps most obviously comically large, as with the aforementioned label, the GI Joe badge measuring 21 centimetres × 12 centimetres, and the U standing in for 'University' of the preppy sweater that, once enlarged at the same rate of the rest of the garment, measures an unlikely 17 centimetres × 12 centimetres (Fig. 27). In addition, the shapes of the garments themselves are off-kilter because of their literal enlargement. Jackets and vests are short and boxy, their widest point uncharacteristically across the lower part of the ribcage, while sleeves appear too long in relation to the rest of the garment and of unequal width. The jeans are also very wide, possibly to account for the fact that the rigid Barbie body would be inflexible while being fitted. Thus, Margiela's doll clothes appear doubly ironic, as they unveil the inherent 'disproportions' of garments belonging to a model body – that of Barbie – metonymically calling into question the idealised body of the doll.

That Barbie, despite her own disproportions, ultimately represents an ideal and aspirational body type has been amply discussed and debated across the humanities and social sciences. A substantial number of books and articles have focused on Barbie's representation of normative racial, class and gender categories as well as her embodiment of unattainable bodily ideals. Much of the debate has focused on whether this translated into negative body image and gender ideals among young girls and, more recently, to what extent, if

Fig. 27 Martin Margiela, enlarged GI Joe badge, spring/summer 1999, courtesy of Firstview

at all, the Barbie doll allows for alternative and queer readings through processes of play.[50] It is, however, precisely because of its anatomical unreality and impossibility that Barbie's body 'has been naturalized as ideal'.[51] As Carol Ockman points out, Barbie has successfully embodied 'ideal femininity' for the past 40 years, thanks in great part to 'the phantasmatic ideal body' she represents.[52] Or, to use Bakhtinian terminology, Barbie's body – literally sealed and without openings – epitomises the contained 'classical' body. This point is perhaps best exemplified by the range of artists' work focusing on breaking the sealed body of the doll and rendering it thus grotesque, since as Stewart points out: 'The miniature world remains perfect and uncontaminated by the grotesque, so long as its absolute boundaries are maintained.'[53]

Margiela's doll pieces also highlight how the body, particularly the female one, is transformed through the capitalist system of production and consumption into a commodity. This point, which Evans discusses at length in her section on 'living dolls',[54] is further complicated by Margiela's pieces, which animate clothes belonging to a fully commodified and inorganic body – that of Barbie – and pair them with another prime example of body as commodity – that of the fashion model. But this doubling of commodified femininities (or in Evans's terms 'ghosting')[55] actually breaks down processes of commodity fetishism, rendering both Barbie's body and the models' bodies absurdly humorous and ultimately grotesque.

Martin Margiela questions the ideal body of the doll through the carnivalesque technique of inversion, thus emptying it of its 'ideal' qualities. He inverts usual processes and deminiaturises the miniature to bring it to human size, yet renders it in actuality gigantic and, in the process, further questions and complicates notions of norms and deviations and ideal bodies versus grotesque ones. He arrives at the gigantic departing from the miniature in one of its most typical forms – that of the doll. In the process, he exposes the disorder, incompleteness, disproportions and lack of balance of the miniature, which historically has represented the idealised world (and, particularly in relation to the doll, the idealised feminine.) As Stewart points out, the miniature, unlike the gigantic, has been traditionally associated with attributes of balance, symmetry and containment, with 'the body as container of objects, perpetual and incontaminable'. Stewart argues that from the late nineteenth and early twentieth century, the doll came to symbolise more specifically the contained and controlled world of bourgeois interiority and ideal femininity (the 'petite feminine')[56]: 'But while the miniature presents a mental world of proportion and balance, the gigantic presents a physical world of disorder and disproportion. It is significant that the most typical miniature world is the domestic model of the doll house.'[57] One could argue that Margiela, by highlighting the disproportions inherent in the miniature via processes of enlargement exposes as a travesty the perfect world of bourgeoisie interiority – the 'incontaminable' world of symmetry perfection and balance. More specifically, he renders the ideal body of the Barbie doll and the perfect feminine it articulates irremediably grotesque.

In addition, by being produced and distributed in the context of contemporary global systems of exchanges, Margiela's work knowingly, or perhaps unwittingly, unveils how the 'perfection' and 'seamlessness' of late capitalist global societies is in fact upheld by the cheap, unskilled, mechanised labour magnified in the hastily made stitches and loose threads of Margiela's enlarged version of garments belonging to such quintessentially American symbols as the Barbie doll and GI Joe.[58] This point is further corroborated by the fact that Margiela, particularly in his 1990s collections, showed a recurrent interest in unveiling and rendering visible his production processes, a realm rigorously kept separate from presentation and sale, the borders between the two often being heavily 'policed'. This can be observed in his spring/summer 1997 collection, where 'a video showing two women wearing the collection walking through the streets and metro adjacent to the showroom is intercut with segments showing the production of pieces at [Margiela's] atelier'.[59]

Ultimately, different subject positions correspond to the gigantic and the miniature, as they refer to the grotesque and the classical body respectively. The miniature, in contrast to the gigantic, allows and perhaps even invites a transcendental subject position – a distanced and sovereign subject that can contain the world of the miniature at once. As Stewart points out in her discussion of miniature books, 'they allow the reader to disengage himself or herself from the field of representation as a transcendent subject'.[60] In fact, one can argue that the miniature validates the omniscient ideal of the Western Cartesian subject, which is denied by the grotesque world of the gigantic. 'While fantasy in the miniature moves toward an individualised interiority, fantasy in the gigantic exteriorises and communalises what might otherwise be considered "the subjective".'[61] The gigantic ultimately returns us to previous discussions of subjectivity, and particularly to the concept of the subject-in-process as inherently related to the becoming unfinished and excessive aspect of the grotesque canon. Thus, Margiela's work, by going from the miniature to the gigantic, refutes a stable and closed subject position, and, just like Kawakubo's, Bowery's and Godley's work, aligns itself with fashion's potential for the promotion of a subject-in-process: a heterogeneous and open subject which is in a constant state of becoming.[62]

In a further twist in Margiela's complex and multi-referential collections, the enlarged doll garments are based on remakes of 1950s and 1960s versions of Barbie dolls, which were marketed under the evocative name 'Nostalgic Barbie' (Fig. 28). These references not only introduce Margiela's interest in complex temporalities, which will be discussed at greater length in the next chapter, but also suggests a camp reading of his work, which

Fig. 28 Photographs of 'Nostalgic Barbie' alongside Margiela's 'Doll Collection', ModeMuseum, Antwerp, 2008 © RST

places it on a continuum with that of Bowery's and Willhelm's, despite their obvious aesthetic differences.

Camp has been theorised as being heavily reliant on 'the outmoded, the out of date, the artefact past its prime'[63] for its effect, and it has perhaps relied and depended most often on the recent past of popular culture, as camp's reading of 1930s Hollywood has made most evident. The cultural studies theorist Andrew Ross writes in 'Uses of Camp' how it

> is a rediscovery of history's waste. Camp irreverently retrieves not only that which has been excluded from the serious high-cultural 'tradition', but also the more unsalvageable material that has been picked over and found wanting by purveyors of the 'antique'.[64]

As a result, one of camp's effects is that of 'ironic nostalgia'. This stands opposed to 'more conventional forms of nostalgia, which mandate a much more earnest consumption of texts'.[65] And it is in this vein that Margiela's doll garments, based as they are on remakes of 1950s and 1960s Barbie dolls, fall within the realm of camp and engage in what could be defined as 'ironic nostalgia'. The possibility of this reading is made further possible by the fact that Barbie could be reminiscent of one's childhood, but as she becomes gigantic (at least metonymically through her clothes), more earnest nostalgic readings are disrupted.

The proclivity of camp to engage with the immediate past and with obsolete artefacts dovetails more generally with Margiela's interest in recycling. In the following chapter, these strategies will come to the fore in discussions of some of his earliest collections. As Caryl Flinn writes: '[t]hrough its investment in detritus, in used-up things, camp might be seen as a critical response to planned obsolescence',[66] something that characterises Margiela's work through his use of recycled garments and fabric and, even more obviously, through the frequent recycling of his own past collections. The repeated re-use of the same collections goes against the accepted fashion norms, as it is predicated on a cyclical model of time as opposed to the linear, sequential and seemingly progressive time of fashion. As next chapter's discussion highlights, this reconception of the temporality of fashion characterises much of Margiela's work and further aligns it with the Bakhtinian grotesque.

FARCICAL DISCREPANCY

The processes of enlargement and alterations of scale that characterised the aforementioned Margiela collections often denied and/or played with the garments' functionality, due to the excessive weight deriving from the huge weave, as is the case with the Barbie clothes, or to their sheer gigantic size, as is the case with the oversized collections. Many of the garments, as illustrated earlier in the chapter, go from shirt to dresses, or from caplet to pea coat, in the process of enlargement, often weighing as much as a prohibitive five kilos. As a result, the carnivalesque aesthetic achieved by the incongruity between garments and bodily proportions is reinforced by the play with and/or denial of a garment's traditional function.

This play with functionality is particularly common in relation to items of clothing used to cover the body's extremities, such as socks, shoes and gloves. Perhaps the best-known item in Margiela's vocabulary is the split-toe shoe, introduced in his very first show (spring/summer 1989) and recurring in endless variations throughout his collections. Inspired by the Japanese footwear *tabi*, they emphasise a relatively hidden body part: the intersection between the big toe and the adjacent one, veering between the

Fig. 29 Martin Margiela, *tabi* shoes, photograph by Ronald Stoops, courtesy of MoMu, Antwerp

unsettling, the comical and the grotesque (Fig. 29). As Caroline Evans points out, their unfamiliar shape (at least to a Western audience) makes reference to the animal world, rendering them 'goatish' – 'cloven hooves imported from a different symbolic system'.[67] Their grotesque and unsettling quality, however, diminishes as they become increasingly part of the current vocabulary of Western shoe design. As Frances Connelly notes, non-Western aesthetic practices are often read as grotesque and perceived as 'deformation of European rules of representations'[68] when initially introduced into the Western vocabulary or as long as 'they troubled an established boundary';[69] yet they tend to become assimilated over time. For instance, the split-toe shoe was eventually popularised by athletic footwear sporting a similar shape to Margiela's *tabi* shoes, and in particular by the Nike Air Rift, which was inspired by another non Western culture, 'the barefoot style of Kenyan distance runners'.[70]

The shoes' 'goatish' shape was later transported to gloves, where it articulates more explicitly a play with functionality. The *tabi* glove constitutes a hybrid between a mitten and a five-fingered glove, making one aware of different configurations of human anatomy and different possibilities of bodily

DECONSTRUCTION AND THE GROTESQUE: MARTIN MARGIELA

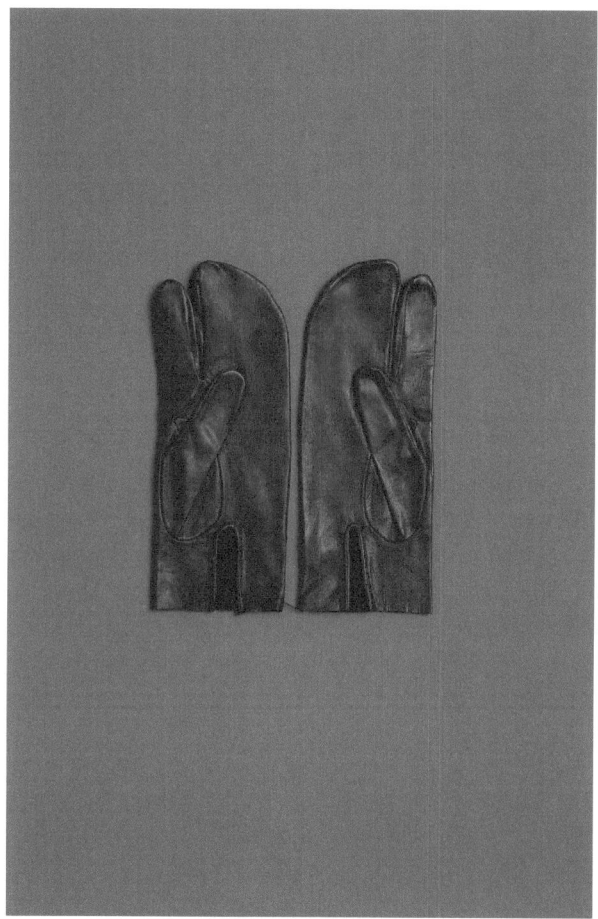

Fig. 30 Martin Margiela, *tabi* gloves in the ModeMuseum collection, courtesy of MoMu, Antwerp

movement by upsetting traditional relations of body and clothes (Fig. 30). This is a quintessential aspect of the grotesque in fashion, as perhaps best observed in relation to Rei Kawakubo's spring/summer 1997 collection, whose amorphous shapes changed the wearer's relation to their own body and to the body of the other.

As these designers explore different relations of bodies and clothes, they also implicitly question what constitutes a 'normal' body and what abilities such a body has. What remains hinted at in this work, as well as in Kawakubo's and Godley's clothes, are references to differently-abled bodies, whose configurations are not in line with the ableist norm. As much as fashion in its standardised pattern and sizing is in line with bodily norms, it also leaves itself open for such a norm to be hacked, manipulated and questioned.

Subtle and not so subtle plays of functionality recur so frequently in the Belgian designer's work that it would be impossible to mention them all. Examining the enlarged and doll collections more specifically, one finds black leather gloves transformed into purses, which were then worn as necklaces in the spring/summer 1999 presentation. On other occasions, socks are reworked to create gloves, while both socks and gloves are employed to create shirts and sweaters. In the third of Margiela's enlarged collection (spring/summer 2001), for instance, tops made of leather gloves were paired with oversized skirts, thus augmenting the sense of comical incongruity introduced by the size of the skirts. In the first enlarged collection (spring/summer 2000), nude stockings become belts and heels are removed to transform stiletto shoes into flats, or what Margiela more precisely describes as 'heel-less stiletto shoes'. Margiela's processes of transformation are, however, in no way seamless. The designer does not hide the garments' or accessories' original function, but rather integrates it into their new iterations, as visible, for instance, in the excessive arch of the 'heel-less stiletto shoe'. It is precisely from the co-existence between their original and new functions that these objects derive their incongruity and their comical effect. An eminent example of these processes, now in the archives of the ModeMuseum, is a fur coat that Margiela produced for his autumn/winter 2002–03 by joining two used fur coats together to create one single piece. Its patchwork nature remained evident in the variations of the pelts and, more obviously, insofar as the combined coats retained all of their sleeves so that no matter how the piece is worn, two extra sleeves dangle from the front and back of the torso respectively.

These practices are also reminiscent of techniques common to Surrealism,[71] an artistic movement that has been amply discussed in relation to the grotesque. In her assessment of the relation between the grotesque and Surrealism, the art historian Kirsten A. Hoving points out that the grotesque:

> lies at the very core of Surrealist thought ... André Breton and his Surrealist followers sought ways to redefine beauty *as* grotesque ... At the heart of the Surrealist enterprise was the need to trespass boundaries in order to discover the hidden meaning at the core of human existence,

and the artists and writers sought ways to free themselves and redefine reality.[72]

Hoving proceeds to sketch out the relation between Surrealism and the grotesque as it played out on the human body, through the medium of photography: 'As the traditional site of the grotesque the body and its norms were the starting point for the blurring of distinctions between things, leading to misshapen and complete disintegration.'[73] Although Hoving discusses these interventions on the body primarily in relation to Surrealist photography, one could easily trace them to the medium of fashion, where they appear very much in line with Margiela's grotesque alteration of the body and its extremities through clothes and accessories.

This relation between fashion and Surrealism, which perhaps becomes most evident in Margiela's work, is present in a number of the designers discussed, as they not only employ techniques common to Surrealism in their transformations of the body (and in particular the female body) and the juxtaposition of incongruous objects and images, but they also refer, more or less explicitly, to particular Surrealist works and figures. This can be observed in Kawakubo's reference to the Surrealist photographer Claude Cahun and in Georgina Godley's and, as will be later discussed, Bernhard Willhelm's references to the work of Elsa Schiaparelli.[74]

This constant play with garments' traditional function, and its attendant disruptions of expectations, reinscribes an irreverent and humorous tone to contemporary fashion via a series of 'carnivalesque' inversions and reversals. Margiela's work is in line with the logic of the 'wrong side out' and 'the farcical discrepancy' between 'the various objects and the way in which they are used'[75] that characterised, according to Bakhtin, 'the choice and use of carnival objects'. Just like these objects, Margiela's garments and accessories are 'turned inside out, utilised in the wrong way, contrary to their common use'[76] and, at times, they are denied any functionality altogether. These strategies were central, as Bakhtin notes, to carnival humour and its temporary disruption of hierarchies: 'A highly important role is played [within carnival imagery] by negation in time and space expressed in forms of the contrary – the backside, the lower stratum, the inside out, and the topsy-turvy.'[77] As noted by Bakhtin in relation to the carnivalesque use of a number of objects in Rabelais's narrative, Margiela's constant play with functionality allows for a reassessment of certain objects and their respective significance and value: 'This new standard invites the reader to look at the object in a different light, to measure it, so to speak, for its new use. In this process the object's form, material and size are reconsidered.'[78]

And it is through these endless inversions and reversals that one can argue that the Belgian designer's work retains a carnivalesque and grotesque element, one that is, in a further ironic turn, very deliberately and carefully achieved, as exemplified by the precise and consistent alterations of scale in the collections discussed. Thus, ultimately, the analytical and the humorous do not necessarily cancel each other out in Margiela's work, but they coexist and are dependent on one another for their full effect.

5

CARNIVALISED TIME
Martin Margiela

MARGIELA'S WORK AND ALTERNATIVE TEMPORALITIES

Bakhtin argued that cyclical time played an extremely important role within the carnival and the culture of folk humour and was opposed to official time, which was characterised by an apparent stability and pretensions to eternity:

> Carnival celebrated temporary liberation from the prevailing truth and from the established order: it marked the suspension of all hierarchical rank, privileges, norms, and prohibitions. Carnival was the true feast of time, the feast of becoming, change, and renewal. It was hostile to all that was immortalised and completed.[1]

'The culture of folk humour', Bakhtin added, 'conceives all these false pretences of immovable stability and eternity in the perspective of ever-changing and renewed time'.[2] This conception of time expounded by Bakhtin in relation to carnival and the ever-becoming nature of the grotesque brings to mind the constantly changing nature of fashion time characterised by ephemerality as opposed to the stability and immortality traditionally claimed by other cultural forms. Thus, one could argue that, to some extent, all fashion partakes of carnival and the grotesque in its relation to time, yet Margiela's work makes this argument most convincingly. By recycling his own collections, as well as old clothes from various past decades, he highlights the cyclical nature of fashion, which is sometimes denied by the linear and progressive teleological narrative of traditional history and traditional fashion histories. The latter often follow long-established art history and art historical survey texts in their dependence on strict chronology and suggestions of progress.[3] Margiela's interest in transience and in the recycling of old garments, however, is shared by a great number of artists and designers of this period and, as has been discussed in preceding chapters, can be partially read as a response to anxieties surrounding ever-accelerating times of production and consumption as well as a rejection of the aesthetic of excess characterising the preceding decade.[4]

As Julia Kristeva points out, cyclical time stands in opposition to 'time as project, teleology, linear and prospective unfolding time; time as departure, progression and arrival – in other words the time of history'.[5] She adds that cyclical time is 'traditionally linked to female subjectivity', a point that further strengthens the link between fashion, the feminine and the grotesque. The concept of cyclical time, in fact, dovetails with Kristeva's discussions of the subject-in-process and the maternal, which presupposes constant and endless change. This temporal modality is also central to the 'ever-becoming' grotesque body of carnival, while the cyclical nature of fashion history, which contradicts popular understandings of fashion as a chronological progression in search of the *new*, can be observed in Barbara Burman Baines's account of fashion's endless revivals, which she explored within the context of English dress in her book *Fashion Revivals from the Elizabethan Age to the Present Day*.[6] This concept has also been theorised in three-dimensional form by Judith Clark's exhibition 'Malign Muses: When Fashion Turns Back', which was dialogically developed with theorist Caroline Evans. The exhibition employed a system of interlocking cogs on which garments from different periods were placed to explore the cyclicality and non-linearity of fashion time.[7]

Margiela, however, takes this process a step further and produces what could be described as a carnivalised time. I use the expression 'carnivalised time' as a further elaboration of Bakhtin's theories of carnival to mean not only the cyclical time of carnival festivities but more specifically an inverted and topsy-turvy time where temporalities of past, present and future are reversed and/or thoroughly confused.[8] Margiela denies the ineluctable linearity of Western industrial time, and literally inverts past and future, thus carnivalising time. Margiela's garments and performances invert and accelerate time, as well as confound both the ageing process of the garments and the historical time of fashion history. He inverts and refutes teleological and progressive notions of time and history by making the old anew and rendering the new as old. These tendencies, although present in the majority of his work, can be best observed in his spring/summer 1993 and spring/summer

1996 collections – two collections that have been largely ignored within the literature on the designer – and culminated in his exhibition/performance in Rotterdam in 1997.

'THEATRE COSTUMES' COLLECTION: SPRING/ SUMMER 1993

The designer's spring/summer 1993 collection presented 'historically inspired underwear and skirts' alongside 'reworked and over-dyed jackets of Renaissance and eighteenth-century style theatre costumes in velvet and brocade worn on bare torsos, closed with safety pins or belted with Scotch Tape'.[9] Besides the obvious irony of using Scotch Tape and safety pins to 'style' historical theatre costumes, their inclusion adds another layer to Margiela's plays with temporalities. These costumes, which were transformed and further aged through an over-dyeing process, in fact already carry a reference to historical time. Not unlike historical film costumes, they approximate an historical past, often by resorting to established conventions of how the past has come to be represented (i.e. puffed sleeves and velvets become a shorthand for the Renaissance, neck ruffs for the Elizabethan era).

Theatre costumes, in fact, perhaps even more so than cinematic ones, present a simplified and emboldened version of 'history' distilled in a few immediately readable signs, which need to be recognisable by an audience at a distance. As a result, they often shed more light on contemporary rather than past fashions and on the way the conventions according to which we represent and imagine various historical periods are rooted in the present. This is particularly evident in the theatre costumes that Margiela included in his 1993 collection, whose historical approximation and vagueness is furthered by the reworking of the garments, which ultimately look rather contemporary and vaguely pan-historical. The reworked theatre costumes, having been taken out of the context of an entire ensemble and having undergone photographic close-up, give away their lack of historical accuracy: snap buttons, which are often used in theatre costume to allow for quick changes, are visible on 'Renaissance' jackets worn open and on a vaguely military eighteenth-century jacket. A waistcoat, once taken out of context, conveys a nineteenth-century riding habit, such as a Redingote à la Hussarde. Stomachers and corsets paired with exposed belly buttons underscore contemporary mores rather than whatever period they were originally meant to represent (Figs 31 and 32).

Fig. 31 Martin Margiela, 'Theatre Costumes' collection, spring/summer 1993, photograph by Anders Edstrom, courtesy of the artist

Margiela's spring/summer 1993 collection brings to mind the complex filmic time of historical movies where the past is imagined via the present. Historical films – such as the 1967 gangster/romance film Bonnie and Clyde and its portrayal of 1930s America – merge fashion from different decades and convey how a decade, be it our own or, in the case of Bonnie and Clyde the 1960s, represented a particular past. This process is in great part achieved via costumes and mise en scène, alongside social mores. Similarly, Margiela's reconstructed theatre costumes highlight the ways in which history is constructed and makes visible how the past is mediated and available only through the

Fig. 32 Martin Margiela, 'Theatre Costumes' collection, spring/summer 1993, photograph by Anders Edstrom, courtesy of the artist

present. They reinforce an understanding of history – or better histories – as reflexive, interpretative and thus necessarily mediated and culturally constructed rather than being a stable and unmediated reconstruction of the past, which could be fully disinterested or objective.

The Belgian designer's pieces constitute a visual and material theorisation of 'new history' and its attendant historiographical methods, which developed with particular force from the 1970s onwards to debunk the so-called 'master narratives' and the traditional paradigm of history.[10] Written from a Western vantage point, this paradigm was highly dependent on official documents in its quest for causality and objectivity, and characterised by an interest in the chronological unfolding of national and international political events. (Needless to say, it had very little space for fashion.) Margiela's reconstructed theatre pieces instead forcefully point to the ways reality is socially and culturally constructed and one 'cannot avoid looking at the past from a particular point of view'.[11] This opens up the field of inquiry and suggests new theoretical models for the study of fashion histories, more fluid in their approach to temporalities and understand histories as inevitably mediated. Thus, ultimately, Margiela's reworking of theatre costumes provides further evidence that fashion is itself theoretical and not an inert matter to which theories are merely applied. As Alison Gill warned, fashion should not be thought of 'as a passive reflection and measure of agencies found elsewhere in (deeper) social concerns',[12] but rather as having a theoretical dimension which intervenes and influences the theoretical discourse.

Under closer scrutiny, and as the suspension of disbelief afforded by the stage is removed, Margiela's garments reveal themselves for what they are: obviously 'fake' replicas and approximations of an historical past often achieved by quoting more recent pasts. This is visible in the case of a small fur jacket invoking the eighteenth century, which seems to be adapted from a 1940s garment, and a Renaissance-like garment whose laced sleeves seem to be quoting the nineteenth century and are possibly of that period. Frequently, due to budgetary restrictions and the unavailability of materials such as old laces, theatre costumes adapt old clothes and materials from a more recent past to refer to an older past. For instance, nineteenth-century lace is often used for Renaissance costumes, as might have been the case with the Renaissance jacket from the 1993 collection. These layering of pasts in Margiela's garments is confirmed by Richard Martin and Harold Koda's research for the exhibition 'Infra-Apparel', in which they date one of Margiela's reconstructed eighteenth-century theatre costumes to the 1940s.[13] And as Alexandra Palmer has shown by unveiling the complex pasts retained in eighteenth-century garments from the collection of the Ontario Museum, clothes often retain a layering of histories.[14]

Rendering the conflation of various historical periods explicit, Margiela's pieces dismantle the illusion of a stable and 'authentic' past that the theatre costumes are meant to represent. The reconstructed theatre costumes deny fixed and stable origins. They carnivalise linear history and, in their obvious inauthenticity and inverted complex time, question a historical past that is stable and unmediated. They show the complex temporalities of dress history where, at closer scrutiny, one finds a palimpsest of historical periods within a single garment.

'TROMP-L'OEIL' COLLECTION: SPRING/SUMMER 1996

This theme of denying and subverting notions of authenticity and origin is recurrent in Margiela's work. Another collection that brings this theme to

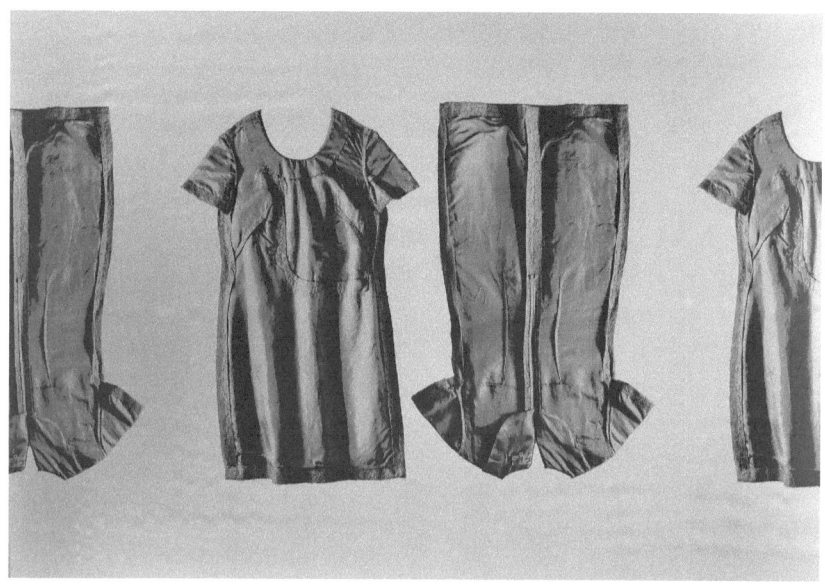

Fig. 33 Martin Margiela, 'Tromp-l'oeil collection', spring/summer 1996, photograph by Guy Voet, courtesy of MoMu, Antwerp

the fore is his spring/summer 1996 collection, for which photographs of garments, often vintage garments alongside ones from previous collections

> are printed on light and fluid fabrics and made up into garments of very simple construction ... A photograph of a 1930's heavy man's, half belted, overcoat is printed on a light viscose, 1940's checked skirts to the knee are shown in silk chiffon. A second-hand army surplus jacket is printed on stretch cotton and a lighter viscose.[15]

and so on (Figs 33 and 34). These printed garments instil a temporal and material confusion, so that the viewer is not sure, at least at first sight, whether they are in fact vintage pieces and/or pieces from Margiela's previous collection – which, in a further twist, were often replicas of vintage pieces to begin with. This is the case, for instance, with the garment from this collection that was included in the 1997 Rotterdam exhibition: 'A photograph of the original lining of the 1950s cocktail dress the reproduction

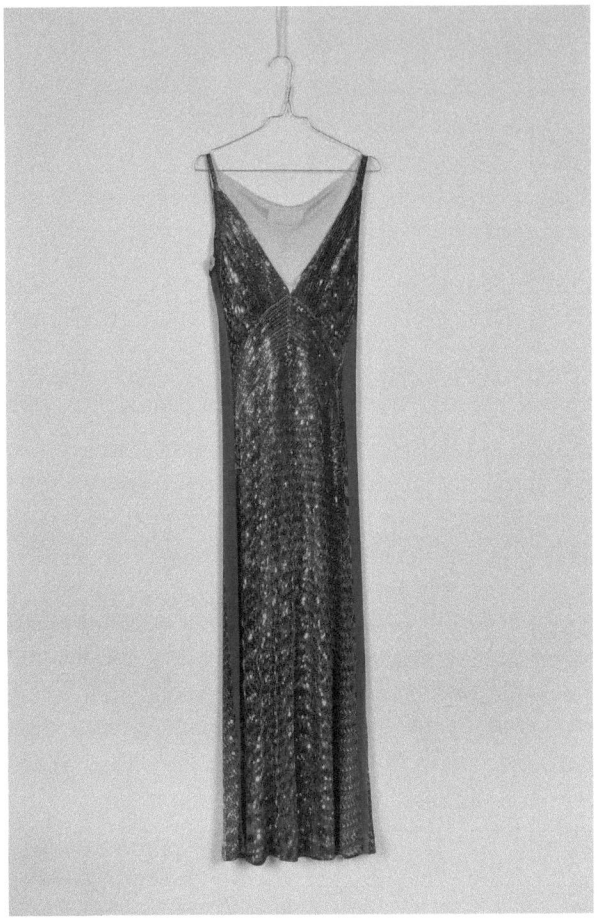

Fig. 34 Martin Margiela, 'Tromp-l'oeil' collection spring/summer 1996, photograph by Guy Voet, courtesy of MoMu, Antwerp

of which appears in outfit 14 (part of the autumn/winter 1995–96 collection).'[16] Furthering the sense of confusion, the garments photographed are of a different material from the one on which the photographs are printed. This creates a *tromp-l'œil* effect that disorients and upsets expectations. In this, Margiela's work is once again reminiscent of Surrealist techniques, especially as articulated within fashion design by Elsa Schiaparelli who, for instance in her 'Tear Dress' from 1938, which she created in collaboration with Dalí, used such techniques to give the suggestions of tears in an otherwise 'whole' garment.[17]

Additionally, as is underlined by the Maison Martin Margiela press release, 'the colours of old photographs – black and white, sepia and tones of brown – are maintained throughout'. These tones are perhaps more obviously visible in the 1950's cocktail dress lining (included in the Rotterdam exhibition) which, in its yellowish colour, carries the patina of an heirloom, and is thus prone to inducing nostalgia and offering the illusion of a direct relation to an authentic past. This strategy would seem to align Margiela with much contemporary fashion and fashion merchandising, which employs reference to bygone times and milieu in order to induce nostalgia and activate an emotive consumption.[18] However, what these goods create is in actuality an 'imagined nostalgia', a longing for an imagined past that was neither experienced nor lost. Referring primarily to fashion advertisements, Arjun Appadurai writes that '[they] teach consumers to miss things they have never lost. In thus creating experiences of losses that never took place, these advertisements create what might be called 'imagined nostalgia'.[19] To which he adds:

> The viewer need only bring the faculty of nostalgia to an image that will supply the memory of a loss he or she never suffered. This relationship might be called armchair nostalgia, nostalgia without lived experience or collective historical memory.[20]

Yet Margiela, in fact, denies or at least, ironises these processes of 'imagined' nostalgia. He does so by isolating and doubling up various elements that are supposed to induce nostalgia, such as the old clothes and the old photographs, and putting them back together in ways that render obvious their artificiality. By printing artificially aged photographs of old clothes onto new fabric and leaving the processes readable, he questions notions of authenticity and unveils how nostalgia – and particularly nostalgia for consumer goods – can potentially be constructed and fabricated.[21]

According to the theorist Linda Hutcheon, processes of ironising nostalgia are common to contemporary cultural productions. She qualifies this claim, however, by arguing that irony and nostalgia were, in fact, associated well before the late twentieth century, and brings up the example of *Don Quixote*, which is, according to Bakhtin, a quintessential carnivalesque novel. Discussing architecture, Hutcheon writes:

> the *postmodern* architecture does indeed recall the past, but always with the kind of ironic double vision that acknowledges the final impossibility of

indulging in nostalgia, even as it consciously evokes nostalgia's affective power. In the postmodern, in other words (and here is the source of the tension) nostalgia itself gets both called up, exploited, *and* ironised.[22]

Hutcheon makes a distinction between these practices of ironising nostalgia versus unironic and potentially conservative invocation of an idealised past partially in response to Fredric Jameson's pessimistic view of 'late capitalist' society. Jameson, in fact, sees all contemporary nostalgic cultural production as a failure to engage with history. He discusses the phenomenon according to which style and periodisation are used to invoke past as a testament to the fact that contemporary cultural production has done away with real history in lieu of historicism, in the negative sense of the term:

> Yet everything in our culture suggest that we have not, for all that, ceased to be preoccupied by history; indeed, at the very moment in which we complain as here, of the eclipse of historicity, we also universally diagnose contemporary culture as irredeemably historicist, in the bad sense of an omnipresent and indiscriminate appetite for dead styles and fashions: indeed for all the styles and fashions of a dead past.[23]

However, as many theorists, including Hutcheon, have commented, Jameson's writings on history are themselves nostalgic – namely for a view of history understood as more coherent and less fragmented which, according to Jameson, allowed for a greater level of political consciousness.[24] Hutcheon asks whether 'Jameson's implicit mythologising and idealising of a more stable pre-*late*-capitalist (that is modernist) world is not in itself perhaps part of an aesthetic (or even politics) of nostalgia'.[25] The way in which Hutcheon's and Jameson's debates ultimately depend on two different understanding of history is discussed by Susannah Radstone in her writing on the representations of history in film. Like Hutcheon, Radstone ultimately suggests the need for a qualification of different types of nostalgia and the way they operate within different cultural output:

> The dispute between Hutcheon and Jameson rests on two conflicting understandings of, and attitudes to, history. Jameson clearly mourns the loss of a Marxist history, with its capacity for transcendence and 'objectivity', while Hutcheon celebrates postmodernism's problematising of such claims for history.[26]

PERFORMING GARMENTS: MARTIN MARGIELA'S ROTTERDAM EXHIBITION

Margiela's ironisation of processes of nostalgia became perhaps even more evident in the designer's retrospective at the Museum Boijmans Van Beuningen, a museum of art and design in Rotterdam organised by the Maison Martin Margiela itself in 1997. As noted by fashion scholar Marco Pecorari in relation to the ModeMuseum in Antwerp, the practice of designers taking an active role in retrospectives of their work has since become commonplace, with all the potential pitfalls in terms of objectivity and critical point of view and benefits in terms of access to the designer and its archives.[27] The potential conflict of interest of such arrangement is probably the reason the Metropolitan Museum of Art has not allowed a retrospective of a living designer since the exhibition of Yves Saint Laurent by Diana Vreeland in 1983. However, in the late 1990s, the role of designers as curators – at least explicitly stated – was still a fairly novel approach, as the field of fashion curation itself was not nearly as developed as it has since become. For instance, the ModeMuseum did not officially open until 2002.

In the case of the Rotterdam retrospective, it would be more precise to call the exhibition a performance, as it constituted an event that unfolded over time, and where (rather uncharacteristically) the main subjects were garments as opposed to the people wearing them. The Rotterdam retrospective entered the realm of performance art as the garments became performing 'subjects'. The clothes came alive or, rather, their organic life and lifespan was made manifest. Pink yeast, red or yellow bacteria and green mould were applied onto clothes from Margiela's past collection, which had been treated with the growing medium agar. The application of these organisms accelerated processes of ageing and decomposition, particularly as the clothes were placed 'in incubating structures' in the museum's garden.

Thus, unlike the hagiographic fashion exhibitions that have since become prominent, Margiela's self-destructing retrospective is in line with what design theorist Linda Sandino described as a shift towards recycling, transience and ephemerality in contemporary art, craft and design of the 1990s, which developed in direct response to the 1980s and to 'cultural and material anxieties arising from the economic excesses of consumer culture and [was] expressed ... through the use of material means'.[28]

The use of bacteria is also suggestive of disease and contagion – a reference that was, however, subverted by the beautiful pattern obtained through

Fig. 35 Dress forms installed outside the museum's pavilion, Margiela retrospective at the Museum Boijmans Van Beuningen, Rotterdam, 1997, courtesy of Caroline Evans

their applications. This reference to disease and medicalised spaces is reminiscent of Godley's and Bowery's work. An undercurrent to experimental fashion produced through the 1980s and 1990s, it can be read as meditating anxieties and obsessions with bodily borders surrounding the AIDS crisis.

This technique allowed for the fabrication of signs of ageing and of patina onto the clothes across a relative short span of time. Once the bacteria had grown on the garments' fabric and achieved the desired effect, the clothes were exhibited on dress forms alongside the perimeter of the museum's garden to further age them. They were visible to the museum-goers from both inside the exhibition hall and, in rear view, from the museum garden in which the visitors could walk. The mannequins were placed on a plinth outside, but facing in as if looking through the glass walls of the exhibition space at the visitors in the empty space inside. This initiated the first of a series of inversions by switching the traditional placement of mannequins vis-à-vis viewers and playing with categories of inside and outside (Fig. 35).

Thus what appeared at first sight as a dejected and abandoned site (especially once the garments were taken out of the enclosures and exposed to the elements) was in actuality painstakingly produced, and was documented in the book accompanying the exhibition. The garments were aged according to a scientific process in a controlled environment so that the process of fabricating imagined histories and a sense of nostalgia was literally deconstructed and put on display.

In the exhibition, one encounters once again Margiela's penchant for carnivalising time and playing with the order of temporalities. Almost overnight, he ages garments that had withstood the passage of time and in the process he shreds them to pieces. Moreover, he does so in the context of the museum, a place traditionally engaged in conservation rather than destruction of objects. Margiela inverts the temporality of the retrospective that is supposed to anoint a designer's or most often an artist's oeuvre into the 'eternal' and stable time of the museum. The designer inverts the relation of the museum to permanence versus transience. As Linda Sandino points out in her discussion of contemporary art works, incorporating ephemeral elements, museums are 'complicit in the transition of transient to durable', as they are 'dedicated to preserve the fiction that works of arts are fixed and immortal'. As a result, 'transience [which well-describes Margiela's entire retrospective] subverts the presumed timeless significance and value of the museum collection'.[29]

The instant patina acquired by the garments on display in the Rotterdam exhibition disrupts 'the symbolic capital' of patina, with its associations with the objects surrounding the upper classes. Patina is, in fact, supposed to bear testament to the fact that certain objects have not been recently acquired, but have a genealogy and history reflecting that of their owners.[30] Moreover, as Evans points out regarding Margiela and other designers of the period who heavily use patina in their work, they invert the relation according to which fashion stands in opposition to patina, the latter's symbolic capital having been threatened and in part eroded by the advent of the industrial consumer revolution, according to which the new – epitomised by fashionable garments – is meant to represent social status.[31] Here, Evans is referring to Grant McCracken's notion that patina's relation to social status declined after the eighteenth century. However, as Appadurai points out, the process was in no way complete, as patina retains a social value to the present day.[32]

Barbara Vinken also comments on how Margiela's use of garments to register the passage of time stands in opposition to a more conventional understanding of fashion's association with the new. 'Time', Vinken writes clings to Margiela's work. His clothes carry the traces which time leaves behind, and are themselves signs of time. Time has entered into them in two respects: 1. as the time of the production process: and 2. as traces, which time leaves behind in the fabric in the course of use.[33]

Another central inversion that took place during the Rotterdam exhibition is that the clothes become animated via the application of bacteria, yeast and mould to the fabric. To this end, Margiela employs a scientific method, which is fully documented in the catalogue accompanying the exhibition. As discussed in the previous chapter, this brings him in line with nineteenth- and early twentieth-century attempts to unveil the secret life of objects and imbue them with subjectivities, an interest in large part spurred by the development of new optical and recording devices. It also puts Margiela in the role of the magician or the carnival trickster who makes objects come to life through an alchemical process. Evans succinctly sums up the designer's peculiar abilities while discussing another of his alchemical processes, his ability to transform discarded objects into high end garments, by referring to Margiela as 'a kind of "Golden Dustman"' of the fashion world, converting 'base material into gold'.[34]

Margiela's work is reminiscent of early cinema's fascination with what remains invisible to the human eye. This exploration, discussed at length in early fashion theory and in particular by the French theorist and filmmaker Jean Epstein,[35] was shared by the Surrealists, including Salvador Dalí, who was fascinated by the possibilities opened up by the world as seen through the microscope. This interest is perhaps most evident in one of his later cinematic works, *Impressions of Upper Mongolia – Homage to Raymond Roussel* (1975). Inspired by the early scientific film by Jean Painlevé, *Impressions* was structured around the extreme close-ups of the brass band of a pen from the St Regis (a luxury hotel in New York), whose 'patterned or mottled patina' had been achieved, as Dalí explains in the film, through the carnivalesque process of applying the artist's uric acid on the pen or, as he more plainly described to the film director José Montes-Baquer:

> In this clean and aseptic country I have been observing how the urinals in the luxury restroom of this hotel have acquired an astounding range of rust colours through the interaction of the uric acid on the precious metals. For this reason, I have been regularly urinating on this brass band of this pen over the past week, to obtain the magnificent structures that you will find with your cameras and lenses.[36]

And as the film's voice-over concludes, it is through this rather simple 'experiment' that Dalí, much like Margiela, claims to have achieved his own alchemical transformation:

> This ballpoint contains the whole homage to Raymond Roussel, the whole voyage, the whole expedition to Upper Mongolia, and the microstructures which my team filmed in a castle in Germany, a castle worthy of alchemists of the Middle Ages. This is what you have just seen.[37]

Finally, in the Rotterdam exhibition there is an inversion of the usual relation between body and clothes. Here, the clothing is animated whereas the wearer, as represented by the dress forms, remains inanimate.[38] A similar reversal of categories has been discussed in relation to digital photography by the fashion theorist Karen de Perthuis. What she defines as the 'synthetic ideal' of digital photography allows, similarly to Margiela's exhibition, for a breaking down between 'subject and object, inside and outside, animate and inanimate, organic and inorganic' and it does so by 'realising a form that announces the idea of a continual becoming'.[39] According to de Perthuis, this breaking down between the category of body and clothing cements a new, wholly artificial being, which she theorises as constituting fashion's imaginary realised.

Albeit within drastically different media and through different processes, it could be argued that Margiela's 'animated' garments are also intent on fully exploring fashion's potential for problematising fixed categories of inside/outside, animate/inanimate, body/clothing and its potential for continual change and transformation. Margiela's garments, in fact, appear not only to be animated but also generative as is underlined by the Maison description of the first stage of the exhibition as 'the gestation period'. The garments' fecundity stands in opposition not only to the inanimate nature of the clothes but also to the traditional sterility of the body of fashion, which epitomises the sealed ungenerative classical body.

The Belgian designer's interest in the maternal body alongside bodies that do not align themselves with the classical bodies of fashion is also explored in one of his very early collections (autumn/winter 1993–94), for which he produced a short film. Shot in black and white film stock, the film, titled *Seven Women*, bestows a lyrical quality to its subjects, which is reinforced by the use of soft environmental light, and the repetitive and hypnotic sound of a film projector as the only soundtrack to an otherwise silent film. The amateurish camera work gives the film a homemade quality, which matches its subject matter: it shows an intimate glimpse of women of different age groups, one of them pregnant, another with her young child, modelling in a spontaneous and unconventional manner some of Margiela's clothes in either their apartments or the streets of Paris.

Much as in the short film, the exhibition's 'fecund' dresses go against the understanding of fashion (and the woman of fashion) as 'profoundly inorganic and anti-maternal'[40] and once again bring us back to experimental fashion's exploration of the generative potential of the body and of different models of subjectivities. These processes of growth and becoming bear further testament to late twentieth-century fashion's ability to articulate a model of a subject-in-process and render Margiela's garments in their relation to reproduction and in their instability undoubtedly grotesque. In their 'gestation' and growth, Margiela's garments, stand-ins for the generative body, closely resemble Kenneth Clark's gynophobic definition of the non-classical body:

> Roots and bulbs pulled up into the light, give us for a moment a feeling of shame. They are pale, defenceless, unself-supporting. They have the formless character of life that has been both protected and oppressed. In the darkness their slow, biological gropings have been the contrary of the quick, resolute movements of free creatures ... and have made them baggy, scraggy and indeterminate ... The bulblike women and rootlike men seem to have been dragged out of the protective darkness in which the human body had lain muffled for a thousand years.[41]

This is the same bulbous, indeterminate body that characterised the work of Kawakubo, Godley and Bowery, as well as that of Bernhard Willhelm, which will be discussed in the following chapter.

6

CARNIVAL ICONOGRAPHY
Bernhard Willhelm

According to Freud, repression occurs when instinctual impulses are kept from entering the conscious mind through a 'persistent expenditure of force', because they threaten the integrity of the ego or are incompatible with ethical standards imposed on it by the superego. However, in the long run, these repressed impulses tend to return and surface to consciousness via mechanisms of condensation and/or displacement. In an interesting parallel with the fashion I discuss, these returns often take on 'extreme forms', since, according to Freud, what is prevented from entering consciousness 'develops with less interference ... It proliferates in the dark, as it were, and takes on extreme forms of expression'.[1] This Freudian image of repressed impulses as proliferating in the dark to then surface as distorted and potentially horrific is reminiscent of Kenneth's Clark description of the non-classical canon. Clark, albeit not using a psychological framework, also describes a process according to which something is buried and grows in the dark to surface later as something disturbing and unsettling to the classical aesthetic – a fact that, according to Clark, makes this class of imagery irremediably ugly.

Both Freud and Clark relate the mechanism of repression to the grotesque canon. However, in their focus on images of growth and proliferation, their descriptions suggest a maternal reference and thus a gynophobic subtext.[2] In Clark's writings, this relation is perhaps more explicit, as the concept is visually translated into the image of a bulb which grows underground, an image that strongly resembles that of the cave, invoked by the grotesque etymology. Additionally, Clark points to a relation between the grotesque and northern European representational tradition, which he defines as the alternative (to the classical) canon, and traces contemporary examples of the alternative canon back to the northern Gothic.

The work of the German-born and Belgian-trained Bernhard Willhelm fulfils these readings of the grotesque as a return of the repressed in a number of ways. Willhelm's work is reminiscent of Clark's discussion of the alternative canon, as the designer employs grotesque imagery, frequently rooted in the northern European representational tradition, while making direct references to carnival iconography. His work also explores an important site – according to Freud's theories – for the articulation of repressed impulses in its constant melding of humour and horror, often within the same collection, garment or fashion show.

Moreover, Willhelm's work defies conventions of symmetry and proportionality, which could be understood as classical and neoclassical, not only by making references to northern European representational traditions of the late Middle Ages, which have been defined in opposition to the classical model of the Italian Renaissance, but also through references to the southern German tailoring traditions. He evokes the grotesque via references to the bodies of contemporary pornography and horror which, following Bakhtin's definitions, defy borders as they couple with other bodies and become unsealed. In its over-abundance of references and varied and excessive imagery, the work of Bernhard Willhelm can be read as a catalyst for various strands of the grotesque in contemporary fashion.

Willhelm, originally from Ulm – a prosperous, conservative city in southern Germany-studied fashion design in the mid-1990s at the Royal Academy of Fine Arts in Antwerp. Upon graduating, he worked for the Belgian designer Walter Van Beirendonck, and was obviously influenced by Van Beirendonck's humorous and colourful pieces that often investigated and subverted normative understanding of bodily anatomy and parodied bodybuilding culture. In collaboration with Jutta Kraus, his close childhood friend and current business partner, Willhelm set up his company in Antwerp in the late 1990s, and later moved, first to Paris and eventually to Los Angeles. It was and remains a small independent company; it operates without any outside backing, and its products are primarily sold in specialist boutiques in the US, Europe and Asia (especially Japan) in particular. The company has, however, gained visibility through its collaboration with visual artists such as Olaf Breuning and musicians, such as Björk.

CARNIVAL ICONOGRAPHY

Willhelm's company label succinctly introduces the themes of the grotesque and northern European culture that characterises his work as a whole. The drawing of a hand, the label is meant to symbolise the hand of the giant, a quintessentially grotesque figure after which the city of Antwerp – in Flemish Antwerpen, from *Hand Werpen* (throw a hand) – is said to take its name.³ According to a local legend, a giant exacted a toll for people crossing the river of Antwerp, and would cut off the hands of those who refused. Eventually, a local hero whose statue is in the city's main square, cut off the giant's own hand and threw it in the river.

Of all the work discussed in this book, Bernhard Willhelm's is perhaps the most explicitly carnivalesque: the German designer makes direct references to actual carnival iconography throughout his work, where themes from the *commedia dell'arte*, the farcical genre developed in Italy in the sixteenth century, after medieval carnivals, are recurrent. Moreover, differently from Margiela, Willhelm's fondness for inversion and disruption of order and symmetry does not stop at garment construction, but is also visible, and often most evident, in his prints and embroideries. Among the collections that best exemplify this aspect of Willhelm's work is his spring/summer 2005 women's collection, which – in its blatant reference to Hermès' traditional equestrian prints and its use of gold lamé, paisley print, quilted textiles and oversized silhouettes – can be read as a subversion of 1980s status dressing. Willhelm's collection was a rebuke to status dressing at a time when a revival of the 1980s, both politically and stylistically, could be observed. This is perhaps most explicit in two looks that are reminiscent of Godley's work from the late 1980s in the way that they make a mockery of corporate greed and financial self-help rhetoric through prints and machine embroidery of what appear to be financial advertisements and newspaper headlines. The pieces in question are two oversized jackets made of heavy cotton and cotton jersey, cut in an intricate diamond pattern to create a gathered effect in front, and paired with a mid-length skirt and jersey leggings (Figs 36 and 37). All the pieces sported printed or embroidered texts in different fonts inciting the readers 'to plunge into the investment ocean', while promising a dubious '97% profit in three months'. It also reminded them 'how the rich don't get richer by putting their money in the bank', while referring to the housing boom, which peaked at the time of the collection (Figs 38 and 39).

The bombardment of seemingly contradictory and overlapping financial advice blanketing the garments is reminiscent of spam email, in both its exaggerated claims and its repetitiveness. Like Godley's 1988 Corporate Coding collection, these pieces were conceived and produced at the height of a market boom, and mock the greed, affluence and sense of euphoria characterising the period. Through the self-help rhetoric of the text, the

Fig. 36 Bernhard Willhelm, financial adverts top and leggings, spring/summer 2005, photograph by Shoji Fujii, courtesy of Bernhard Willhelm

garments invoke enterprising models of the self, which were solidified in the period since the 1980s, and allowed a shift of responsibility from society to the individual for one's well being.[4] At the turn of this century, enterprising models of subjectivity bloomed as a self-empowering rhetoric, perhaps best epitomised by the *Oprah Winfrey Show*, was coupled with the solidification of neoliberal governments in both the US and much of Europe, which

Fig. 37 Bernhard Willhelm, financial adverts top and skirt, spring/summer 2005, photograph by Shoji Fujii, courtesy of Bernhard Willhelm

successfully promoted individual accountability over social and government responsibility.[5]

By contrast, much of Willhelm's spring/summer 2005 women's collection is not as overt in its critique of wealth and affluence but, rather, makes a critique by subverting 1980s status dressing, in a testament to its persistence

Fig 38 Bernhard Willhelm, detail of financial adverts prints in the ModeMuseum collection, spring/summer 2005, photograph by the author, courtesy of MoMu, Antwerp

Fig 39 Bernhard Willhelm, detail of financial adverts prints in the ModeMuseum collection, spring/summer 2005, photograph by the author, courtesy of MoMu, Antwerp

as a symbol of the ostentatious display of wealth. In an interview with Hint from 2005, Willhelm discusses his distaste for power dressing:

> The one thing I don't like is fashion as a status symbol. I don't buy things to look rich. I have no respect for that. I'm not into the power that fashion can bring. I'm really against power dressing. Fashion is too linked with status and money. It's obvious and false. It kills the creativity. It kills everything, even your personality.[6]

This critical and mocking attitude is particularly evident in a number of garments, also from spring/summer 2005, that are now in the collection of the ModeMuseum in Antwerp, to which Willhelm donated the entirety of his archive. For these pieces, the designer reworked and ironised fox-hunting scenes by literally inverting them, as the clothes were sewn so that the riders in the prints appear upside-down. One of these pieces, which is identified in the accompanying garment tag with the name of 'Ms Behaviour', appears at first sight to be a conservative drop-waisted dress made of quilted fabric (Fig. 40). Its ostensibly conservative look is mirrored by the seemingly formal fox-hunting attire worn by the riders portrayed in the prints (Fig. 41). However, just as the inversion of the print undermines the primness of the dress, the rider's 'gentlemen hunter' attire is ironised by the use of a pointed conical hat in lieu of the top hat generally worn with the formal fox-hunting outfit.

The pointed conical hat – also known as the fool's hat, was later developed into the so-called dunce hat – is a common trope in carnival iconography, where it is often used to mark the court jester. The relation between the pointed hat and the category of 'the fool' can be best observed in the history of northern European art, where pointed hats were often used alongside 'unusual physical features' to mark the court jesters, as well as witches and Jews, in a revealing collapse of categories of otherness.[7] The art historian Ruth Mellinkoff presents a number of examples of the ways pointed hats were used in northern art of the late Middle Ages as a mark of otherness alongside physical typology and facial features, which markedly diverged from the classical canon. This was particularly evident in depictions of Jews and jesters from the period, such as those in the Conrad Laib's Crucifixion (1449), where red cone hats are used to identify two grown men and a child, disparagingly portrayed as 'sneering Jews'; while in the Scene from the Life of Young Tobias (Florentine artist, c.1500), the fool is identified by the pointed conical hat and his small stature.[8]

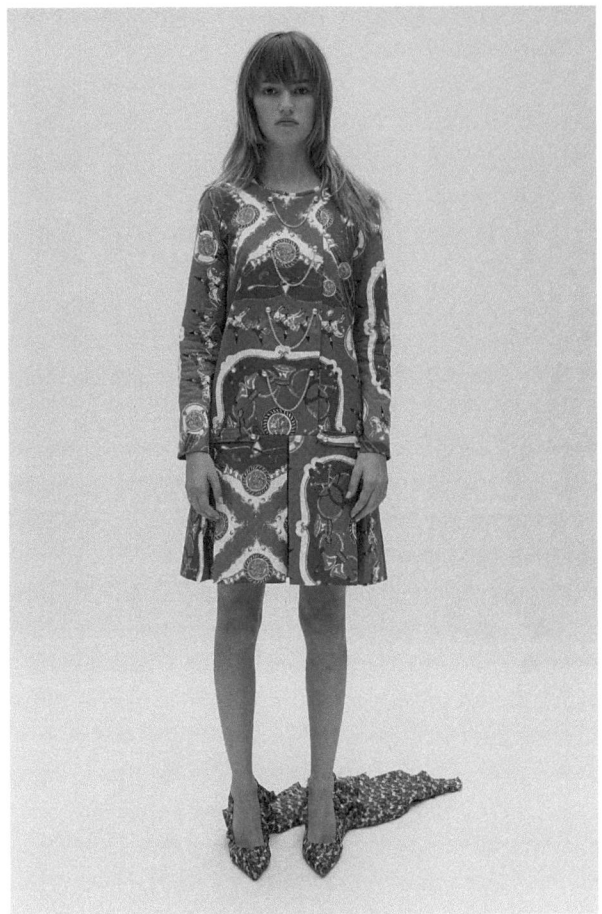

Fig. 40 Bernhard Willhelm, 'Ms Behaviour' dress, spring/summer 2005, photograph by Shoji Fujii, courtesy of Bernhard Willhelm

These two works display the ambiguous nature of the carnival and carnival iconography and the way in which it can be understood, as Bakhtin suggests and Willhelm practices, as having a liberating and subverting quality in its mockery of positions of power and authority. Yet carnival and its associated iconography can also be used as a mark of difference to single out and disparage those with less power in the social formation, as Conrad's and the Florentine artist's portrayals make evident. This phenomenon has been described by Stallybrass and White as 'displaced

CARNIVAL ICONOGRAPHY: BERNHARD WILLHELM

Fig. 41 Bernhard Willhelm, print detail from 'Ms Behaviour' dress in the ModeMuseum collection, spring/summer 2005, photograph by the author, courtesy of MoMu, Antwerp

abjection': 'the process whereby "low" social groups turn their figurative and actual power, *not* against those in authority, but against those who are even "lower" '.[9]

Returning to Willhelm's equestrian prints, these depictions of the hunt further subvert the rigidly codified ritual of fox hunting by having all of the riders depicted in the prints wear the red jacket known as the *pinque*, which is generally only worn by the master of the hunt, and by 'inverting' their gender, as the riders are uncharacteristically portrayed as women. This spirit of carnivalesque inversion is further emphasised in the leggings from this collection, where the equestrian prints are arranged so that the riders circle around the crotch. Thus, Willhelm's iconography, much like Bowery's costumes and performances, strongly brings to mind the carnivalesque practice of inverting social codes, bringing the high to the low, and the 'topographical logic' of shifting top to bottom.[10] According to Bakhtin, in medieval culture this function was actualised by the jester, also known as the clown or fool, whose main attribute 'was precisely the transfer of every high ceremonial gesture or ritual to the material sphere'.[11] Like the designer, the clown accomplished this through humour: 'It is the popular corrective of laughter applied to the narrow-minded seriousness of the spiritual pretence' which 'degrades and materialises.'[12]

That Willhelm explicitly references the medieval jester's attire via his use of the conical hat – a trope which recurs through his collections – points to the fact that his interest in carnivalesque practices of inversions is perhaps more explicit and conscious than in the case of the other designers discussed. This has been pointed out by the German journalist Ingeborg Harms who, in the catalogue accompanying Willhelm's exhibition at Antwerp's ModeMuseum, describes Willhelm himself as a modern-day clown or fool who brings down fashion's pretensions. She goes on to describe Willhelm as the court jester of high fashion who 'holds up [a mirror] to the courtiers' in order to mock them.[13] This description echoes the designer's self-image as he lays claim to 'the jester's freedom', because, according to Willhelm, the jester 'was always the exception, the only character who could say whatever he wanted'.[14]

Willhelm's interest in carnival iconography is further illustrated by his many references to *commedia dell'arte* characters and particularly to the figure of Harlequin – a quintessentially grotesque character and a clown figure who was understood in medieval cosmology as a 'comic devil'.[15] According to Bakhtin, Harlequin represented the desecrating and renewing spirit of 'the material bodily lower stratum'; as a result the *commedia dell'arte* – alongside other popular comic genres – had a 'revitalising effect on objects, positions, professions'.[16]

The Harlequin's diamond pattern is disseminated throughout Willhelm's collections: for instance, it adorns the skirt of a female Superman (spring/summer 2006) and a futuristic androgynous look from his autumn/winter 2003–04 collection, which sports a skirt and blouse with daggered unfinished edges, leggings and a bi-coloured hood partially covering the model's face (Fig. 42). However, references to the *commedia dell'arte* characters became most evident and explicit in Willhelm's autumn/winter 2002–03 collection, which featured female versions of Harlequin and Pierrot alongside the lesser known character of Doctor Balanzone. As such, the collection also revisits the theme of gender inversion, which is a recurrent trope in his work. While not wearing the grotesque masks characteristic of many *commedia dell'arte* characters, a number of models wore heavy and colourful make-up covering

CARNIVAL ICONOGRAPHY: BERNHARD WILLHELM

Fig. 42 Bernhard Willhelm, Harlequin inspired look, autumn/winter 2002–03, photograph by Shoji Fujii, courtesy of Bernhard Willhelm

much of the face, which did suggest a masked appearance.[17] (Willhelm's autumn/winter 2002–03 was not, however, the first designer's collection to be directly inspired by the *commedia dell'arte*. Such a collection was produced as early as 1938 by the French-based Italian designer Elsa Schiaparelli.)

In some cases Willhelm creates an almost literal rendition of the *commedia dell'arte* costumes, as with the grey coat with a ruched collar, characteristic of

Balanzone's attire, while the white Pierrot blouse becomes striped and the harlequin's diamond patterns adorns a daggered skirt, a full-sleeved blouse and various kinds of headgear. One of the hats is open on top, thus lacking functionality, a characteristic of carnival attire. Moreover, many of the elements that Willhelm adds to the traditional *commedia dell'arte* costumes – striped motif, daggered edges – were historically used as marks of otherness to identify fools, minstrels and jesters across Western fashion history, and with particular insistence in northern European attire from the early Middle Ages onwards.[18] Thus, in Willhelm's case, there is a more literal and direct engagement with the history of carnival costumes and iconography than in Margiela's, where the carnivalesque is primarily referenced via garments' inversion and play with scale and functionality.

CARNIVALESQUE PRACTICES

Willhelm's autumn/winter 2002–03 collection not only included actual carnival iconography but also introduced carnivalesque practices of 'farcical discrepancy'[19] and comical incongruity, which characterise the German's designer work throughout. It did so through the fashion show accompanying the collection, as well as through the garments' prints and embroideries. Both, under a light-hearted and childlike façade, belied incongruously dark themes of war and death.

The fashion show, which was staged in Paris in March 2002, was accompanied by the recording of a German television news broadcast.[20] Thus, the models were walking to the reporting of hard news of terrorist bombings and corruptions in the SPD (Sozialdemokratische Partei Deutschlands – Social Democratic Party), as well as soft news of weather conditions and sports events, while wearing incongruously brightly patterned and coloured outfits. Recounted in German, the news was probably incomprehensible to the majority of the audience. However, it could be argued that the clash between a spoken German soundtrack and a fashion show – particularly considering the association of German radio to World War II narratives – might have been apparent to the non-German speaking members of the audience. This contrast was highlighted by the clothes' harlequin patterns and humorous prints, thus imbuing the show with a visual cacophony and a sense of the absurd. Willhelm's exploration of comical incongruity reveals a darker undertone than Margiela's, and introduces a coalescence of humour and horror. This theme was then fully explored in the designer's collaboration

Fig. 43 Bernhard Willhelm, embroidery of a man hanging from a sweater in the ModeMuseum collection, autumn/winter 2002–03, photograph by the author, courtesy of MoMu, Antwerp

with the video artist Olaf Breuning, with whom he produced a mock horror short film/fashion show.

If the incongruous and, at times, disturbing narrative accompanying the fashion show could not have been fully comprehensible to the majority of the audience, the garments' prints and embroideries would have been, as they articulated a pictorial language of sorts. The embroidered and print pieces in this collection reveal some of the recurrent motifs in Willhelm's iconography, which veer from the religious-inspired (i.e. angels ascending a ladder, the all-seeing eye of God), to the comical (i.e. Aladdin coming out of a shoe, a circus animal playing with a frog), to the more ominous motif of a hanging man (Fig. 43). Here, once again, we encounter an incongruity, in this case, between the style of the prints and embroidery – which are

Fig. 44 Bernhard Willhelm, aerial bombing embroidery from a sweatshirt in the ModeMuseum collection, autumn/winter 2002–03, photograph by the author, courtesy of MoMu, Antwerp

rendered in a naive childlike style reminiscent of outsider art – and what they represent. However, if we read these images in the context of the collection as a whole, it could be argued that Willhelm is borrowing the conception of death characteristic of the *commedia dell'arte* spectacles and puppet theatre, 'where death can be a comic episode and a murder parody'.[21] According to Stam, within the context of the *commedia dell'arte* these themes would have been perceived 'not as the death or suffering of real people, but in a spirit of carnival and ritual'.[22] These attitudes towards death are indebted to carnival traditions, where the cycle of life and death was celebrated, thus allowing both to be perceived within the festive atmosphere of the carnival and narratives of rebirth. This is perhaps most evident in the *Totentanz*, the dance of death, which was widespread in northern European visual culture of the late Middle Ages, and to which Bernhard Willhelm also makes reference. However, there were risks involved in the spectacularisation and distancing of death in the context of actual historical carnivals, as made clear by Stallybrass and White's discussion of 'displaced abjection' – the risk of actually demonising those weaker in the social structures, as opposed to mocking figures or authority.[23]

One of the most heavily embroidered pieces in the collection is a cotton sweatshirt which, according to the accompanying garment tag, is called 'Angel Eyes', and was produced in white with black embroidery and in the opposite combination of black background and white embroidery. This piece recalls the television news that accompanied the fashion shows, as it includes on one of the sleeves a machine-embroidered scene of an aerial bombing, (Fig. 44). The scene, which is rendered in the simplified drawing style characteristic of most of Willhelm's embroidered pieces, goes almost undetected at first look, as it is placed across the right sleeve and overwhelmed by the diversity and sheer amount of embroidery on the sweater. However, like the show accompanying the collection, at closer look the piece relays a sense of the absurd, as some of the figures escaping the bombing are portrayed as smiling. The embroidered motifs on the shirt as a whole alternate between the humorous and the unsettling. Among the discordant scenes represented in the piece are a figure clad in medieval garb resting by a tree, a cathode ray tube television, a number of angels ascending a ladder, a tree being cut down, a portrayal of Michael Jackson, as well as the designer's initials sweetly rendered in cross stitch.

In its use of embroidery to portray motifs taken from popular culture and/or to explore themes of war and environmental destruction, Willhelm's work is also in line with a number of artists, often men, who use traditionally feminine crafts, historically associated with the domestic sphere, against what is perceived to be their proper use, thus creating a tension between the art form and what is depicted. The pervasiveness of these practices is evidenced by the exhibition 'Pricked: Extreme Embroidery', which surveyed contemporary European and US artists using embroidery in their practice, as well as by the revived interest in the work of Alighiero e Boetti, the Italian artist associated with *arte povera* and best known for his embroidery of world maps.[24]

Absurd

In its quest for the absurd, understood as something 'out of harmony with reason or propriety; incongruous, unreasonable, illogical',[25] Willhelm's prints, embroidery and fashion presentations present a close affinity with various carnival genres. As Bakhtin discusses in *Rabelais*, the sense of the absurd was characteristic of the comic speech popular in the Middle Ages, and particularly the genre known as *coq-à-l'âne*, which translates as 'rooster to ass'. This form of comic speech, unhinged from rules of grammar and logic, allowed for new and unexpected relations to be formed between words and for an exploration of their potential and multiple meanings:

> This is a genre of intentionally absurd verbal combinations, a form of completely liberated speech that ignores all norms, even those elementary logic ... It is as if words had been released from the shackles of sense, to enjoy a play period of complete freedom and establish unusual relationships among themselves. True, no new consistent links are formed in most cases, but the brief coexistence of theses words, expression, and objects outside the usual logical conditions discloses their inherent ambivalence. Their multiple meanings and the potentialities that would not manifest themselves in normal conditions are revealed.[26]

A similar effect could be said to have been achieved by Willhelm through his equally illogical and seemingly random visual juxtapositions. However, a more historically proximate reference in Willhelm's work, and particularly in his fashion presentations, can be found in their relation to performance art, especially as this relates to the early experiments within Dada and Surrealism. The presentation for his autumn/winter 2007–08 collection was based on the image of George Grosz as Dada Death (Figs 45 and 46). This costume, which consisted of a white over-sized skeleton mask, a long coat and cane, was worn by Grosz in a performance from 1918, in which he walked the Kurfürstendamm in Berlin. Willhelm's work refers most directly to the Berlin iteration of Dada, as this has been theorised as a darker expression of the 'movement' than the previous Swiss-based one.[27] Developing in the aftermath of World War I, Berlin, Dada explored themes of war and death in their alternately ominous and humorous performances. The incongruity of Willhelm's autumn/winter 2002–03 presentation, combined with a certain humour and darker undertones, points to an indebtedness to these strategies.

It is interesting to notice how Dada and Surrealism have been conversely theorised as descendants of carnival. According to Stallybrass and White, as actual European carnival waned, carnivalesque practices went underground and one of the ways they resurfaced was through the European artistic avant-garde:

> The elimination of carnival as a real social practice led to development of salon carnivals, compensatory Bohemias offering what Allon White calls 'liminoid positions' on the margins of polite society. Thus movements such as expressionism and surrealisms took over in displaced form much of the grotesque bodily symbolism and playful dislocations – exiled fragments of the 'carnivalesque Diaspora' (White) – which had once formed part of the European carnival. Carnival, in this modified and somewhat hostile form, is present in the provocations of Dada, the dislocation of surrealism, in the travesty-revolts of Genet's *The Maids*, or *The Blacks*, and indeed in the avant-garde generally.[28]

Willhelm's fashion shows also point to the general relation between fashion shows and performance art. Time-based and process-oriented, it has never been defined with a level of consensus but, like the grotesque, it has been discussed through its association with liminality, in-betweenness and border crossings. According to performance art theorist and historian RoseLee Goldberg, it can be understood as 'a medium that challenges and violates borders between disciplines and genders, between private and public, and between everyday life and art'.[29]

And, as has been discussed by a number of performance studies scholars, notions of borders and liminality are central to the field, so much so that the efficacy of performance has come to be measured 'in terms of liminality – that is, a mode of activity whose spatial, temporal and symbolic 'in-betweenness' allows for social norms to be suspended, challenged, played with, perhaps even transformed'.[30] Here, the performance theorist Jon McKenzie borrows his definition of liminality from cultural anthropology, and in particular from Victor Turner. Starting with Arnold van Gennep's theories of rites of passage – 'rites which accompany every change of place, state, social position and age',[31] and during which the subject occupies a transitional state – Turner discusses liminality's relation to ambiguity and in-betweenness:

> The attributes of liminality or of liminal *personae* (threshold people) are necessarily ambiguous, since this condition and these persons elude or

Fig. 45 George Grosz as Dada Death, Berlin, 1918, courtesy of VAGA

slip through the network of classifications that normally locate states and positions in cultural space. Liminal entities are neither here nor there; they are betwixt and between the positions assigned and arrayed by law, costume, convention, and ceremonial. As such, their ambiguous and indeterminate attributes are expressed by a rich variety of symbols in the many societies that ritualise social and cultural transitions, Thus, liminality is frequently likened to death, to being in the womb, to invisibility, to darkness, to bisexuality, to the wilderness, and to an eclipse of the sun or moon.[32]

The striking resemblance between definitions of carnival and of performance in their relation to liminality allows for similar criticism to be made of performance as that made about carnival. Both are understood as functioning as

CARNIVAL ICONOGRAPHY: BERNHARD WILLHELM

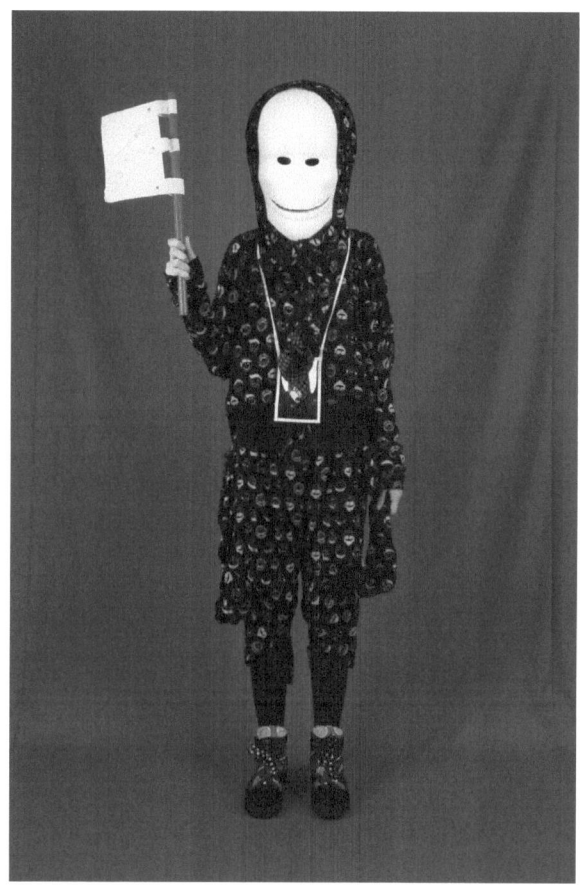

Fig. 46 Bernhard Willhelm, look inspired by George Grosz, autumn/winter 2007–08, photograph by Shoji Fujii, courtesy of Bernhard Willhelm

means to maintain social structures by allowing a temporal release, yet also as a way to suggest and, at times, foster different structures and social hierarchies. Thus, like carnival – a liminal state in its own right – performance could be either normative or transgressive.[33]

Willhelm's work, and in particular his fashion presentations, can be understood on a continuum with performance practice, as the designer not only upends a range of social norms, particularly norms of gender and propriety associated with fashion, but does so by taking on the role of the court jester, a quintessentially liminal figure. Much like Bakhtin, Turner describes the jester as a privileged marginal figure who, thanks to his liminal status of neither insider nor outsider, is able to 'strip off the pretensions of high rank and office and reduce them to the level of common humanity and mortality'.[34]

In its affinity with performance art, Willhelm's work is in line with more general discussions of the relation between performance art and the fashion show, but also fashion exhibition, as we have seen in the case of Margiela. This relation, which I will discuss at greater length in Chapter 7, has been tackled by Caroline Evans' writings on experimental fashion in *Fashion at the Edge*, as well as by Ginger Gregg Duggan's article in *Fashion Theory*, 'The Greatest Show on Earth: A Look at Contemporary Fashion Shows and their Relation to Performance Art', which traces a series of comparisons between a number of artists' performances and contemporary fashion shows.[35]

Humour and horror

Willhelm's melding of contemporary and historical codes in his exploration of the grotesque can be perhaps best observed in their collaboration with the New York-based Swiss artist Olaf Breuning, with whom Willhelm made a mock horror film shown in lieu of his spring/summer 2004 presentation. Produced and later shown at the Palais de Tokyo in Paris in 2003, the six-minute short, titled *Ghost*, combines humour and horror – a quintessential characteristic of the grotesque. *Ghost* starts with a shot of teenagers in Paris sitting on the steps of a building. They are eventually approached by what appears to be a drug-addled vagrant, who sells them Ecstasy. Upon taking the pills, the teenage girls start hallucinating and are abducted by ghosts, who engage them, against their will, in activities alternatively reminiscent of childhood play and physical subjugation. The ghosts toss the girls about like ragdolls and force them into rough versions of children's games such as leapfrog and potato-sack racing. In the ghost segment, the models are wearing the clothes comprising Willhelm's autumn/winter 2004 collection – colourful garments adorned in what Willhelm has described as Aztec-like prints – yet make reference to a number of ancient cultures ranging from Greek to Etruscan. The ghosts' costumes, on the other hand, are made of white sheets with printed-on facial features. In their simplicity, they read as a parody of high-tech costumes and effects, particularly to an audience accustomed to technologically advanced images of horror.

The film makes more or less explicit reference to conventions characteristic of the horror genre, and particularly the slasher subgenre. Despite the lack of bloodied victims, *Ghost* repeats the conventional narrative of the slasher film, which places disobedient and/or precocious teenagers and particularly girls in the role of victims. (In *Ghost* their transgression is having bought drugs from a stranger.) References to horror can be observed as much in the narrative as in the film's formal characteristic, such as sound editing, and its *mise en scène*, lighting and costume in particular. Breuning makes a direct reference to B-horror movies and uses the trite and cheap techniques of backlighting to mark the ghost apparition alongside the smoke machine for special effect. Both are such dated and recognisable signs of horror that they end up calling attention to the film's artificiality and thus preventing any fear response, transforming it instead into one of laughter.

In punctuating the artificiality of various elements comprising horror films, Breuning's and Willhelm's film falls within camp – or at least what the American cultural critic Susan Sontag identifies as 'deliberate camp':[36] a self-aware intentional parodic. The fact that they do so by employing obsolete techniques and artefacts – evident in the lighting, special effects and costumes – further aligns the film with camp in its investment with the 'outmoded, the out of date, the artefact past its prime'.[37] As discussed in relation to Bowery, camp, as defined in Susan Sontag's 'Notes on Camp', is understood by 'its love for the unnatural: of artifice and exaggeration'. Camp actualises a theatricalisation of life and art and is characterised by a rejection of seriousness.[38] This places it on a continuum with carnival and performance. Sontag describes camp as 'the sensibility of failed seriousness, of the theatricalisation of experience. Camp refuses both the harmonies of traditional seriousness, and the risks of fully identifying with extreme states of feeling'.[39] However, unlike the carnivalesque potential to challenge power positions and the social order, Sontag claims camp to be apolitical and exclusively concerned with the aesthetic realm. Her argument, however, only stands if the aesthetic realm is understood to be sharply divided from the political, an argument that has been repeatedly rebuffed by later theorists of camp.

The subversive potential of camp, particularly in its relation to gay culture, has, in fact, been discussed subsequent to Sontag's article, which was first published in 1964. In 'Taking out the Trash: Camp and the Politics of Parody', Chuck Kleinhans argues that camp can, in fact, operate as a critique of dominant ideology through a parodic stance. This becomes particularly evident in light of Bourdieuian understanding of aesthetic sensibility and taste as socially and culturally constructed.[40] Discussing low camp, Kleinhans writes:

> In defiance of Kantian aesthetics and high culture prejudices, a trash imagination understands that aesthetic pleasure can be found in diverse ways, including the marginalised and excluded. When employed intentionally as a strategy for production, Camp – whether its source is gay subculture or nongay appropriation–relies for its effect of casual excess, deviant decorum, and libidinal obviousness. Camp pushes a poorly done form (poorly done by conventional standards of technique and social manners) to the limits so that its very badness is what the work is about … In other words, low camp deliberately celebrates bad taste and often intentionally offends aesthetic and social sensibility in order to make a statement.[41]

Thus, camp, in this more obviously politicised form, can easily be understood in relation to the grotesque strategy of debasement, as it brings the high to the low domain through parody and carnivalisation. As a result, not only is the film Willhelm produced with Breuning aligned with camp in its 'poorly done form', but much of Willhelm's work, similarly to Bowery's in its excessive quality and affront to good taste, falls within the realm of low camp.

Debasement

This allegiance with low camp becomes more obvious in the work's strategy of debasement and degradation, a recurrent carnivalesque technique of bringing the high to the low domain. According to Bakhtin, 'the essential principle of grotesque realism is degradation, that is, the lowering of all that is high, spiritual, ideal, abstract; it is a transfer to the material level, to the sphere of earth and body in their indissoluble unity'.[42] Carnivalesque humour – what Bakhtin often refers to as laughter – was of central importance to processes of degradation, as it allowed the dethroning of the high domain to the lower sphere and the reassessment of value categories, hierarchies and accepted truths.

These themes of degradation and debasement through humour can once again be observed in Willhelm's use of prints and embroidery. For instance, a shirt from the spring/summer 2005 collection pairs a depiction of a toilet with the neoclassical architecture characteristic of repositories of official

Fig. 47 Bernhard Willhelm, embroidered skirt and shirt, spring/summer 2005, photograph by Shoji Fujii, courtesy of Bernhard Willhelm

power and knowledge (i.e., universal survey museums, libraries and government buildings) (Figs 47 and 48). Other motifs that adorn the accompanying skirt are the depiction of a rat on a fully set plate, a dung beetle and the carnivalesque motif *par excellence* of buttocks being bared (Figs 49 and 50). Thus, here we see the topographical logic of the grotesque at work, the shift from top to bottom, quite literally achieved through the act of

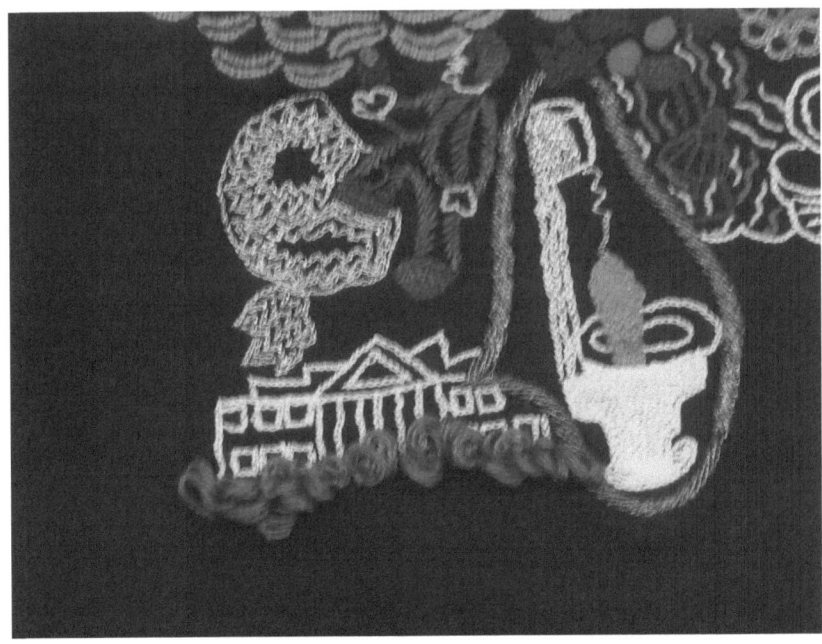

Fig. 48 Bernhard Willhelm, embroidery of toilet and neo-classical building, detail of shirt from the ModeMuseum collection, spring/summer 2005, photograph by the author, courtesy of MoMu, Antwerp

mooning belonging 'to the cycle of themes in which the face is replaced by the rump'.[43]

This shift from top to bottom is also more symbolically enacted by the image of a rat, an animal most related to the city's sewer, and here presented as the main course of a formal meal, a central trope of the 'civilising process'.[44] The centrality of images of rats as a metaphor of debasement and contamination is underscored by Stallybrass and White's discussion of rats as central metaphors of contagion between different parts of modern cities and the social classes that inhabited them.[45] According to Stallybrass and White, the rats, which symbolised the underbelly of the city, together with bodily images symbolising debased body parts (i.e. the buttocks) were central to the formation of the proper bourgeois subject, which was formed in opposition to such symbols of 'debasement'. Thus, starting in the nineteenth-century modern urban centres, a transcoding occurred between the 'topography' of the body and that of the city:

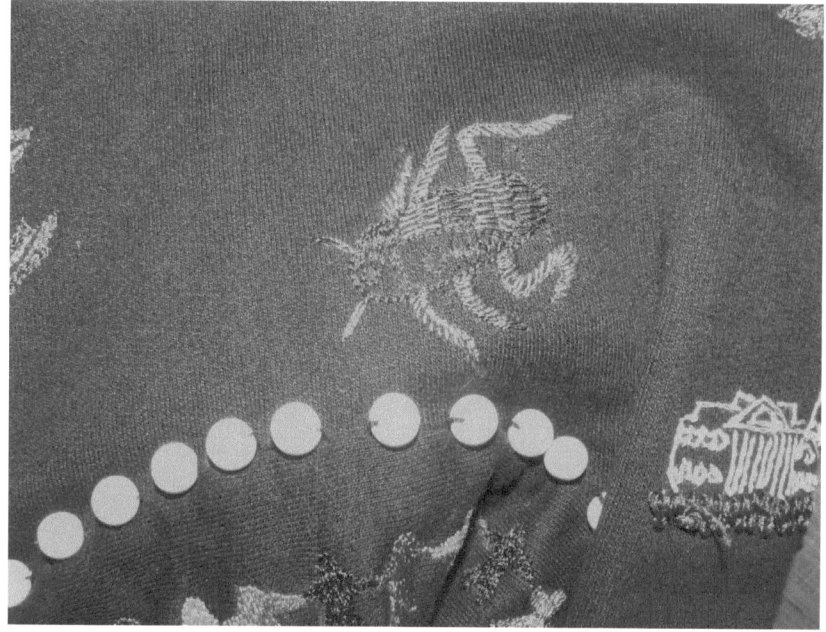

Fig. 49 Bernhard Willhelm, embroidery of a dung beetle, detail of skirt from the ModeMuseum collection, spring/summer 2005, photograph by the author, courtesy of MoMu, Antwerp

The vertical axis of the bourgeoisie body is primarily emphasised in the *education* of the child: as s/he grows up/is cleaned up, the lower bodily stratum is regulated or denied, as far as possible, by the correct posture ('stand up straight', 'don't squat', 'don't kneel on all fours' – the postures of servants and savages), and by the censoring of lower 'bodily' references along with bodily wastes. But whilst the 'low' of the bourgeois body becomes unmentionable, we hear an ever increasing garrulity about the *city's* 'low' – the slum, the rag-picker, the prostitute, the sewer – the 'dirt' which is 'down there.' In other words, the axis of the body is transcoded through the axis of the city, and whilst the bodily low is 'forgotten', the city's low becomes a site of obsessive preoccupation, a preoccupation which is itself intimately conceptualised in terms of discourses of the body.[46]

In an interesting parallel between Stallybrass and White's theories and Willhelm's work, a number of the prints discussed do, in fact, pair images of

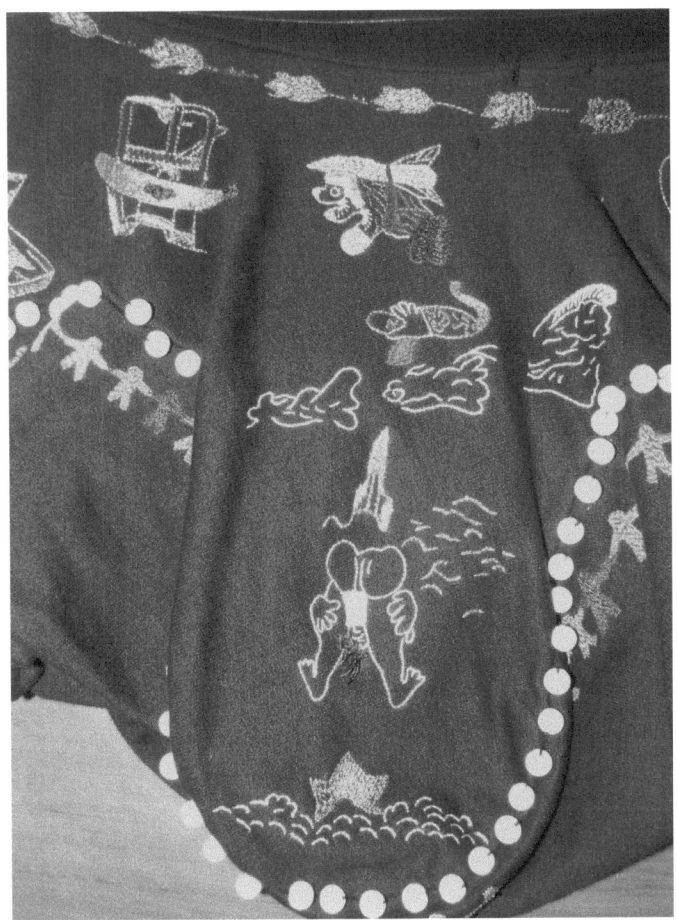

Fig. 50 Bernhard Willhelm, embroidery of person mooning, detail of skirt from the ModeMuseum collection, spring/summer 2005, photograph by the author, courtesy of MoMu, Antwerp

what appears to be a fantastical depiction of 'savages' with those of rats and 'the lower bodily stratum'.

This theme of debasement had been perhaps even more fully explored in an earlier Willhelm collection, autumn/winter 2001–02, which was entirely dedicated to the rituals of the dung beetles. These are exhaustively recounted in the literature accompanying the collection, which described in detail the behaviour of the dung beetle, a species that feeds primarily on faeces:

> The sacred scarab beetle, like many other related scarabaeidae, takes very good care of its brood. The scarab and other dung beetles feed on dung, their wide horns not only enable them to process this material perfectly, but they can also prepare the soil for their burrow. If the food is for the beetle itself it makes a vertical corridor in the burrow, in which it hides its food; this corridor also functions as a larder. When it is taking care of its young the scarab beetle acts totally differently, first it makes walnut-sized balls out of the dung, then it rolls them over and over until they become as big as a man's fist ... The ball is then buried in a suitable place and the female scarab will lay an egg in a specially prepared space in the ball. As we know now, these complicated preparations for their offspring are completely instinctive, but the ancient Egyptians thought supernatural powers were at work and they believed that scarab beetles were exceptionally clever and wise. This is why they venerated them.[47]

This passage is strongly reminiscent of Bakhtin's writings on the role of excrement in the grotesque cosmology. This is recuperated in Bakhtin's work and understood as an important link between cycles of birth and death and thus connected to the sacred. In more than one passage, Bakhtin discusses the ambivalence of faecal matter and its representation in Rabelais' novels:

> The images of faeces and urine are ambivalent, as are all the images of the material bodily lower stratum; they debase, destroy, regenerate, and renew simultaneously. They are blessing and humiliating at the same time. Death and death throes, labour and, childbirth, are intimately interwoven.[48]

These views are corroborated by Susan Signe Morrison's study on the function and meaning of excrement in the late Middle Ages, which, partially relying on Bakhtin's theories, explores the ambiguity of faeces throughout the period.[49] A similar discussion of the ambivalence of dung is advanced by Julia Kristeva in *Powers of Horror*, where she describes dung, together with a range of other bodily fluid, as an ambiguous matter at the border between life and death, which, through its elimination, allows one to be. 'Dung', Kristeva writes, 'signifies the other side of the border, the place where I am not and which permits me to be'.[50]

This exploration of borders through bodily excretions traces a direct parallel between Willhelm's work and Leigh Bowery, whose performances were perhaps even more directly engaged with these explorations, as they melded excrements (i.e. fake urine and faeces) and birth processes. At times Willhelm's work seems to make almost direct allusions to Bowery's oeuvre in his references to bodily fluid and to the points of entry and exit of the body. This is particularly true of photographs accompanying the men's spring/summer 2008 collection, which depict the French gay porn star François Sagat wearing the designer's garments in lewd yet humorous poses, which read, at times, as spoofs of gay pornography and, like Bowery's work, point to a playful understanding of sexuality. In one of the photographs Sagat is portrayed mooning the viewer, a bouquet of flowers budding out of his buttocks, while in another he is clad in Willhelm's gold spandex attire, seemingly spurting liquid from his anus, actually a fountain geyser (Fig. 51). This image strongly brings to mind Bowery's catwalk in London, where he performed a similar feat, after having administered himself an enema. In their combination of explicit sexuality, grotesque anatomy, allusions to bodily fluid and inversions, these images are prime examples of carnivalesque debasement in the service of mocking pervasive moral codes and social conventions. The images were collated in a calendar, a clear attempt at mocking the quintessential fashion/erotica pin-up calendar: the Pirelli calendar that is created annually by the Italian tyre company and until recently presented its scantily clad female models in exotic localations photographed by different prominent fashion photographers. Thus Willhelm invokes and queers gay and straight erotica and porn imagery through the choice of subject, garments and poses. However, Sagat's photographs were shot and circulated at a time not characterised by the intense policing of gay men's bodies characteristic of the 1980s and early 1990s, when Bowery was active, and consequently appear far less threatening to its contemporary audience.

An equally humorous take on male sexuality and pornography is articulated in Willhelm's spring/summer 2007 Tyrolean collection, where the specifically southern German and Austrian tradition of lederhosen, which is associated with the conservative Tyrolean region, is reworked and ironised. Willhelm's shorter and tighter versions of the traditional garment not only pokes fun at traditional Bavarian culture, but also brings out the garments' latent eroticism. This has since been famously explored by Sacha Baron Cohen's 2009 film Brüno, whose wearing of an albeit more drastically abbreviated version of lederhosen seems a direct reference to Willhelm's collection. On the occasion of this collection, the designer staged a performance,

Fig. 51 Bernhard Willhelm, François Sagat clad in Willhelm's gold spandex jumpsuit, men's, spring/summer 2008, photograph by Lukas Wassmann, courtesy of the artist and Bernhard Willhelm

which once again pokes fun at porn imagery, as he boarded a tram wearing lederhosen holding a giant bratwurst, obviously reminiscent of a penis. The designer's interest in playing with the codes of pornography and upending accepted ideas of male sexuality was indicated by his being the first cover subject of Butt from May 2001, for which he posed naked for the photographer Wolfgang Tillmans.[51] A Dutch-based magazine printed in a zine-like format on pink newsprint, Butt has since become well known for its frank and humorous exploration of gay men's sexuality through candid portrayals and interviews with both famous and non-famous subjects. Again, the circulation of magazines like Butt within a relatively wide young urban audience further points to the way anxieties surrounding the bodies of gay men, which reached an apex in the 1980s, had by this time substantially subsided.

7

THE PROLIFERATION OF THE GROTESQUE
Lady Gaga

LADY GAGA AND EXPERIMENTAL FASHION

As I have shown throughout the book, the grotesque became increasingly visible in fashion from the 1980s onward. However, it was only starting in 2009 that experimental fashion, and particularly its grotesque manifestation, took centre stage, if only briefly, through Lady Gaga. At times, the pop phenomenon wore some of the most experimental ensembles produced by the designers discussed, as with Rei Kawakubo's Comme des Garçons; in many other instances, she conspicuously made reference to experimental work, especially that of Leigh Bowery.[1]

I would argue, in fact, that Lady Gaga's fame is very much dependent on the fashions articulated in her on- and off-stage performances and videos. It is in great part her ensembles that have made her a compelling figure, rather than her music, which, by comparison, seems stylistically conservative. Indeed, it was only in 2009, when she started actively collaborating with Nick Knight (a fashion photographer and founder of SHOWstudio) and Nicola Formichetti (then a stylist and creative director for *Dazed and Confused*), that the singer achieved greater fame. And it is through her collaborations with these fashion insiders – already at the forefront of British experimental fashion – that Gaga claimed the spotlight. Notably, her pop dominance and cultural relevance began to wane in 2013, around the same time these collaborative synergies ended. I believe that it is through her fashion, rather than her music, that her most experimental and thought-provoking work can be found. In fact, Gaga can be understood as the culmination of the proliferation of grotesque fashion discussed throughout this book.

Lady Gaga's outlandish costuming can find a lineage in pop stars – particularly Björk, more than Madonna, with whom Gaga is often equated. However, the Icelandic musician, who has often collaborated with experimental fashion designers including Bernhard Willhelm, could not scale the charts to the same extent that Gaga did, in part because her experiments in fashion were matched by those in music. (Notably, Björk's collaboration with Willhelm took place within the pages of *Dazed and Confused* for its October 2007 issue, while Nicola Formichetti was the magazine's creative director.) In a more spectacular and American 'showbiz' move, Gaga blew up the references to reproduction and eggs that were coyly embodied in Björk's much maligned 'swan' dress, worn to the 2001 Academy Awards. Gaga made her entrance at the 2011 Grammy awards fully enveloped in an egg-shaped pod designed by the Cypriot/British experimental designer Hussein Chalayan, and wearing prosthetic make-up in a Thierry Mugler-designed latex costume. This outfit is perhaps emblematic of Gaga's piling on of references to the grotesque as previously articulated in visual culture through experimental fashion and art, particularly performance art.

Births and embryos were called into being through Chalayan's egg, which was a reiteration of a similar construction the designer completed for *Place to Passage*, a video on border-crossing screened at the Centre Pompidou. References to bodily modifications and alternative standards of beauty were enacted through prosthetic make-up, which very literally resembled the French artist Orlan's actual bulges (so much so that the artist eventually sued Gaga for copyright infringement). Unlike Gaga, Orlan achieved her bulges through more permanent methods. The French artist hacked plastic surgery by having implants normally used to enhance cheekbones grafted onto her forehead, creating two horn-like protuberances. In her commentary on standardised female beauty and 'technologies' for self-improvement and self-optimisation, Orlan's art follows a trajectory of feminist art and figures such as Hannah Wilke, but it also relates to Godley's and Kawakubo's feminist experimentations with bumps and bulges in the collections I have discussed. Gaga's references to Orlan's 'carnal art', however, may have been further mediated via the French artist's collaboration with Walter Van Beirendonck, where models for his autumn/winter 1998–89 collection wore bulges achieved through prosthetic make-up.[2]

The relation of prosthesis, augmented bodies and fashion is central to many of Lady Gaga's looks and performances. It is most successfully articulated in her 'Bad Romance' video from 2009 – the first video on which Formichetti worked. A number of her ensembles, in fact, point to the porous line between fashion and bodily augmentation and how clothing, particularly shoes and undergarments, often constitute technologies of bodily modification, albeit older and much lower-tech ones than plastic surgery. In the video, which was released at Alexander McQueen's 2010 show, a series of facial masks making references to medical devices such as braces or neck casts are worn by the back-up dancers, while the singer herself wears a series of structured garments by McQueen and Haus of Gaga and progressively more extreme footwear designed by McQueen, which culminates in the now famous Armadillo shoes. Sporting staggering ten-inch heels, the shoes resemble platform point shoes with heels; from a technical viewpoint, they are reminiscent of Bowery's practice of wearing high-heeled shoes in men's boots.

The abundance of prosthesis alongside very constructed garments in Gaga's looks and performances questions not only bodily boundaries but also the dividing lines between body and dress, as well as dress and medical devices and technologies. While the Orlan-inspired facial bumps place various techniques of beautification from make-up to cosmetic surgery on a continuum, the Armadillo heels and facial masks call into question the division between medical prosthesis and dress. However, Gaga's exploration of these themes with Knight and McQueen has a more thought-provoking precedent. It is reminiscent of the photographer's and designer's earlier collaboration with the athlete-turned-model Aimee Mullins, which led to a more sustained exploration of bodily borders. Mullins's *wearing* of below the knee prosthesis on a semi-permanent basis, as she is a below-the-knee double amputee, prompted McQueen to design functional prostheses/boots that questioned and problematised categories of body and clothes, medical devices and dress, and the functional and aesthetic.[3]

Thus Gaga's experimentation also points to possible further areas of study and the future of what experimental fashion might entail. As her collaboration with McQueen suggests, a fertile area of research would be the interaction between medical history and fashion history and the way these two powerful discourses conceive and visualise the body. As my discussion of immunology, conception of the body and fashion in connection to Kawakubo and Bowery points out, Bakhtin's thoughts could also be applied to an exploration of medicine fashion and bodily boundaries. This intersection, however, could be read as explicated historically in the shifting borders between the body, medical devices, and clothing.

As Jack Halberstam argues in *Gaga Feminism: Sex, Gender and the End of Normal*, despite the pop star's anthem 'Born this Way', Gaga's male alter-ego Jo Calderone, who first appeared at the MTV Video Music Awards in 2011, pointed to the social construction of gender alongside the artificialities of a host of identity categories and bodily norms.[4] Significantly, in an early interview in *Vanity Fair*, the singer mentioned *Paris Is Burning* – the 1990 documentary on Harlem's ball culture and an important work in gender studies and queer theory – as one of her influences. Gaga can often contradict the very ideas her fashionings point to, and more sustained and poignant explorations can be found in work of the experimental fashion and performance art that predated her. Yet as Halberstam points out, her work is still relevant to a cultural moment where such artificialities and constructions take centre stage and where, as this book has argued, the grotesque as fashion's ultimate incarnation proliferated.

Although explorations of bodily borders and the grotesque canon abound in Lady Gaga's work, the most famous one remains her donning a meat dress, originally to attend the 2010 Video Music Awards (VMAs). Again, this dress is an almost direct quotation of an earlier exploration of the same trope by another artist, in this case the Canadian artist Jana Sterbak in her 1987 piece 'Vanitas: Flesh Dress for an Albino Anorectic', which, like Orlan's work, was rooted in feminist art of the 1980s. An epitome of the grotesque, raw meat destabilises bodily borders and, according to Bakhtin, is intimately related to dress. In *Rabelais* Bakhtin writes:

> The word *habiller* means to 'dress' or 'clothe,' but it can also mean to 'dress' the meat of a slaughtered animal. Thus, when the guest speaks of 'the calf I dressed this very morning,' he means in the first place himself, dressed for the occasion, but also the calf that was dismembered, dressed and consumed [...] The dividing line between man's consuming body and the consumed animal's body is once more erased.[5]

Kristeva discussed raw flesh, central to Judeo-Christian dietary prohibitions, as 'the propitious place for abjection where *death* and *femininity, murder* and *procreation, cessation of life* and *vitality* all come together'.[6] And it is because of this destabilising effect on bodily boundaries of inside and outside and its implicit reference to cannibalism, pollution and contagion that even in Lady Gaga's cartoonish rendition, the pairing of flesh and body remains unsettling.

LADY GAGA AND FAT DRAG

Interestingly, it was the very conflation of Gaga's meat outfits with her less disciplined flesh that caused the most consternation in the press – once again reminding us, as Mary Russo writes in *The Female Grotesque*, that there are risks involved in women aligning themselves with the grotesque, as women's bodies are already marked by such associations. And although one cannot equate Gaga's off- and on-stage performances of transgression with the daily embodiment of difference experienced by bodies that deviate from the norm, the two eventually overlapped. During her 2012 tour, Lady Gaga visibly gained weight; it was a photograph of her onstage performance in Amsterdam depicting the performer – overweight according to the standards of female pop stardom – and donning a (this time faux) meat corset that caused a flurry of criticism in the press.[7] The image conflated one too many references to bodies-out-of-bounds. The negative responses to the performance and to this look in particular render obvious the power of norms and the way bodies are constantly policed, particularly those of female celebrities.

That a relatively slight weight gain incited such a level of scrutiny in the press and across social media, on a par with some of her most extreme looks, points to the policing of female bodies and celebrity female bodies, where fatness remains one of the most problematic and 'revolting' transgressions. The 'fat' body, and particularly the 'fat' female body, is, in fact, an undisciplined one. Not only does it defy contemporary beauty standards but it also reads as a failure to perform successfully the daily and incessant work on the body that one is required to undertake in neoliberal society in order to be a good subject. As Nead discussed in *The Female Nude*, and much of fat studies literature has since explored in depth: 'Within this [contemporary Western aesthetic] "fat" is excess, surplus matter. It is a false boundary, something that is additional to the true frame of the body and needs to be stripped away.'[8]

However, Gaga employed fashion, a potentially regulatory discourse, as a response to the criticism.[9] A few days after the September 2012 concert in Amsterdam that prompted most of the criticism over her weight gain, Gaga wore a cartoonish pink and blue dress from Rei Kawakubo of Comme des Garçons's 2012 flat collection (Fig. 52). Reminiscent of the Japanese designer's ongoing experimentation with pattern cutting and body shapes in her 'Body Meets Dress' collection, the dress was made of felt, with the seam allowance left uncut. Much like Margiela's enlarged garments, it created an oversized shape irrespective of the wearer's size, and – especially as worn by Gaga, covering her entire body down to the ankles – was reminiscent of a fat suit. The singer employed experimental fashion as a tongue-in-cheek response to the press's negative commentary and used humour to upend the criticism in what was one of her most successful performances.

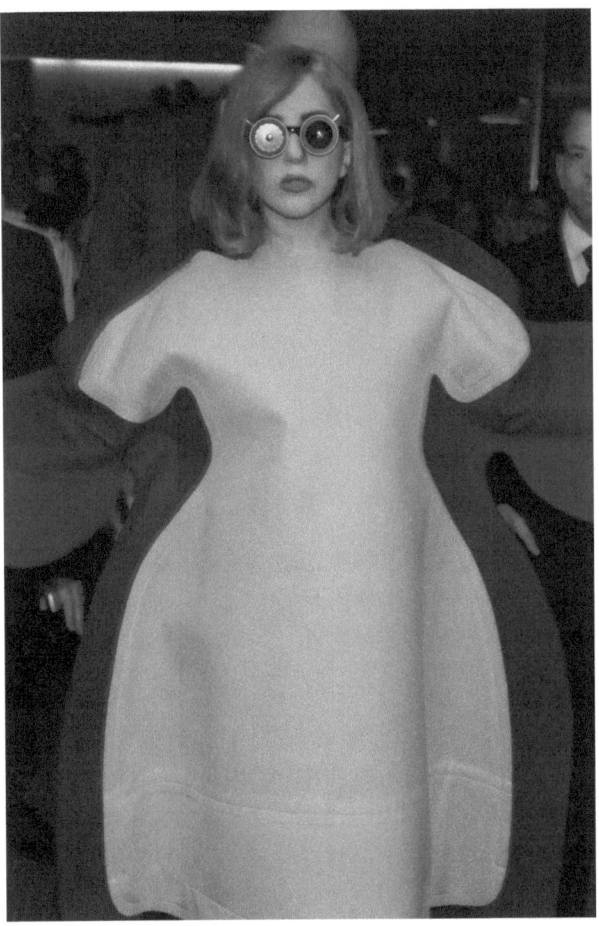

Fig. 52 Lady Gaga in Comme des Garçons outside the Park Hyatt Paris Vendôme Hotel, 22 September 2012, photograph by Marc Piasecki, © Getty Images

By *performing* fatness or 'fat drag' via a fat suit at a time in which she was accused of being 'fat', Gaga problematised and denaturalised identity categories and questioned the boundaries between reality and performance. Gaga's performance, in a fashion familiar from Judith Butler's writing, complicated ideas of origins and stable identities and pointed to the artificiality and construction of the body by rendering a parodic version of her own weight gain with a gargantuan garment that further built her body.

In her Comme des Garçons look, Gaga took up the call by cultural theorist Kathleen LeBesco to enact a potentially disruptive performance of 'fat drag' achieved through the fat suit.[10] Her performance, much like the work of Bowery, falls in the realm of camp, or 'fat camp', which plays with excess and parodic artificiality. If only temporarily, Gaga re-appropriated the association of women, excess – in this case excessive flesh – and the grotesque to make a carnivalesque critique that challenges regulatory norms.

FASHION, PERFORMANCE AND PERFORMATIVITY

What are we to make of this mainstreaming, however temporary, of the grotesque in modern image culture, and fashion in particular? That graphic, humorous and potentially disturbing imagery, which explores bodily norms and borders and, by extension, gender and social norms, eventually entered the mainstream through Lady Gaga can be seen as symptomatic of what has been discussed in this book.

It could be most clearly attributed to the narrowing of the boundaries among fashion, performance and other visual disciplines that occurred since the 1980s. This narrowing was, in turn, related to general shifts in models of subjectivity, as bodies became more porous and fixed subject positions came under threat most clearly as they related to gender categories, performance and performativity started to occupy centre stage. The changes as discussed throughout the book were precipitated by feminism and the AIDS crisis, both of which problematised stable gender identities and sexualities. They granted fashion, or at least experimental fashion – a discipline defined by constantly permuting subject positions – an increasingly central role within cultural expressions.[11]

A parallel can be traced between the increasing relevance of performance and fashion and their attendant field of studies. To a great extent, they both developed in relation to changes in systems of thought that gave increasing attention to the performative – theorising gender and identity as inherently performative – as well as to appearances and surfaces.[12] Performance studies theorist Richard Schechner's argument for the centrality of performance could, in fact, also be employed as an account for the increasing centrality of fashion:

Accepting the performative as a category of theory makes it increasingly difficult to sustain a distinction between appearances and reality, facts and make-believe, surfaces and depths. Appearances are actualities – neither more nor less so than what lies behind or beneath appearances. Social reality is constructed through and through. In modernity what was 'deep' and 'hidden' was thought to be 'more real' than what was on the surface (Platonism dies hard). But in postmodernity, the relationship between depths and surfaces is fluid; the relationship is dynamically convective.[13]

Moreover, if we understand gender identity as a performative act repeatedly enacted through time, we clearly see the importance of fashion as a tool for upholding gender norms and, more generally, normative processes of identity formation, yet retaining the potential for subversion. Fashion, as the work of the designers discussed in this book highlights, could allow for the expansion of 'the cultural field bodily through subversive performances of various kinds'.[14]

Thus, performative genres, to which fashion undoubtedly belongs, have the potential for transgression, as is particularly the case with grotesque fashion in its affinity with liminality, yet they can also be highly normative. This ambivalence is partially mirrored in Butler's discussion of the performative vis-à-vis performance scholars' understanding of the concept. While a number of performance scholars, in particular Schechner, focus on its transgressive potential, Butler focuses more closely on its normative power. As Jon McKenzie writes: 'What Butler creates ... is a theory that poses performativity not only as marginal, transgressive, or resistant, but also a dominant and punitive form of power, one that both generates and constrains human subjects.'[15]

Mirroring this dichotomy, fashion, most often in its mainstream variety, can be part of the performativity of gender, understood as punitive and normative repetitions of gender norms, upholding through continuous performances a range of social norms and hierarchies, while it can allow for breaks and interjections of those norms. The more or less lasting disruptions produced by the fashions discussed in this book ripple through these normative systems, they can upend certain norms and hierarchies while enforcing others.

For instance, Bowery's subversive 'performance' of a heterosexual wedding, despite his being openly gay, translated into a traditional arrangement after his death, where his widow acquired full control of his estate, thus simplifying the complex social network that Bowery was part of in his lifetime. Godley's and Kawakubo's disruptive pregnant bodies were partially superseded by fashion media's representation of pregnancy in the new millennium – and in particular celebrity pregnancy – as a discreet and temporary accessory. Or, as perhaps most simply articulated by Margiela's use of Japanese shoe tradition in his *tabi* shoes, such disruptions, in this case of bodily norms, are not only culturally but also historically contextual. As these 'foreign' sartorial traditions and their attendant conceptions of the body become more and more widespread, they become accepted within European and American fashion vocabulary.

Experimental fashion's disruptions are highly contextual and often impermanent. Butler, while discussing the resurfacing of the abject – a discussion which echoes Stallybrass and White's discussion of the grotesque as a return of the repressed – as the other in opposition to which acceptable subjects and social norms are formed and maintained, argues that the challenge is:

> to consider this threat and disruption not as a permanent contestation of social norms condemned to the pathos of perpetual failure, but rather as a critical resource in the struggle to rearticulate the very terms of symbolic legitimacy and intelligibility.[16]

FASHIONING THE GROTESQUE

The reasons behind the proliferation of out-of-bounds bodies and subjects at the turn of the twenty-first century are numerous. Following Stallybrass and White's argument that the repressed returns through disciplinary discourses, which a certain kind of fashion could be seen to embody, then the widespread use of grotesque and carnivalesque imagery in fashion of this period can be understood as a return of the repressed grotesque body, the 'low-Other' against which the classical body is created. The grotesque returns in those sites of negation as a result of the excessive energy generated by the labour of exclusion. Making sense of the process of creation of the classical canon in literature, they write: 'The production and reproduction of a body of classical writing required a labour of suppression, a perpetual work of exclusion upon the grotesque body and it was that supplementary yet unavoidable labour which troubled the identity of the classical.'[17] Here, Stallybrass and White are borrowing Freud's psychological model of repression, according to which what is repressed is not allowed to enter the conscious mind through great and constant 'expenditure of force'. As a result, it proliferates in the unconscious where it takes on extreme forms.[18] Thus, if one understands a certain kind of mainstream fashion as part of civilising discourses, the grotesque, which resurfaces through the experimental fashion of this period, could be understood as its repressed unconscious.

Another explanation is that fashion might be inherently grotesque. A concept that surfaced throughout is the relation between tenets of the grotesque as an aesthetic category and fashion; both are in a constant state of becoming and dependent on perpetual change. They have also both been disparaged within Western aesthetic history and hierarchies of knowledge due to their instability and their relation to the feminine. This is the feminine of both the decorative and the detail and of the maternal-grotesque and horrifically unsealed. Discussing the centrality of the grotesque canon in modern and contemporary visual culture, Connelly writes:

> Although nineteenth and twentieth-century imagery engages and expands the grotesque more than ever before in Western imagery, modernist theory and history have (until recently) almost completely written out the grotesque and its association with the material, the flesh, and the feminine.[19]

The grotesque, in its instability and change, could be understood as fashion manifest destiny. This makes for a particularly pertinent argument, as it raises the question of whether fashion, once unleashed from constraints (as is partially the case with experimental fashion), is prone to the grotesque. Borrowing de Perthuis's term, one could argue that the grotesque constitutes fashion imaginary realised. The 'synthetic ideal' of digital photography, which de Perthuis discusses as fashion's imaginary realised, is, in fact, very much in line with the Bakhtinian grotesque as it breaks down the boundaries between 'self and other, subject and object, inside and outside, animate and inanimate, organic and inorganic' and it does so by 'realising a form that announces the idea of a continual becoming'.[20]

If, therefore, fashion is understood as an integral part of contemporary culture which takes part in, mediates and affects cultural meaning, the work discussed corroborates an understanding of subjectivity as 'in process' and of identity, and in particular gender identity, as performative and thus constructed. It also advances an understanding of complex non-teleological linear temporalities that are related to the feminine, in the words of Kristeva, and to carnival time according to Bakhtin. Thus, in turn, it corroborates fashion's centrality to contemporary culture. As identity and gender become performative and conceptions of time become cyclical, fashion-and particularly grotesque fashion, in its unstable, changing, protean nature-becomes central to culture. This suggests a reason for fashion's pervasiveness within contemporary culture and its spillage into other disciplines, most clearly performance art.

The designers and artists whose work I discussed throughout the book clearly interjected and mediated the cultural politics that surrounded them in an attempt to shift, or at least critique, the grounds of acceptable norms in fashion. For instance, Godley and Kawakubo intervened in feminist theory through a reconception of the body of fashion, and in the process provided a critique of 1980s neoliberal enterprising culture. Bowery, and in a different way Willhelm, mediated the increasing visibility of queer bodies, and in the case of Bowery challenged fears surrounding bodily borders at the height of the AIDS epidemic in the West. Bowery, Godley and Kawakubo re-inscribed the pregnant body with all of its potential for ruptures of borders, immunological instability and a new conception of subjectivities to fashion of the 1980s and 1990s. Margiela, throughout the period I discuss, criticised the normative body of fashion via his ingenious play with sizing. His garments' disregard for symmetry and proportionality upend and question Western ideals of beauty and classical aesthetics, while his presentations and exhibitions make reference to processes of birth, growth and contagion. Willhelm mediated the shifting borders of masculinity as well as providing a commentary on material excess and rampant neoliberal rhetoric of the new millennium. This proliferation of bodies-out-of-bounds culminated in the advent of Lady Gaga, who popularised experimental fashion and its relation to the grotesque canon.

The repressed that returns in fashion of this period can be understood in terms of difference, as it is articulated through non-normative bodies, through sexualities which do not conform to dominant sexual mores, as well as through what is culturally other. The experimental fashion discussed articulates physical, sexual and cultural otherness. Fashion's traditional disengagement with the political – understood in the narrow sense of electoral politics – and its allegiance with the contingent and the frivolous is precisely what gives it a privileged position in precipitating and engendering such re-articulations of norms. Its pervasiveness within contemporary society, combined with its lesser status vis-à-vis other forms of cultural output, could be seen as a tool, as opposed to a hindrance, to experimental fashion in its articulation of the grotesque – that which lies beyond the boundaries of the proper. Thus, the work discussed in this book, precisely because it falls within the realm of fashion, is often not taken seriously as a form of contestation and is consequently allowed to permeate a greater variety of symbolic domains. As a result, fashion, and particularly experimental fashion, proves valuable for a re-articulation of norms and deviations.

APPENDIX

INTERVIEW WITH NICOLA BOWERY

I visited Nicola Bowery, widow of Leigh Bowery, in her Brighton, England, home in the summer of 2006 to discuss Bowery's fashion and performances from the 1980s and 1990s. Nicola was extremely kind in taking the time to show me a number of her husband's elaborate costumes. Having been painstakingly made to measure to Bowery's large girth, the costumes appeared eerily empty – particularly as a complex system of understructures kept them in shape, further highlighting Bowery's absent body. Nicola also discussed her role as the slime-covered baby in the humorous, unsettling 'birth scenes' that Bowery staged as part of his performances with his band Minty, from the early 1990s until his untimely death in 1995.

> *Francesca Granata:* Bowery seemed really interested in manipulating his body through his increasingly complex costumes and accentuating parts of the body, like the belly, which tend to be restricted and de-emphasised. Do you know why he was he so interested in accentuating the belly in some of his looks?
>
> *Nicola Bowery:* Because he had one! When he first came to London, he was quite conscious of his weight and he dieted at some point as well. Then he started to use his body for the fashion that he was making at the time. In the early 1980s, he started emphasising his body (particularly his better points) and squeezing himself into corsets that you couldn't really see from the outside, so a lot of his garments were a more restrictive look. It was probably after he started sitting for Lucian Freud and Lucian was so into his body and thought it was so fantastic. They had this mutual thing going on: they both loved his body and so Leigh started to use more of it in his costumes. It started with his bum in the very early 1980s, with a lot of jackets which exposed the bottom with knickers or frilly knickers and then he got into breasts because he had

quite a lot of blubber up there so he could make boobs. He wasn't like every other drag queen, he didn't want to be like a woman but he just liked to emphasise certain parts of his body and he was a big bloke and he did have a belly and some of the things he wore later on that was the shape of the belly so he would emphasise it even more…

FG: You said this particular one [a brown look with protruding belly] came about by looking at robots?

NB: This one, it's a spin-off from the book of robots he got from Japan, sort of the next stage. The one with the tutu head – that one was influenced by the book of robots and transformers. All of these shapes were made using foams so they'll end up looking very robotic. This one had a foam ball in it. The foam came in different shapes, but there was a guy he was working with for the costumes at the time – his name was Lee Benjamin – and he was very good at sculpting, so they'll get lumps of foams and then shape them. I am not sure if that was a foam ball which was bought like that or whether Lee actually sculpted it to make a round shape.

Leigh was very productive all the time and some of his looks came from mixing his old looks. He would use old things to make new things. He eventually used that look [the brown one, Look 9], to which he added a foam head, to make two other looks [Look 32 & 33]. See, it is the same garment underneath, but he is also wearing a foam headpiece He just made an overgarment for it. He made one with Lycra and the other with velour. We called the one with velour the Fraggle Rock because it was like a quite big rock, a mossy rock. Leigh was always full of ideas: costumes would come from other costumes and he would try things out to see if they worked and they usually did.

FG: You mentioned how the birth performance, in which you played the baby, was inspired by Divine in *Female Trouble*. Did Leigh talk to you about being the baby before planning the piece?

NB: He didn't really talk about his ideas so much. He would just get on and do them and then tell me what I'll be doing with it, you know. In the movie *Female Trouble*, Divine was wearing a yellow and black striped dress and a head scarf and glasses just before she gives birth to little Taffy. For the very first performance he did of the birth scene, Leigh remade that dress and he wore a headscarf and bought glasses. We did a performance at Kinky Gerlinky and he enacted part of the bit where Divine is in the telephone booth and she is telling her boyfriend that she is pregnant and he tells her to get the hook, and so he re-enacted that bit and I was rolled in a ball inside it at the time. It was the first birth that we ever did and nobody knew I was underneath him. Leigh had to go up on the table to give birth to me and I came out and I can say it did shock a lot of people. You can tell by the audience reaction – they were like, fucking hell! People were very shocked because nobody was expecting it at all. There is a man called Dick Jewel who filmed the very first performance at Kinky Gerlinky.

FG: I'm guessing the audience wasn't made of straight stuffy people?

NB: Not necessarily. Kinky Gerlinky was a major nightclub event every month and everybody dressed up to the hilt to go there. All the drag queens would look fantastic, strike out, look amazing.

FG: Was it hard to shock that type of audience?

NB: Yes, it was hard to shock, plus they were used to Leigh wearing some sort of extravagant costume. They obviously didn't realise there was a person underneath, but it wasn't unusual for him to have a sculpted belly.

FG: How were you able to hang upside down?

NB: We used a system of harnesses and tights, that's how I was able to hang upside down for such a length of time without him dropping me. When he got up on the table, there were two ribbons which I pulled and it would come apart. Then I'd be able to get free....

FG: Did you have to break the stockings to come out?

NB: No, it was Velcroed so all you had to do was pull the Velcro.

FG: How long did you stay upside down?

NB: We tried to minimise the amount of time I was upside down. I suppose the performance was about half an hour from the time I got into the custom. The stage time itself was only seven to eight minutes. Actually, to be honest, I am not sure how long they were and as they started getting more involved they became longer, so he wouldn't put me in the harness until the last minute, because he wanted to minimise the time I was upside down. Sometimes he would get ready in advance and he would lean on the table with me in the harness and when it was time for us to go on, we would just get on with the performance.

FG: So the birth performance came about because he was a fan of Divine?

NB: Yes that's how it initially came about. Leigh absolutely adored Divine. He thought he was excellent.

FG: And then he thought it worked and he continued to build upon that?

NB: Yes and it changed obviously after the very first time when he did the Divine costume. That's the only performance we did with that costume. Afterwards, he made outfits that were more sculpted around the birth. For instance, when we did Wigstock, he made a lovely velvet jacket and a velvet skirt and he constructed these massive bosoms and I used to have to go inside it. Lee Benjamin, the guy who was helping with this, would cut around it. When I would have to go in the harness, the bosom was cut to conceal me so nobody would know I was there and it would all look in proportion. He also had a sculpted face for it. It was a facemask made out of Lycra stockings with these great big lips and cheekbones so he would look like a caricature of a person. That was at Wigstock and after that we did a few performances with this outfit and then he would strip down so people could see me actually inside.

FG: At some point you were doing a performance of the birth as part of a residency and they told you that you had to stop because of Westminster Council.

NB: Yes it was at the Freedom Café. Apparently, you are not allowed to have full frontal male or female nudity in a performance and after Leigh gave birth to me I was obviously nude and he stripped off as well to change into something else.... Well, actually you are allowed to be nude but if you move you are not, so you could be still and be nude. It had to do with the olden days in Soho with strip clubs and things of that sort. It is a really old law that's not usually put into effect. I don't know who, but somebody rung up Westminster Council and warned them that would be the case. They didn't mind about the peeing and the fact that I was drinking his pee – not that I really was, but it looked like it – and they didn't mind Leigh pretending to lick chocolate off of Richard Torry's bottom. But the nudity.

It was a bit of silliness, a bit of a scandal – ridiculous, really. And that was the last performance Leigh did before he died. We got shut down after that first night and then he started to get headaches and he ended up in the hospital with meningitis and died. That was the last performance he ever did.

FG: Did you enjoy performing with Leigh? Did you do other performances with him?

NB: Yes, I enjoyed performing with Leigh. We were great mates, I loved him to death and we enjoyed performing together. Why wouldn't I? It was exciting. The birth performances might have been the only ones, I think. I sang a bit with the band.... Oh no, there was another performance I was involved in, and that is when he did a performance in Holland in this fort called Fort Asperen in which he hung upside down.... I was dressed as a ballerina of sorts and was spraying the audience with air freshener, so I was in that performance too, in that way. I am sure there is something else but I can't really remember.

FG: In Tokyo, from the photos, it looked like you and Leigh were performing together.

NB: In Tokyo, he did a series of performances in a department store called Parco. He did a small performance which included him bending over and puking on me. I was dressed quite normally in black t-shirt and black trousers, and he pretended to puke over me (although it was just mainly soap), but it really freaked out the Japanese audience, because they actually came up to me asking whether he was sick. And Leigh quite liked it. He had a mischievous sense of humour, and definitely liked to confuse people.

FG: What about the Wigstock audience? Were they shocked? I saw the Wigstock tape and the other performers seem to be wearing more traditional drag...

NB: Well I don't know, to be honest. You know how New York drag queens are like: sometimes they love you and sometimes they hate you. I think Leigh always got along with them, because he used to go to New York quite a lot. He went to clubs in New York and that's where he met a lot of drag queens. He had extreme respect for them because he thought they were fantastic, Lady Bunny, in particular. She and Leigh really got on well. I think they had a very similar sick sense of humour and Perfidia is another one he got on really well with. Michael Alig at the time was hosting the nightclub the Limelight, and he'd bring Leigh over to host some nights.

FG: Were there artists he really liked besides Freud?

NB: Charles Atlas, Michael Clark. He liked all the artists he collaborated with. These are people he met through the club scene, but when he actually opened up his own club that's when he got to meet more people.

FG: In New York there was a lot of press on Leigh Bowery on occasion of the Wigstock show. How was the press on him in Britain? Did they take him 'seriously' right away or did it take a while?

NB: Yes, I mean there was a piece about him in *Flash Art*, there was an article in *Lovely Jobly*. A lot of magazines started to take him seriously as an artist in the 1990s. It started after he did the performance at the Anthony d'Offay Gallery in the late 1980s. That's when he realised he wanted to be thought more of as a performance artist.

FG: All the costumes that he did for that gallery performance looked really labour intensive.

NB: Yes, all of his stuff was.

FG: Did you work on a lot of his garments?

NB: I did quite a few of his garments. I was always helping with various bits and pieces but I was mainly known for sewing all the sequins on his garments. I was good at beading.

FG: Did you learn that in college?

NB: No, I studied printed textiles. After I left college, I was just working with some friends of his and they basically just gave me a bag of bugle beads. They were doing a fashion show and asked me, 'Can you make these bras look nice?' And he came around to the studios and saw what I was doing and he really liked me and asked me if I could work with him on some of the Michael Clark costumes.

FG: Did you and Leigh make all the costumes yourself or did you contract it out?

NB: He pretty much did most of the things himself. He never contracted it out. There were three main people that he worked with: Lee Benjamin, Pearl and myself.

FG: Did you do this elaborate costume?

NB: Yes, I stitched all the feathers. It would take six to seven days to sequence something like that because they are tiny bugle beads. It took a long time to do a lot of the costumes. That's all we worked on. We were quite lucky really, because Leigh had a regular amount of money coming in from sitting for Lucian [Freud] and so did I, so we had enough money. Usually sitting for Lucian was at night so we could work on the costumes during the day. And before we started sitting for Lucian, we were on the dole, or self-employed.

FG: Did you continue working on costumes after Leigh's death?

NB: Yes, because I was very good at sewing on sequins, I made a living at it. Together with Pearl, we worked with Christian Lacroix, Thierry Mugler and Vivienne Westwood. We were really good mates, so we worked together on more up-market stuff.

FG: It seems that a lot of designers were influenced by Leigh. Did he mind that?

NB: Well, at times he was influenced by the same people that were influenced by him. He thought Vivienne Westwood was great. Jean-Paul Gaultier was influenced by Leigh, too.

FG: Did he want to sell his garments or did he not really care?

NB: The thing with him is that he was not very materialistic, as long as he had enough to get by. Most of the money he used towards his costumes and living quite simply. He wasn't extravagant, you know, the extravagances were in the work, in the art. And then Lucian would take him out for expensive meals, which he liked.

    He didn't really make much money at all, and the money he made went towards the costumes. We had enough money to live and get by reasonably well. Enough money for him to continue doing his art. Fortunately, because Leigh became so well known as an artist, you know, a performance artist, he was then asked to host clubs and exhibitions and the expenses were paid to go out there, so we travelled a lot. So what would you really want money for: food, living, your art and also to go travelling.

FG: That's strange considering how well known he is.

NB: He was becoming very well known before he died and has become a real name since. Since his death, because I look after the estate of Leigh Bowery, I have had various people ring up and ask if they could have exhibitions of his work, which means I go over and help choose the costumes with them and help set up the costumes and the mannequins. The main exhibition was at MCA [Museum of Contemporary Art] in Australia.

FG: Do people ask you to buy Leigh's garments?

NB: No, I sold one to the MCA in Australia and then donated a costume. I think that's the only one I have sold.

FG: I feel the economics of performance are particularly hard, because there is great visibility, but it's hard to translate that in economic returns.

NB: Apart from the time I sold the garment to Australia, I haven't sold any of his work. And sometimes the curators are very nice and they only have small places to show his work. But if I think they are showing it at the right place and it's a really good exhibition it's worth it, because more than anything Leigh wanted to be seen. He wanted to be remembered and that's at the back of my head the all time. I could say no to the exhibitions and I wouldn't be any worse off, but ultimately I do what he would want, which is to be seen or known. Thanks to the exhibitions I have been doing, he is becoming more and more well known, which is great for his legacy and in years to come I might benefit in some way from it.

    It took some time for people to think of Leigh as an artist, a performance artist rather than a fashion icon, because he started exploring his looks in nightclubs. And as far as he was concerned the nightclub was his gallery and the public who came to the club were coming to see him. Whenever he went out he was doing a performance. The d'Offay exhibition was quite important because they took him out of a nightclub situation and in a proper gallery and then they started to take him more seriously.

FG: I think in New York there is a gallery that represents him (as well as representing Fergus Greer) and there he was well known in the nightclub scene but he wasn't the icon he was in London. So it's probably easier in New York to encounter him for the first time as an artist.

NB: I think it was in their [the gallery's] best interest, because they are selling Fergus Greer's photographs of Leigh and people like to know background information on Leigh. I mean, they are buying artwork that's going to increase in value.

INTERVIEW WITH GEORGINA GODLEY

I visited Georgina Godley at Higher and Higher, where she is currently Director of Creative Enterprise, in London in the autumn of 2008. Godley recounted her work in fashion throughout the 1980s by looking through her old press clippings.

> *Georgina Godley:* I am assuming you are interested in the 'Bump and Lump' collection?
>
> *Francesca Granata:* Well, primarily, but that is because it is the one I found more press about and so that is the collection I became most familiar with. For some of the other collections, I had a hard time understanding which pieces came from where.
>
> GG: Do you want to have the picture book by your side? This is Crolla. This is the collaboration that started in 1981 and it's significant in a way, to put things in context. I was interested in the fact that you talked about feminism in our email exchanges. This [Crolla] is as much a journey into sexuality, as it was the birth of the 1980s dandy and I was very interested in the role-playing that was going on, because women were becoming hidden away sexually and men were coming forward. It was a very interesting time. And also there was huge cross-cultural interest, particularly in London. We had a big Arab presence. There was a mix of cultures. Everyone was using ethnic fabric. It's impossible to understand this work without really understanding how radical this was. Everyone was wearing very tasteful beige, unstructured suits and such. So this was very reactionary, in a way.
>
> FG: Did you have a shop at the time?
>
> GG: Yes, in Dover Street. And it was also playing with the establishment and building something up and then pulling the carpet from underneath. It was very much a clash of cultures and ethnicities, and a rubric of what was correct and what wasn't. In a way, I became a victim of its success in as much as we created a look that was a political and social statement in clothing. And because it was successful, people wanted more of the same. We established a brand identity, so I left and we parted company. And at the time, the biggest fashion lead was swathes of black, unconstructed. Again, it was Yamamoto, it was heavy eyebrows, it was sportswear. So to create something so female was radical. It was extraordinary.
>
> FG: Was Crolla menswear and womenswear?
>
> GG: It was men's. When it came to menswear, this all-floral look hadn't really been looked at. All around, the fashion climate was about black, it was big black nylon, unconstructed, no form, no shape, girls wearing

Dr. Martens, very heavy. So to have something like that was absolutely on the pulse. It kind of just took off.

FG: So was it well received?

GG: Yes, critically as well as commercially. A lot of this imagery was taken by pop culture. This was the first collection I had done after I left Crolla. The climate was Alaïa and body consciousness. And this collection was a response to the body obsession. Datewise I think this is probably 1985. This is pre-'Bump and Lump'. It was called 'Body and Soul' [spring/summer 1986], so it would have been shown in September 1985.

FG: I read that the 'Body and Soul' collection also revolved around the body and it explored body parts, such as the spinal cord.

GG: This look [pointing at a photograph from her archive] was all rubber, and it was the same material you put under a bed. It was made of incontinent sheeting – that weird rubber sheeting, medical rubber. This was actually pre-'Body and Soul', so it must have been autumn/winter 1985–86. It was not a full collection, just a few pieces. This other one was velvet, hand-quilted velvet which looked like muscles. And this was silk jersey. And everything was worked very much like anatomical drawings. I worked it all on the stand and the cutting was in line with the drawings. This other piece was quite amazing. It was a male from the front and female from the back. It had a skirt on the front that you can't see very well. And then.... Well one of the things about these pictures is that very often the stylist styled the clothes. It was an interpretation.

This particular dress – it's in the V&A collection – it was silk jersey [the dress at the V&A is from 'Body and Soul' [spring/summer 1986] and that came after this collection. For 'Body and Soul', I made long dresses that went completely liquid onto the floor. If you imagine liquid pooling at the bottom this is really where it came from. I was trying to keep that constant fluidity. These were made as sheath dresses to be worn alone or with the shaped underwear beneath it, so that was the first collection following the bodyline, and then I made very simple things but made the form as underwear [referring to 'Bump and Lump'].

FG: And the V&A also has one of the underwear pieces from 'Bump and Lump'?

GG: I don't think they do. There were some pieces in the exhibition '100 Years of Fashion and Art' at the Hayward Gallery. The Dome in Brighton showed a piece, but I don't think it's in their permanent collection.

FG: Is it the bustle-like piece?

GG: I think maybe the pregnancy one, but I don't remember. To be honest, I didn't keep tabs on them. This one, for example, had a clear organza panel in the back and I got a short and a long dress. It's all a bit out of order. That's an example of a half-size mannequin. I had all these little mini mannequins made.

For 'Bump and Lump', I also made these padded pieces that went over the top: a padded belt – a kind of farthingale. But the interest, the obsession if you like was, a very hard and aggressive generation of women had evolved through the early '80s period and in America there was a big trend to aerobic Jane Fonda body toning. Everybody had the perfect body. And then there was Azzedine Alaïa. All those clothes angered me, because I found them very hostile to women, I didn't see it as celebrating women at all. In your emails, you mentioned Barbie dolls. I have pictures of those Barbie dolls. Really what I did for this collection ['Bump and Lump'], I did a lot of research into much more primitive cultures and what fecundity meant and what fetish dolls looked like. I did research into African fertility dolls, Egyptians, different shapes of body, different cultures of what men found beautiful as opposed to what we evolved, which was this rather masculine ideal. Partially, I felt angered that we so-called achieved women's liberty, but, in fact, we were not allowing ourselves to be true to our natural form. We should have been beyond all of that and able to celebrate fat, reproduction, all the things that happen to women's bodies…. It makes me laugh now because I am middle-aged and lumpy. It was very easy for me to do it back then, to do a collection like that. I was skinny as a weed and, of course, it all made sense, but I vividly remember this one client saying, "Oh it's all right for you to do this now, you wait till you have children, you wouldn't want to be celebrating it then". Which made me even more angry, because I thought this culture has gone so wrong. And there has been lots written about it, but in economic terms you know the wealthier you are, the thinner you are. The more affluent, the shorter the skirt and the more masculine women become.

FG: Especially at the time that you were making this work, in the 1980s, the silhouette was quite comical – it involved these really big shoulders, this sort of male swimmer body.

GG: Having to apply power rather than knowing that power is within yourself.

FG: The 1980s silhouette looked somewhat distorted.

GG: It was armour. It really was armour and that's why, I think, it was so wonderful. I mean, in the evolution of the role of women that Girl Power could come out in force and the next generation of women weren't afraid to be girly.

[Going back to the photo album] I made very thin sheath dresses and these [pointing at what looks like a padded bumbag], which were kind of bumbags in a way. That one in the picture was stuffed out to the front and there were others that were like bustles.

FG: Were they from the 'Bump and Lump' collection?

GG: I am trying to remember. Yes, this was the autumn/winter collection, which was 'Bump and Lump'. Let me explain all the various options that one had with the collection [meaning 'Bump and Lump']: I sold long sheath dresses and short ones, but I prefer the long ones because the proportions were so much more beautiful. There were padded accessories which went over the top [of the dresses] and they were made out of a really beautiful fabric, and I seemed to remember this was a quasi-silk. They were exquisite things and they were like abstracted farthingales, and they were beautiful to wear, because they exaggerated the female form.... It idealised it in a way, but in a way that people hadn't addressed because it was all masculine, so [by wearing the pieces] you would achieve a beautiful hip or you would have a wonderful rear.

FG: And how were they received? Did people actually wear them, or was it more of a conceptual collection?

GG: I sold a lot of the sheath dresses, of course, but when it came to the underwear and the overpieces, the overpieces were more successful. To be honest, apart from being photographed like mad, I think I sold maybe three padded undergarments that were worn. In a way, maybe it's an achievement, but there weren't a lot of people who were out there doing it. I had a wonderful client who bought a sheath dress, which was a long white one and she wore it without underwear (her father was a vicar). It was made of almost transparent organza in the back virtually bearing her bottom, and she wore it for a white wedding in a church. She didn't wear the lumpy bit, but it was a real statement for her to have worn it as a wedding dress. 'Bump and Lump' was the first collection for which I did a whole range. No, 'Body and Soul' was the first one. I did quite an extensive range for it. Where did I show that? Oh yes, Bloomingdale's in America. They funded it. They were so supportive. They gave me eight windows. This was in the summer of 1986. This other one was before 'Body and Soul'. This was autumn/winter 1985. It wasn't a huge collection. It was about transgender and body and it was made before my pieces started including hoops and growing away from the body.

FG: So did you leave Crolla to explore more conceptual work?

GG: Yes, and what was very frustrating was that it was a bit like you fed the monster. Crolla itself was very successful and many artists when they are successful are recognised for one thing and the commercial demand was to produce the same thing. Now that I am old and wise I realise

I should have just done both [meaning her own collection and Crolla], but I wasn't then. But anyway we were emotional partners when we started the business and we separated halfway through the business and I really needed to be alone.

FG: Were you in your 30s when you started?

GG: No, 26. I was quite young. We had just been out of college. We met at art school. I was studying fine arts but made clothes all the time, and Scott Crolla was doing sculpture, and was doing conceptual photographic work. We came to London and were fortunate enough to find some people to back this concept of the shop. I worked as a picture restorer. I did an MA in Chelsea in conservation in-between. Oh, here are some pictures of the Barbie dolls. They had some extra clay lumps and bumps and things like these.

FG: Did you experiment with the Barbie dolls before you did the collection ['Bump and Lump']?

GG: That was how the whole idea came about, because Barbie is the definition of extreme, almost pervy, femininity. Again, there was this obsession with a boyish figure. So I got a whole line-up of Barbie dolls and played around with body and clay and built them out in different places. At the time, I was studying fertility dolls, which informed this exercise. It was from the reshaped Barbie that I worked on a selection of padded underwear.

FG: Did some of the underwear pieces refer to pregnancy?

GG: Yes, but it wasn't simply a replica of pregnancy. It was rather beautiful because it came in and it had a dip. I could almost model it again. It went down and came out. It was a very organic and rather magical shape actually, but what it had was more of a sense of a Vermeer, it was a very lyrical body to look at. It felt incredibly feminine. What I was trying to do was to look at the body and understand what true femaleness was, to some extent. Trying to cross boundaries of culture and things and come up with a much more natural and beautiful form, I suppose. It was completely asymmetrical. This other one was flat in the front [the one in the shape reminiscent of a bustle] and came around and sort of grazed onto the tie. In a way a lot of the African fertility dolls have big ties and bottoms and they are considered a very erogenous zone, which is so not the case in our culture. The shape of the hip is inspired by fertility dolls, in a way, but it also makes reference to the bustle, which has had its moments of beauty in European history. So that's how it worked: it started from here, it came out like a shelf and came around to the front like that and it was beautiful. It was really beautiful. So these are the pieces and they had padded shoulders as well like that. They were very soft rounded shoulders, again a complete antidote to the square 1980s shoulder. And the padding stopped there, so there wasn't much padding. They were cut all the way around. It was a double layer of cotton Lycra and French seams, and then I literally just stuffed all the webbing onto one layer and stitched it. It was all done like a quilt – a pretty simple quilt.

FG: Was it a conscious response to the 1980s silhouette and the way they used padding?

GG: Yes, but ultimately padding is just a means to the end. They could have gotten angular shoulders any other way. My work was certainly in response to wanting to change the brutal nature of the masculine silhouette.... It was all about changing the perspective of what could be beautiful. It was all the things we learned to consider ugly. I was challenging that. Beauty could be a fleshy arm, because there is something fecund and sensual about it.

FG: Looking back at the 1980s, the shoulder pads seem quite comical from a distance.

GG: Yes, now, going to a second-hand shop, it's hard to believe what one sees. Back then the manufacturers would be sewing three or four shoulder pads together just to put in a jacket.

FG: Do you think anybody might have documentation of the other underwear pieces?

GG: I have an actual example of the pregnancy one and one of the farthingale ones in storage somewhere. This is the 'Recent Decent' collection [spring/summer 1986]. Here I wrote something really pretentious: 'Fabric as a cry against the over portrayed executive woman by adapting a memory of uniform style, interchangeable garments, dresses with boning ....' There was a quite complex tailoring involved in the garments which you can't see from the photographs. There were sculptural shapes but created in the flat. It achieved feminine curves. These pieces had boning in the back so it made a balloon. So that one went right out in a sculptural way in the back. It had a balloon back giving the impression of a big rear, but this time through tailoring rather than padding out.

FG: Despite your use of this complex tailoring, you weren't really trained in fashion.

GG: I always made my own clothes, but no, I trained in sculpture, which is probably the reason why I approached fashion the way I did. I was always able to cobble things together myself, but I had this brilliant crew I worked with: brilliant cutters and seamstresses, who were able to put it together beautifully. I always worked on the stand and I tried it on myself first. To be honest, I am very glad I didn't train because it made me try a number of things other people wouldn't have gone near.

FG: I wanted to ask about things that came later, but I don't have the exact years. There were some pieces you did with logos that I want to talk about, and something you did with prints, with all sort of images: milk cartons, slimming pills and roses... .

GG: That was autumn/winter 1987–88. There was one print in the 'Recent Decent' collection and that was a smock top. That was the first photographic print. I called it photographic embroideries. I was interested in the idea of fast couture. To have all the impression of decoration but it was done with photographic prints. Well now it's commonplace, but it wasn't really done back then. I laid out a top smock pattern on the beach and found all those salvaged bits from the beach and shells and seaweed and ropes and I photographed it and printed it and it formed the pattern like an engineered print. That was the one we just looked at, 'Recent Decent'.

GG: And then there was this collection. It must have been autumn/winter 1987–88. This was bits of rubbish: nappies, plastic bags, bits of old bleached pots and pills and roses. The pair was made out of pills. This collection was called 'School Colours' and it was shown in the Victoria and Albert Museum and there was a presentation with slides of all the work that had gone into it. The collection split the people in half. I got a huge amount of press from it, but I heard that many editors thought, 'How arrogant of her to think that we might be interested in the inspiration behind the collection', which is strange considering how many people have done it since.... I think I was just the first.

FG: Did you show the clothes as well?

GG: Oh yes, I didn't want to do the up on a catwalk, pure sex in your face. I wanted a sensitive engagement and an intimacy, and I wanted to have a woman talk about each piece. And the problem many people had is that it didn't have the sex appeal people expect from seeing fashion. Generally speaking a lot of the audience felt they had been patronised and felt uncomfortable.

FG: Do you think the setting had to do with it?

GG: I was trying to undo the sexually alluring aspect associated with fashion, and that's why I didn't really want to put it on a catwalk. A parallel would be presentations by designers who came later, such as Hussein Chalayan. He did put on productions like that, but because it was categorised as a cultural statement, it was acceptable. But at the time I did it, nobody was doing that in fashion really, so it was thought of as weird and they were nervous, because they couldn't place it.

FG: And did you have a relation with the Victoria and Albert or did you just use their space?

GG: No, they were very supportive and it was fine. Actually they were glad to do it; it was in the lecture theatre and they had their main curator read from the pages. She was quite turgid. Maybe I wouldn't do it like that now, but I was young, I was angry and I had lots to say. It was a very complicated collection. It was a huge collection: there were photographic velvets, there was this extraordinary technique of rubber printed on silk that gave a couture finish. It looked like it was beautifully hand-quilted, but actually it was just rubber printed. What I really wanted to do was to bring in labour and couture but make it very modern. I called it fast couture after fast food. This was also a print. It was velveteen and it was made into a dress as well. It was looking at femininity and the jacket was shaped at the back like that. Among the things I was looking at, at the time of this collection, were Russian dolls and iconic female images. I got a lot of orders. This was a very successful collection. I did a lot of work on innovative fabric after this collection.

I was also asked to design a dress for Margaret Thatcher, alongside other designers. I gave her an academic gown. It was quite curious because the various responses gave you the impression of what was going on at the time. The look was still very 1980s, while I was changing the silhouette completely. I was doing the soft cocoon shapes and then you had the Bodymap thing.

FG: Did you cross paths with other designers?

GG: I had a studio on All Saints Road and a whole gang – Leigh Bowery, Rachel Auburn, Tom Dixon – who I was very close to at this time.

FG: Did you feel like you were exchanging ideas with the people you were in touch with?

GG: Always. I didn't necessarily exchange ideas with fashion designers. My best friends were furniture designers, painters – by friends I mean the people who enjoyed each other's company. We did belong to a community and had similar interests. There was actually a community.

FG: I am also writing about Leigh Bowery. I was wondering if you knew his work.

GG: Well he was a little bit younger than me. In the house that we lived in at that time, there was this girl Rachel Auburn – she is around, she lives in London and she will be able to tell you more. She is now a DJ. She is kind of fabulous and I was at college with her before that time. And my last year at Crolla [1985], we went to a trip called 'London Goes to Tokyo'. Japan supported it and Bowery was there and Trojan and Rachel Auburn, they were all there at the time, and that's when Bowery was just starting out as a club character.

FG: Like you, Bowery did a lot with padding and body manipulation.

GG: My understanding of his work is that his pursuit was.... He was about a pumped-up aesthetic, as well as agonising on issues of sexuality. His intention was perhaps more about undoing masculinity than making femininity.

FG: I read somewhere that you did make a power suit, but it was made of throwaway materials like towels.

GG: That was a 'Recent Decent' piece. It was made of tea towels and yellow dusters all sewn together – the actual things – and piqué towels, the really absorbent waffle towels.

[Again pointing at the lookbook]. This is spring/summer 1988. This season was called 'Corporate Coding'; it was a summer collection. One must imagine the climate at the time. London was so incredibly affluent, and the City boom and all the yuppies. Margaret Thatcher and the whole corporate culture were overwhelming and I had the sense that the bubble had to burst. I had a weird feeling that it can't go on. For 'Corporate Coding' I made working suits, all in one bodysuits with leather gloves. Everything was sort of based on a kind of sportswear meets City shirting striped fabric – what all the City Boys would wear – but they were empire lines, very feminine jumpsuits. These were shirting striped dresses, but they had ballooned back, again very soft shapes over the shoulders, very feminine so again addressing the power balance, trying to make things more feminine. They were formal, but very feminine. These were trousers, padded at the hips and bum, like pantaloons Pierrot style.

FG: But they were padded at the hips?

GG: Yes, padded at the hips and the bum, so it stuck right out and it was made of gazar, white gazar. It was beautiful. This was a jacket made out of that blocking material you make hats out of. I don't know how you call – it was like a gauze that I did on a mannequin, and then she took it off and she was bare-breasted. 'Corporate Coding' also included print. They were based on the home. Again, I was discussing this thing: 'what has happened to female power?' I commissioned the artist Tim Head, who at the time was very interested in logos. There was one print called home security, which was an alarm bell in blue and yellow, whose meaning was: 'Keep your home alarmed.' There was the test tube one, which made an allusion to condoms and test tube babies. Then there was one called Deep Freeze, meaning one was a slave to the freezer, and a TV dinner print. At the time there was this embrace of modernism, meaning new technologies. People didn't tend to know about organic vegetables and slow food. This collection was done in spring/summer 1988. A week later there was a major crash in the City.

FG: Were you at the fringe of the fashion business then?

GG Yes, there was only mainstream and fringe. Yes, I was in the fringe, constant fringe. I was bigger in Japan, because they bought into concepts more in Japan. My work was bought mainly by Japanese buyers, but I also sold at Harrods and Whistles. I produced in England. It wasn't unusual at the time, I was manufacturing in Wales.

Later on – but really all along – I was experimenting with fabric, metal, geological matter. 'Earthly Mater' was the name of this collection. It was looking back into motherhood and female forms. It was a cocoon shape, bare-breasted Amazon look.

I didn't have a fashion show then, because I lost my Japanese clients. The financial crisis had hit Japan by then, so I stopped the fashion shows, it was the beginning of the recession. I retrenched and showed in my showroom. In this period, I also did sport couture: very sculptural work made of Gore-Tex, goose-filled jackets. I was looking for a meeting of the practical and the conceptual. I wanted things to work and be easy. The wearability aspect was always important to me. In 1991 I did the last collection. There were no Japanese buyers and I married Sebastian Conran in 1989 and started doing more and more consultancy. I carried on doing couture in my studio. Well, actually in 1998 I did an exhibition at Joseph and it was about women of different sizes. It was called 'Dolly's Date'. I worked with antique textiles and dresses.

Then in 1999, there was the exhibition at the Hayward Gallery, which included pieces from the 'Bump and Lump' collection. And it was interesting how Rei Kawakubo's work was included and specifically her 'Dress Becomes Body' collection – which explored similar themes – and at the last minute the gallery had to call me to ask me if it was okay for my piece to be moved, because Kawakubo refused to be hung near me, or even in the same room.

FG: That is sort of problematic. It shows a certain insecurity on her part.

GG: Yes, I mean obviously those themes were part of the collective consciousness at the time. Women in the 1980s were either hiding under seven layers or adopting a masculine silhouette. Both disguised their femininity and to present yourself in the workforce you had to hide your femininity.

NOTES

Introduction

1 Mikhail Bakhtin, *Rabelais and His World*, trans. Hélène Iswolsky (Bloomington, IN: Indiana University Press, 1984), 322–23.
2 Ibid., 320.
3 Ibid., 322–23.
4 The grotesque is explored within fashion design earlier than the 1980s, and particularly in the work of surrealist designer Elsa Schiaparelli, produced in the 1930s.
5 Michel Foucault, *The History of Sexuality*, Vol. 1: *An Introduction* (New York: Random House, 1978), 139.
6 Susan Sontag, *Aids and its Metaphors*, (New York: Picador, 1988), 114
7 For a summary of the history AIDS, see Victoria A. Harden, 'AIDS as a Cultural Phenomenon', *AIDS at 30*, (Dulles, VA: Potomac Books, 2012), as well as Paula A. Treichler, 'AIDS, Homophobia, and Biomedical Discourse: An Epidemic of Signification', in *How to Have Theory in an Epidemic: Cultural Chronicles of AIDS*, (Durham, NC: Duke University Press, 1999).
8 Ibid.
9 Ibid., 3.
10 The normative 'classical' body of mainstream fashion of the period was also predominantly a white body. However, the discussion of race within fashion of this period could not be sufficiently unpacked in this work, given its length, and thus remains beyond the scope of this book.
11 The term 'experimental' generates debates within art history and cannot be easily and unproblematically transported to the realm of fashion, where it does not have the centrality it has achieved within the history of art and the history of modernism in particular. For a discussion of the avant-garde and the neo-avant-garde in the twentieth century, see Hal Foster, *The Return of the Real: The Avant-Garde at the End of the Century* (Cambridge, MA: MIT Press, 1996); Benjamin H.D. Buchloh, *Neo-Avantgarde and Culture Industry: Essays on European and American Art from 1955 to 1975* (Cambridge, MA: MIT Press, 2001).
12 The intersection between feminism, queer theory and performance became perhaps most evident in the NEA controversies of the early 1990s surrounding the work of the performance artists Karen Finley, Holly Hughes, John Fleck and Tim Miller. For a recent

account of the relation between feminism, and performance in North America, see Jayne Wark, *Radical Gestures: Feminism and Performance Art in North America* (Montreal: McGill-Queen's University Press, 2006). For an earlier account of the relation between feminism, the body and performance, see Lynda Nead, *The Female Nude: Art, Obscenity and Sexuality* (London: Routledge, 1992). On queer theory and performance, see Ivy I-Chu Chang, *Queer Performativity and Performance* (Taipei: Booksmann Books, 2003).

13 RoseLee Goldberg, *Performance Art: From Futurism to the Present* (New York, NY: Thames and Hudson, 2001). On the relation between performance and borders, see also Marvin Carlson, *Performance: A Critical Introduction* (London: Routledge, 1996); Richard Schechner, 'What Is Performance Studies Anyway?', in *The Ends of Performance*, ed. Peggy Phelan and Jill Lane (New York, NY: New York University Press, 1998), 357–63; and Jon McKenzie, 'The Liminal Norm', in *The Performance Studies Reader*, ed. Henry Bial (London: Routledge, 2004), 26–31.

14 Paul Du Gay et al., *Doing Cultural Study: The Story of the Sony Walkman* (London: Sage and the Open University, 2013), 68.

15 Robert Stam, *Subversive Pleasures: Bakhtin, Cultural Criticism, and Film* (Baltimore, MD: Johns Hopkins University Press, 1989), 122.

16 Caroline Evans, *Fashion at the Edge: Spectacle, Modernity, and Deathliness* (New Haven, CT: Yale University Press, 2003); Rebecca Arnold, *Fashion, Desire, and Anxiety: Image and Morality in the Twentieth Century* (New Brunswick, NJ: Rutgers University Press, 2001).

17 For an in-depth discussion of the interaction of the mainstream and the experimental aesthetic in fashion of the 1990s, see Evans, *Fashion at the Edge*, 5–7.

18 According to Freud, repression occurs when instinctual impulses are kept from entering the conscious mind through a 'persistent expenditure of force', because they threaten the integrity of the ego or are incompatible with ethical standards imposed on it by the superego. However, in the long run these repressed impulses tend to return and surface to consciousness via mechanisms of condensation and/or displacement. See Sigmund Freud, 'Repression', in *The Standard Edition of the Complete Psychological Works of Sigmund Freud*, vol. XIV, trans. and ed. James Strachey (London: Hogarth Press, 1958), 149; see also 'Unconscious' (1915), reprinted in the same volume.

19 Norbert Elias, *The Civilizing Process* (Blackwell: Oxford, 1994). For a discussion of Elias's theories in relation to contemporary fashion, see Evans, *Fashion at the Edge*, 3–14.

20 Ibid., 3.

21 On the romantic grotesque, see Wolfgang Kayser, *The Grotesque in Art and Literature*, trans. Ulrich Weisstein (Bloomington, IN: Indiana University Press, 1963).

22 Evans, *Fashion at the Edge*, 6.

23 Judith Butler, *Gender Trouble: Feminism and the Subversion of Identity* (New York, NY: Routledge, 2006), *Bodies that Matter: On the Discursive Limits of 'Sex'* (New York, NY: Routledge, 1993).

24 Judith Butler, 'Performative Acts and Gender Constitution', in *The Performance Studies Reader*, ed. Henry Bial (London: Routledge, 2004), 187–88.

25 Ibid., 197

26 Butler, *Bodies That Matter*, 7.

27 Arnold, *Fashion, Desire, and Anxiety*, 48–62, 80–94. Arnold's reading conforms to arguments that have been made in relation to contemporary horror movies, and particularly the slasher film sub-genre. (For a discussion of gender and the slasher film, see Carol J. Clover, 'Her Body, Himself: Gender in the Slasher Film', in *The Dread of Difference*, ed. Barry Keith Grant (Austin, TX: University of Texas Press, 1996), 66–113.

28 Arnold, *Fashion, Desire, and Anxiety*, 93.

29 Arnold, 'Flesh', ibid., 89–95.
30 Here, I am paraphrasing Prown's definition. Jules David Prown, 'Mind in Matter: An Introduction to Material Culture Theory and Method', in *Art as Evidence: Writings on Art and Material Culture* (New Haven, CT: Yale University Press, 2001), 70 (this essay was originally published in *Winterthur Portfolio* 17, no. 1); and Prown, 'The Truth of Material Culture: History or Fiction', in *American Artifacts: Essays in Material Culture*, ed. Jules David Prown and Kenneth Halthman (East Lansing, MI: Michigan University Press, 2000), 11.
31 The *mise en scène* – which is made up of those aspects overlapping with theatre and performance such as 'setting, lighting, costume and the behaviour of the figure' – represents the most important element of the fashion show films and videos.
32 David Bordwell and Kristen Thompson, *Film Art: An Introduction*, rev. ed. (1979; repr. Boston, MA: McGraw Hill, 2004).
33 See for instance, Angela McRobbie, 'Fashion and the Image Industries' in *British Fashion Design: Rag Trade or Image Industry?* (London: Routledge, 1998).
34 Both *Visionaire* and *Six*, which tend to be difficult to find, were made available to me by the Costume Institute library at the Metropolitan Museum of Art.
35 Amy Spindler, 'Coming Apart', *New York Times*, 25 July 1993.
36 Daryoush Haj-Najafi, 'Bernhard Willhelm: Maverick with a Mission', *Hint Magazine*, 2005, accessed 7 November 2008, http://www.hintmag.com; Katie Shillingford, 'Outer Limits', *Dazed and Confused* 2, no. 54 (October 2007): 122–31; Peter de Potter, 'Interview with Bernhard Willhelm', *Butt* 1 (2001): 14–8.
37 Linda Sandino, 'Oral Histories and Design: Objects and Subjects', *Journal of Design History* 19, no. 4 (2006): 280. For a more general discussion of oral history, see Paul Thompson, *The Voice of the Past: Oral History* (Oxford: Oxford University Press, 1988); while on oral history and fashion, see Lou Taylor, 'Approaches Using Oral History', in *The Studying of Dress History* (Manchester: Manchester University Press, 2002), 242–71.
38 Robert Proctor, 'The Architect's Intention: Interpreting Post-War Modernism through the Architect Interview', *Journal of Design History* 19, no. 4 (2006): 302.
39 See, in particular, Barbara A. Babcock, 'Introduction', in *The Reversible World: Symbolic Inversion in Art and Society*, ed. Barbara A. Babcock (Ithaca, NY: Cornell University Press, 1978).
40 Bakhtin, *Rabelais and His World*; Peter Stallybrass and Allon White, *The Politics and Poetics of Transgression* (Ithaca, NY: Cornell University Press, 1986). In turn, Bakhtin's writings, and particularly *Rabelais and His World*, have been influential to cultural anthropology.
41 Peter Burke, *What is Cultural History?* (Cambridge: Polity Press, 2004), 3. For an introduction to the discipline, see his *Varieties of Cultural History* (Ithaca, NY: Cornell University Press, 1997).
42 Breward, *The Culture of Fashion*, 1–2.
43 Caroline Evans's *Fashion at the Edge* is a recent example of a use of 'applied theory', which takes into account 'the material facts of fashion and fashion design', within academic writing about fashion. Evans, *Fashion at the Edge*, 3.

Chapter 1 Against Power Dressing: Georgina Godley

1 For an overview of returns of past fashions throughout Western fashion history, see Barbara Burman Baines, *Fashion Revivals: From the Elizabethan Age to the Present Day* (London: Batsford, 1981).

2 See Joanne Entwistle, '"Power Dressing" and the Construction of the Career Woman', in *Buy this Book: Studies in Advertising and Consumption*, ed. Mica Nava et al. (London: Routledge, 1997), 311–23. For an analysis of power suits in the context of African-American culture of the 1980s, see Siobhan Carter-David, 'Wearing it to "Work It" or Wearing it to Work: Fashions in the Making of The Black Professional', in 'Fashioning *Essence* Women and *Ebony* Men: Sartorial Instruction and the New Politics of Racial Uplift in Print, 1970–1993', (PhD diss., Indiana University, 2011)
3 John T. Molloy, *Women: Dress for Success* (New York, NY: Peter H. Wyden, 1980).
4 For a discussion of Vivienne Westwood's work, see Claire Wilcox, *Vivienne Westwood* (London: V&A, 2004); Caroline Evans and Minna Thornton, *Women and Fashion* (London: Quartet Books, 1989); and Rebecca Arnold, 'Vivienne Westwood's Anglomania', in *The Englishness of English Dress*, ed. Caroline Cox, Christopher Breward and Becky Conekin (Oxford: Berg, 2002).
5 For a recent assessment of the term, see Emily Apter, 'Reflections on Gynophobia', in *Coming Out of Feminism*, ed. Mandy Merck et al. (Oxford: Blackwell Publishing, 1998), 102–22.
6 Mary J. Russo, *The Female Grotesque: Risk, Excess, and Modernity* (New York, NY: Routledge, 1995), 1–6.
7 On the exclusion of the grotesque from Western art history, see Frances S. Connelly, 'Introduction', in *Modern Art and the Grotesque*, ed. Frances S. Connelly (Cambridge: Cambridge University Press, 2003), 1–19.
8 Russo, *The Female Grotesque*, 1.
9 Barbara Maria Stafford 'Conceiving', in Connelly, *Modern Art and the Grotesque*, 81.
10 Ibid., 81, quoting Antoine-Raphael Mengs' *Sämmtlicje hinterlassene Schriften*.
11 Mavis Kirkham, ed., *Exploring the Dirty Side of Women's Health* (London: Routledge, 2007).
12 Mary Douglas, *Purity and Danger: An Analysis of Concepts of Pollution and Taboo* (London: Routledge, 2002), 2, 36–37.
13 Helen Callaghan, 'Birth Dirt', in *Exploring the Dirty Side of Women's Health*, ed. Mavis Kirkham (London: Routledge, 2007), 16.
14 I thank Maureen Brewster for pointing this out to me through her MA thesis 'Bump Watch: Fashioning Celebrity Pregnancy as Performance and Product' (MA thesis, The New School, New York, 2014).
15 Mikhail Bakhtin, *Rabelais and His World*, trans. Hélène Iswolsky (Bloomington, IN: Indiana University Press, 1984), 118.
16 Ibid., 25–9.
17 Kenneth Clark, *The Nude: A Study of Ideal Art* (London: John Murray, 1956), 317–18.
18 Ibid., 333
19 Bakhtin, *Rabelais*, 240.
20 Russo, *The Female Grotesque*, 63.
21 Ibid., 10–12.
22 Georgina Godley, interview with author, London, September 2008 (see Appendix, 178).
23 Maria Luisa Frisa and Stefano Tonchi, eds, *Excess: Fashion and the Underground in the 80s* (Milano: Charta, 2004), 344.
24 Richard Martin, *Fashion and Surrealism* (New York: Rizzoli, 1987), 17. Here Martin uses the term in its art historical significance, as he discusses Godley's pieces in the context of surrealism: 'Biomorphic art is a form of abstract art which purports to take

its abstract forms from living organisms rather than from the geometrical basis of such abstract movements as constructivism' (from the definition in the *Oxford English Dictionary* Online Edition).
25 Godley, interview with author (see Appendix, 177).
26 Ibid. See Appendix, 176.
27 Ibid. See Appendix, 169.
28 Ibid. See Appendix, 169.
29 Alistair O'Neill, *London – After a Fashion* (London: Reaktion Books, 2007), 188.
30 Godley, interview with author (see Appendix, 172).
31 Unfortunately, most garments from Georgina Godley's various collections were not systematically archived and/or photographed, so that often the only documentations are photographs of the pieces in style and fashion magazines of the times, and/or quotes from journalists and Godley herself. This renders a detailed description of many pieces impossible.
32 Elizabeth Wilson, 'Fashion and the Postmodern Body', in *Chic Thrills: A Fashion Reader*, ed. Juliet Ash and Elizabeth Wilson (Berkeley, CA: University of California Press, 1993), 12.
33 Steve Beard and Jim McClellan, 'Cerebral Couture', in 'The Surreal Issue', special issue, *i-D Magazine* 1, no. 57 (April 1988): 72–6, 78.
34 Godley, interview with author (see Appendix, 172).
35 Exhibition label for padded undergarment by Georgina Godley, 1986 (remade 1998) in the Brighton Museum's Body Gallery.
36 Museum catalogue entry for Godley's green hooped silk jersey dress (1986) in the Victoria and Albert Museum's collection.
37 Liz Jobey, 'Designing Women', *Vogue UK*, July 1987: 111.
38 Godley, interview with author (see Appendix, 171).
39 Ibid.
40 A more detailed discussion of Barbie and bodily ideals and the way she embodies normative racial, class and gender categories can be found in my discussion of Martin Margiela's Barbie clothes. Among the books discussing Barbie, the ideal body and normative femininity, see Mary F. Rogers, *Barbie Culture* (Thousand Oaks: Sage Publications, 1999); Erica Rand, *Barbie's Queer Accessories* (Durham, NC: Duke University Press, 1995); Yona Zeldis McDonough, ed., *The Barbie Chronicles* (New York: Touchstone Books, 1999); and Jeannie Banks Thomas, *Naked Barbies, Warrior Joes and Other Forms of Visible Gender* (Urbana, IL: University of Illinois Press, 2003).
41 Lynda Nead, *The Female Nude: Art, Obscenity and Sexuality* (London: Routledge, 1992), 7.
42 Ibid., 7.
43 Godley, interview with author (see Appendix, 171).
44 Hannah Rechowicz, 'Extract from an Interview with Georgina Godley', in 'Exploring the Connection between Artistic "Creativity" and Childhood Play through the Examination of the Work of Four Diverse Artists' (BA diss., Central Saint Martins, London, 1996), 1. Also see an interview with the designer in Beard and McClellan, 'Cerebral Couture'.
45 This is perhaps most evident in 1970s cultural/radical feminism, which viewed women as sharing a female essence or nature; see, for instance, Mary Daly, *Gyn/Ecology: The Metaethics of Radical Feminism* (Boston, MA: Beacon, 1978); and Adrienne Rich, *Of Woman Born: Motherhood as Institution and Experience* (New York: Bantam, 1976).

46 For a thorough critique of essentialism as exclusionary, see Elizabeth Spelman, *Inessential Woman: Problems of Exclusion in Feminist Thought* (London: The Women's Press, 1988).
47 See Judith Butler, *Bodies that Matter: On the Discursive Limits of 'Sex'* (New York: Routledge, 1993).
48 On attempts to recuperate essentialism, see, for instance, Naomi Schor, 'The Essentialism Which is not One', in *The Essential Difference*, ed. Naomi Schor and Elizabeth Weed (Bloomington, IN: Indiana University Press, 1994).
49 For a thorough account of this debate within the feminist movement, on which my summary is partially based, see Alison Stone, 'Essentialism and Anti-Essentialism in Feminist Philosophy', *Journal of Moral Philosophy* 1, no. 2 (2004): 135–53.
50 Ibid., 136.
51 Here, I use the term alterity to indicate a condition of otherness after Kelly Oliver's writings on Kristeva, which will be discussed in the following chapter.
52 Rechowicz, 'Interview with Georgina Godley', 2.
53 In the interview I conducted, Godley mentions having researched African art and visual culture, yet she no longer has the specifics of her research. Godley, interview with author (see Appendix, 169–78).
54 Godley, interview with the author, London, September 2008 (see Appendix, 173)
55 See Paul Heels and Paul Morris, eds, *The Values of the Enterprise Culture: The Moral Debate* (London: Routledge, 1992).
56 Nikolas Rose, 'Governing the Enterprising Self', ibid., 146.
57 Entwistle, 'Power Dressing', 318–19.
58 On the negative reception of Godley's collection, see Richard Buckley and Anne Bogart, 'London: That Brit Wit's Missing', *WWD* 153 (March 16 1987): 1.
59 The reference to historical images and flower motives is also an echo of her previous work at Crolla: see, O'Neill, *London – After a Fashion*, 177–97.
60 Michel Foucault, 'Technologies of the Self', in *Technologies of the Self: A Seminar with Michel Foucault*, ed. Luther H. Martin, Huck Gutman, and Patrick H. Hutton (Amherst, MA: The University of Massachusetts Press, 1988), 18.
61 Godley, interview with the author, London, September 2008 (see Appendix, 177).

Chapter 2 Fashioning the Maternal Body: Rei Kawakubo

1 This point is also made in Caroline Evans' discussion of Martin Margiela's early work and his recycled aesthetic, and Rebecca Arnold's study of the 'heroin chic' look of the 1990s. Caroline Evans, *Fashion at the Edge: Spectacle, Modernity, and Deathliness* (New Haven, CT: Yale University Press, 2003), 35–9; Rebecca Arnold, *Fashion, Desire, and Anxiety: Image and Morality in the Twentieth Century* (New Brunswick, NJ: Rutgers University Press, 2001), 48–55. On design more generally, see Linda Sandino, 'Linda Sandino, 'Here Today, Gone Tomorrow: Transient Materiality in Contemporary Cultural Artefacts', *Journal of Design History* 17, no. 3 (September 2004): 283–93.
2 Nead refers to female bodybuilding as 'a mixed blessing for feminism'. She discusses it as being aligned with feminism insofar as it produces a different kind of body image and allows for the development of female muscular strength, but ultimately she see it as being easily co-opted within strategies of containment. Lynda Nead, *The Female Nude: Art, Obscenity and Sexuality* (London: Routledge, 1992), 9.

3 Ibid., 8–9.
4 Maria Luisa Frisa and Stefano Tonchi, eds, *Excess: Fashion and the Underground in the 80s* (Milano: Charta, 2004), 38.
5 Ibid., 15.
6 Hilton Als, 'Bump and Mind', *Artforum* 35 (December 1996): 21 (italics mine).
7 The press of the period did not fail to notice Kawakubo's questioning of female standards of beauty. On this point, see Lynn Yaeger, 'Material World', *Village Voice*, 1 April 1997, 16.
8 See Caroline Evans, '"Dress Becomes Body Becomes Dress": Are You an Object or a Subject? Comme des Garçons and Self-Fashioning', *032c Magazine* (Special edition 'Embrace Instability'), no. 4 (October 2001); see also Lynn Yaeger, ibid., who quotes one of the store clerks at Commes saying that customers 'are taking the pads out'.
9 On the glamorisation of pregnancy in contemporary visual culture, and particularly Hollywood films, see Kelly Oliver, *Knock Me Up, Knock Me Down: Images of Pregnancy in Hollywood Films* (New York, NY: Columbia University Press, 2012)
10 On response to the cover, see, for instance, Leslie Scriviner, 'Nude and Pregnant: Is it Pretty or Porn?' *The Toronto Star*, 4 August 1991: A1
11 Deyan Sudjic, *Rei Kawakubo and* Comme des Garçons (New York, NY: Rizzoli, 1990), 80
12 Eva Respini, 'Will the Real Cindy Sherman Please Stand Up?', in *Cindy Sherman* (New York, NY: Museum of Modern Art, 2012), 35.
13 On Sherman and AIDS and feminism, also see ibid., 35–8.
14 Through direct observation of a number of 1980s garments by Kawakubo in the Metropolitan Museum of Art's Costume Institute collection, I was able to ascertain that even when she did use shoulder pads, they were modest – especially by 1980s' standards – and could be easily removed.
15 Arnold, *Fashion, Desire, and Anxiety*, 94–5.
16 Julia Kristeva, *Revolution in Poetic Language*, trans. Margaret Waller (New York, NY: Columbia University Press, 1984), 137–9.
17 Mikhail Bakhtin, *Problems of Dostoyevsky's Poetics*, trans. Caryl Emerson (Minneapolis, MN: University of Minnesota Press, 1984); *The Dialogical Imagination*, trans. Caryl Emerson and Michael Holquist (Austin, TX: University of Texas Press, 1981).
18 Peter Stallybrass and Allon White. *The Politics and Poetics of Transgression* (Ithaca, NY: Cornell University Press, 1986), 175
19 Kelly Oliver, *Reading Kristeva: Unravelling the Double-Bind* (Bloomington, IN: Indiana University Press, 1993), 12.
20 Robert Stam, *Subversive Pleasures: Bakhtin, Cultural Criticism, and Film* (Baltimore, MD: Johns Hopkins University Press, 1989), 6.
21 Oliver, *Reading Kristeva*, 11–2. Kristeva discusses motherhood as exemplary of the subject-in-process in her essay (originally published in 1977) 'Stabat Mater'. It is also in this piece that she advances her theory of a new ethic based on a new understanding of motherhood, which she calls an 'herethic'. *Strangers to Ourselves* (1988) also illustrates the process according to which an understanding and acceptance of ourselves as 'disintegrated' – once again as 'subjects-in-process' – allows for an acceptance of the other: see Julia Kristeva, *Strangers to Ourselves*, trans. Leon S. Roudiez (New York, NY: Columbia University Press, 1991).
22 Emily Martin, 'The Fetus as Intruder: Mother's Bodies and Medical Metaphors', *Cyborg Babies: From Techno-sex to Techno-tots*, ed. Robbie Davis-Floyd and Joseph Dumit (New York, NY: Routledge, 1998), 126.
23 Ibid., 131.

24 See, for instance, Lennard J. Davis, 'Constructing Normalcy', in *Enforcing Normalcy: Disability, Deafness and the Body*, (New York: Verso, 1995).
25 Martin, 'The Fetus as Intruder', 139.
26 For an account of this tension between fashion's tendency to problematise the subject's boundaries vis-à-vis its continued employment in the construction of a bounded self, see Dani Cavallaro and Alexandra Warwick, *Fashioning the Frame: Boundaries, Dress and Body* (Oxford: Berg, 1998).
27 Thurston Moore, Jim O'Rourke and Andrew Russ joined Kosugi in performing the music for the BAM's performances of *Scenario*: see Gia Kourlas, 'Comme Dancing', *Time Out New York*, 9–16 October 1997, 21–3.
28 Ibid., 22.
29 Here, I refer to the Brechtian notion of *Verfremdungseffekt*, which is more often translated from the German as 'making strange', meaning to defamiliarise, to estrange.
30 Kourlas, 'Comme Dancing', 22; and Robert Johnson, 'The Bulges: Merce Cunningham's "Scenario"', *Ballet International*, no. 12 (December 1997): 52–3.
31 I am basing my description of *Scenario* on recordings of the premiere and a performance of excerpts of the dance, which I attended at the Joyce Theatre (New York, 11 October 2006), as well as on reviews of the performance. For the latter see previous note, as well as Leigh Witchel, 'Merce In and Outside Time', *Ballet Review* 35 (Winter 1997): 35–41.
32 A revealing exchange, which took place the night I attended the Mini-Scenario piece, brings further proof to the unmistakable reference of the costumes to birth processes. An older woman, on bumping into the belly of a younger pregnant woman in line to use the restroom, exclaimed: 'Oh it's just like those costumes', to which she added embarrassingly, 'but yours is beautiful, you know, symmetrical not lopsided'. The pregnant woman replied: 'Well, I don't think of it [pointing at the belly] as something which I would *choose* to wear' (Joyce Theatre, New York, 11 October, 2006).
33 For an overview of Merce Cunningham's work, see David Vaughan's *Merce Cunningham: Fifty Years* (New York, NY: Aperture, 1997) and *Merce Cunningham: Fifty Forward* (New York, NY: Cunningham Dance Foundation, 2005).
34 For an in-depth discussion of Ridley Scott's *Alien* and its relation to the maternal, see Barbara Creed, 'Horror and the Monstrous-Feminine: An Imaginary Abjections', in *The Dread of Difference*, ed. Barry Keith Grant (Austin, TX: University of Texas Press, 1996).
35 Sigmund Freud, 'The Uncanny' in *The Standard Edition of the Complete Psychological Works of Sigmund Freud*, trans. and ed. by James Strachey, Vol. XVII (1917–19), 245. On the relation between nostalgia, the uncanny, and the maternal body, especially as it can be articulated in fashion design, see Caroline Evans's 'No Man's Land', in *Hussein Chalayan*, ed. Barbera van Kooij, and Sue-an van der Zijpp (Groningen: Nai Publishers, 2005).
36 Kristeva, *Strangers to Ourselves*, 191–92 (my italics).
37 Stam, *Subversive Pleasures*, 123.
38 For a discussion of hybridity and transcultural design in a Japanese context, see 'The Walkman: How 'Japanese' Is It?' In Paul Du Gay, Stuart Hall, Linda Janes, Hugh Mackay and Keith Negus, *Doing Cultural Study: The Story of the Sony Walkman* (London: Sage Publications and the Open University, 2013), 64–9.

Chapter 3 Performing Pregnancy: Leigh Bowery

1. Peter Stallybrass and Allon White, *The Politics and Poetics of Transgression* (Ithaca, NY: Cornell University Press, 1986), 43.
2. The relation between Kawakubo and Bowery was not completely missed at the time the collection was presented. Though discussed in dismissive tones, it was pointed out by Tamsin Blanchard in the *Independent*, 'Fashion's Bumpy Night of Lumps and Humps', *Independent*, 10 October 1996, 5.
3. Christopher Lambert, Honolulu and Richard Torry, interview with Leigh Bowery in 1989 at Richard Torry's Old Compton Street apartment/studio, Soho, London (posted as audio stream on SHOWstudio and transcribed by the author).
4. A long obituary of Trojan, which discussed his relation with Bowery, was published in the January 1987 issue of *The Face*: 'Trojan's Story', *The Face Magazine*, January 1987.
5. However, he worked on a number of Rifat Ozbek's collections in the early 1990s. See Robert Violette, ed., *Leigh Bowery* (New York, NY: D.A.P., 1998).
6. Details of Leigh Bowery's biography can be found in Sue Tilley, *Leigh Bowery: The Life and Times of an Icon* (London: Hodder & Stoughton, 1997); Violette, *Leigh Bowery*; Charles Atlas's documentary *The Legend of Leigh Bowery* (New York: Atlas Films, 2004); and publications from the time, chiefly the *Face* and *i-D* magazines.
7. *i-D Magazine* 1, no. 57 (April 1988). This same issue also prominently features the work of Georgina Godley.
8. Nicola Bowery, interview with author, Brighton, July 2006 (see Appendix, 161–8).
9. Excerpt from Lambert et al., interview with Leigh Bowery.
10. Mikhail Bakhtin, *Rabelais and His World*, trans. Hélène Iswolsky (Bloomington, IN: Indiana University Press, 1984), 8, 21.
11. Ibid., 8, 21.
12. Atlas, *Legend of Leigh Bowery*.
13. Arnold, *Fashion, Desire, and Anxiety*, 76
14. Nicola Bowery, interview with author, 161–2.
15. John Fiske, 'Offensive Bodies and Carnival Pleasures', in *Understanding Popular Culture* (London, New York: Routledge, 1991), 92–3. The literature on 'fat studies' has greatly expanded since Fiske's article. On this topic, see, for instance, Kathleen LeBesco, *Revolting Bodies?: The Struggle to Redefine Fat Identity* (Amherst, MA: University of Massachusetts Press, 2006).
16. Susan Stewart, *On Longing, Narratives of the Miniature, the Gigantic, the Souvenir, the Collection* (Durham, NC: Duke University Press, 1993), 73. I will discuss Stewart's writings at more length in my next chapter in relation to my discussion of Martin Margiela's enlarged and doll collections.
17. Excerpt from Lambert et al., interview with Leigh Bowery.
18. The performance took place in 1988 in the Parco department store in Tokyo. Information in regard to the performance was gathered through the author's interview with Nicola Bowery.
19. In the catalogue accompanying the exhibition 'Take a Bowery' (which took place in 2003 at the Museum of Contemporary Art in Sydney), Robin Healy referred to this costume as the 'pregnant tutu head'. See 'Where the Sun Shines: Leigh Bowery the Super-Fashion Heavyweight', in Vivienne Webb, *Take a Bowery: The Art and (Larger than) Life of Leigh Bowery* (Melbourne: Museum of Contemporary Art, 2003), 83.

20 I thank Shaun Cole for pointing out to me these looks' resemblance to Gumby. Gumby was a green clay figure that was animated through stop motion techniques and starred in an American 1950s children's TV series, which saw a revival in the 1980s. For a full account see Louis Kaplan, *Gumby* (New York: Harmony Books, 1986).
21 Among the most famous pictures depicting a pregnant women in profile, hand over belly, is Anne Leibovitz's nude photo of a seven months pregnant Demi Moore for the cover of *Vanity Fair* in August of 1991.
22 This was, however, not the only look for which Bowery included a human body. In another one of his looks, he created a very large bustle by harnessing Mr Pearl to his back.
23 Hilton Als, 'Life as a Look', *New Yorker*, 30 March 1998, 83
24 Ibid., 83–4.
25 This information was gathered through Nicola Bowery's interview with the author. See appendix, p. 172.
26 Roger Malbert, 'Exaggeration and Degradation: Grotesque Humour in Contemporary Art', in *Carnivalesque*, ed. Timothy Hyman and Roger Malbert (London: The Hayward Gallery, 2000).
27 Susan Sontag marks a distinction between naive camp and deliberate camp – the former being unintentional, an instance of failed seriousness; see Susan Sontag, 'Notes on "Camp"', in *Against Interpretation and Other Essays* (New York, NY: Anchor Books Doubleday, 1986), 282.
28 Ibid., 275, 280.
29 Ibid., 288.
30 On discussion of camp in relation to gender studies and queer theory, see, for instance, Fabio Cleto, ed., *Camp: Queer Aesthetics and the Performing Subject: A Reader* (Ann Arbor, MI: University of Michigan Press, 1999).
31 Caryl Flinn, 'The Deaths of Camp', ibid., 439 (italics mine).
32 On the politics of camp, see Moe Meyer, ed., *The Politics and Poetics of Camp* (London: Routledge, 1994).
33 Butler, cited in Liz Kotz, 'The Body You Want: Liz Kotz Interviews Judith Butler', *Artforum* 31, no. 3 (November 1992), 84. Butler later expanded this theory, which was meant as a corrective to any misreading of *Gender Trouble* and *Bodies That Matter*.
34 Fiske, 'Offensive Bodies', 94. Butler also has discussed drag as a denaturalisation of gender in *Gender Trouble*.
35 Kelly Oliver, *Reading Kristeva: Unravelling the Double-Bind* (Bloomington, IN: Indiana University Press, 1993), 7.
36 Ibid., 7.
37 Ibid., 6. Kristeva discusses the topic both in her early and late writings. See in particular 'Stabat Mater', originally published in *Tel Quel* in winter 1997, and later translated by Leon S. Roudiez into English as part of *Tales of Love* (New York, NY: Columbia University Press, 1987); and *Black Sun*, originally published in 1987 as *Soleil noir: Depression et mélancolie* and translated into English by Leon S. Roudiez two years later (New York, NY: Columbia University Press, 1989).
38 Judith Butler, *Gender Trouble: Feminism and the Subversion of Identity* (New York, NY: Routledge, 2007), xxii–xxiii.
39 Judith Butler, 'Performative Acts and Gender Constitution', in *The Performance Studies Reader*, ed. Henry Bial (London: Routledge, 2004), 164. (Previously published in *Theatre Journal* 40, no. 4.)
40 Ibid., 164.

41 Elizabeth Wilson, 'A Note on Glamour', *Fashion Theory* 11, no.1 (December 2004): 103.
42 Nicola Bowery, interview with author, 164.
43 Emily Martin, 'The Fetus as Intruder: Mother's Bodies and Medical Metaphors', *Cyborg Babies: From Techno-sex to Techno-tots*, ed. Robbie Davis-Floyd and Joseph Dumit (New York, NY: Routledge, 1998). See also Emily Martin, *Flexible Bodies: Tracking Immunity in America from the Days of Polio to the Age of AIDS* (Boston, MA: Beacon Press, 1994).
44 Fiske discussing Foucault's *The History of Sexuality*: 'Offensive Bodies', 90
45 Ibid., 70.
46 Michel Foucault, 'Body/Power', in *Power Knowledge: Selected Interviews and Other Writings 1972–1977* (New York, NY: Harvester Press, 1980), 56
47 Lambert et al., interview with Leigh Bowery.
48 Als, 'Life as a Look', 85.
49 Norbert Elias, *The Civilising Process*, trans. Edmund Jephcott (New York: Urizen Books, 1978). For a discussion of the 'civilising process' in relation to fashion design, see Caroline Evans, *Fashion at the Edge: Spectacle, Modernity and Deathliness* (New Haven, CT: Yale University Press, 2003), 3–14.

Chapter 4 Deconstruction and the Grotesque: Martin Margiela

1 Suzy Menkes, 'Margiela Quits the Fashion House He Built', Finance Section, *The International Herald Tribune*, 9 December 2009, 17.
2 Bill Cunningham, 'The Collections', *Details*, September 1989, 246.
3 Among the first journalists to use the term in the English language press besides Bill Cunningham are Sally Brampton, 'The Cut High Chic Gets the Boot in Paris,' *Guardian* (14 October 1993), 22; Debbie Buckett, 'Raw Talent Design with a Conscience or King of Destroy Couture?', *Guardian* (29 October 1992), 214; Marion Hume, 'Coming Unstitched, or Just a Stitch-up?', *Independent* (30 September 1993); Amy Spindler, 'Coming Apart', *New York Times*, (25 July 1993), A1, A9; and Bernadine Morris, 'Paris is Glowing, Kindled by Lagerfeld', in the *New York Times* (16 March 1991), 28.
4 Amy Spindler, 'Coming Apart', A1, A9.
5 Significantly, the early 1990s recession not only affected companies that had embraced the 1980s mainstream aesthetic, but also put out of business a number of designers who had been critical of the 1980s' language of excess, as is the case with the British designer Georgina Godley.
6 Harold Koda, 'Rei Kawakubo and the Aesthetic of Poverty', *Dress: The Journal of the Costume Society of America* 11, no. 1 (1985): 5–10.
7 Angela Carter, 'The Recession Style', in *Shaking a Leg: Journalism and Writings* (London: Chatto and Windus, 1997), 132, originally published in *New Society* in 1983.
8 Sally Brampton, 'The Cut: High Chic Gets the Boot in Paris', *Guardian* (14 October 1993), 2.
9 Spindler, 'Coming Apart.'
10 Brampton, 'The Cut', 2.
11 For references to punk aesthetic in some of the press of the time, see Lou Winwood, 'Fashion: Shredded Bliss', *Guardian*, 11 April 1998, 38; Lucinda Alford, 'Fashion: Holed Out', *Observer*, 26 September 1993, 8.

12 Brampton, 'The Cut', 2.
13 I am borrowing the 'self-reception' from Robert Proctor, who discussed the notion in his writings on the architect's interview. Proctor uses the term to describe architects' views of their own work to avoid falling into the intentional fallacy, as the term underlines that those views represent only one of the many possible readings of the work. Robert Proctor, 'The Architect's Intention: Interpreting Post-War Modernism through the Architect Interview', Journal of Design History 19, no. 4 (2006): 302.
14 La Maison Martin Margiela, Martin Margiela (9/4/1615) (Rotterdam: Museum Boijmans Van Beuningen, 1997).
15 Bill Cunningham, 'Fashion du Siècle', Details, March 1990: 206.
16 Alison Gill, 'Deconstruction Fashion: The Making of Unfinished, Decomposing, and Re-assembled Clothes', Fashion Theory 2, no. 1 (1998): 25–49.
17 Mikhail Bakhtin, Rabelais and His World, trans. Hélène Iswolsky (Bloomington, IN: Indiana University Press, 1984), 410–11.
18 Ibid., 218.
19 Peter Stallybrass and Allon White, The Politics and Poetics of Transgression (Ithaca, NY: Cornell University Press, 1986), 18.
20 Barbara A. Babcock, 'Introduction', in The Reversible World: Symbolic Inversion in Art and Society, ed. Barbara A. Babcock (Ithaca: Cornell University Press, 1978), 14.
21 Oxford English Dictionary, 2nd edn. Also quoted in Babcock, The Reversible World, 15.
22 Bakhtin, Rabelais, 410.
23 Babcock, The Reversible World, 17. Here Babcock is referring to Henri Bergson's well-known essay 'Laughter', reprinted in Wylie Sypher, ed., Comedy (New York: Doubleday Anchor Books, 1966), 61–190.
24 According to my research of Italian plus sizes, the so-called taglie forti currently in production extend to size 60. (Information gathered from Italian stores specialising in taglie forti.)
25 On the naval uniform, see Amy Miller, Dressed to Kill: British Naval Uniform, Masculinity and Contemporary Fashions 1748–1857 (London: National Maritime Museum, 2007).
26 Foucault, The History of Sexuality, Vol. 1: An Introduction (New York, NY: Random House, 1978), 144.
27 Barbara Vinken, 'Martin Margiela: Signs of Time', in Fashion Zeitgeist: Trends and Cycles in the Fashion System, trans. Mark Hewson (Oxford: Berg, 2005), 141.
28 Bakhtin, Rabelais, 342.
29 Ibid., 303.
30 Susan Stewart, On Longing: Narratives of the Miniature, the Gigantic, the Souvenir, the Collection (Durham, NC: Duke University Press, 1993), 83.
31 Information gathered from Frances Leto Zangrillo, 'How the Plus-Size Body Proportions Increase per Size', in Fashion Design for the Plus-Size (New York, NY: Fairchild Publications, 1990), 178–83.
32 Caroline Evans, Fashion at the Edge: Spectacle, Modernity, and Deathliness (New Haven, CT: Yale University Press, 2003), 36–9.
33 Linda Sandino, 'Here Today, Gone Tomorrow: Transient Materiality in Contemporary Cultural Artefacts', in Journal of Design History 17, no. 3 (September 2004): 283.
34 Norbert Elias, The Civilising Process (Blackwell: Oxford, 1994), 128–29.
35 John Fiske, 'Offensive Bodies and Carnival Pleasures', in Understanding Popular Culture (London: Routledge, 1991), 99.

36 Ibid., 97.
37 Ibid., 99.
38 Ibid.
39 On the fat suit, see Katherina R. Mendoza, 'Seeing through the Layers: Fat Suits and Thin Bodies in *The Nutty Professor* and *Shallow Hal*', in *The Fat Studies Reader*, ed. Esther D. Rothblum and Sondra Solovay (New York: NYU Press, 2009), 280–88.
40 Stewart, *On Longing*, 101–02.
41 Press release from La Maison Martin Margiela, autumn/winter 1994/1995.
42 Gill, 'Deconstruction Fashion', 42.
43 Richard Martin and Harold Koda, 'Analytical Apparel', in *Infra-Apparel*, ed. Richard Martin and Harold Koda (New York: The Metropolitan Museum of Art, 1993), 94–105.
44 See, for instance, Spindler, 'Coming Apart' and Brampton, 'The Cut'.
45 Gill, 'Deconstruction Fashion', 31.
46 Jacques Derrida, *Deconstruction in a Nutshell*, ed. John D. Caputo (New York: Fordham University Press, 1997), 9–10. I came to this text thanks to Penelope Deutscher's *How to Read Derrida* (London: Granta Books, 2005), which also quotes part of this passage in her discussion of deconstruction.
47 Stewart, *On Longing*, 54.
48 See in particular Jean Epstein, 'Bonjour Cinema and Other Writings [1921–1930]', trans. Tom Milne, *Afterimage* 10 (1981): 9–38; as well as Le Corbusier. 'Spirit of Truth', in *French Film Theory and Criticism 1907–1939*, ed. Richard Abel (Princeton, NJ: Princeton University Press, 1988).
49 For a visual documentation of designers' Barbies, see Frédéric Beigbeder, *Barbie* (Paris: Éditions Assouline, 1998). For a more theoretical and historically grounded account of designer babies, see Juliette Peers, 'Not Only a Pretty Face: Towards the New Millennium with the Designer Doll', in *The Fashion Doll: From Bébé Jumeau to Barbie* (Oxford: Berg, 2004).
50 See, for instance, Mary F. Rogers, *Barbie Culture* (Thousand Oaks, CA: Sage Publications, 1999); Erica Rand, *Barbie's Queer Accessories* (Durham, NC: Duke University Press, 1995); Yona Zeldis McDonough, ed., *The Barbie Chronicles* (New York: Touchstone Books, 1999); and Jeannie Banks Thomas, *Naked Barbies, Warrior Joes and Other Forms of Visible Gender* (Urbana, IL: University of Illinois Press, 2003).
51 Carol Ockman, 'Barbie Meets Bouguereau: Constructing an Ideal Body for the Late Twentieth Century', in McDonough, *The Barbie Chronicles*, 76.
52 Ibid., 75.
53 Stewart, *On Longing*, 68.
54 Evans, 'Living Dolls', in *Fashion at the Edge*, 165–76.
55 Evans uses the term in relation to Viktor and Rolf's 1993 collection; ibid., 166.
56 Stewart, *On Longing*, 62.
57 Ibid., 74.
58 The explicit military nature of the GI Joe – whose clothes and accessories take a back seat to Barbie's in Margiela's collection – makes this point all the more incisively.
59 Margiela, *Martin Margiela*.
60 Stewart, *On Longing*, 45.
61 Ibid., 82.
62 Julia Kristeva, *Revolution in Poetic Language*, trans. Margaret Waller (New York, NY: Columbia University Press, 1984), 137–39.

63 Caryl Flinn, 'The Deaths of Camp', in *Camp: Queer Aesthetics and the Performing Subject*, ed. Fabio Cleto (Ann Arbor, MI: University of Michigan Press, 1999), 435.
64 Andrew Ross, 'Uses of Camp', ibid., 320.
65 Flinn, 'Deaths of Camp', 436.
66 Ibid., 437.
67 Caroline Evans, 'The Golden Dustman: A Critical Evaluation of the Work of Martin Margiela and a Review of Martin Margiela Exhibition (9/4/1615)', *Fashion Theory* 2, no. 1 (March 1998): 79.
68 Frances Connelly, ed., *Modern Art and the Grotesque* (Cambridge: Cambridge University Press, 2003), 5.
69 Ibid., 5.
70 See nike.com, accessed 13 January, 2016 http://www.nike.com/us/en_us/launch/c/2015-04/nike-air-rift
71 I use the term 'surrealism' to refer to the historical phenomenon that developed in France in the 1920s.
72 Kirsten A. Hoving, 'Convulsive Bodies: The Grotesque Anatomies of Surrealist Photography' in Connelly, *Modern Art and the Grotesque*, 220–40. On the relationship between art and surrealism, see also Wolfgang Kayser, *The Grotesque in Art and Literature*, trans. Ulrich Weisstein (Bloomington, IN: Indiana University Press, 1963), 168–73.
73 Hoving, 'Convulsive Bodies', 221.
74 For a discussion of Elsa Schiaparelli's relation to surrealism, see Dyls Blum, 'Fashion and Surrealism', in *Surreal Things: Surrealism and Design*, ed. Ghislaine Wood (London: V&A, 2007), 139–59.
75 Bakhtin, *Rabelais*, 375.
76 Ibid., 410, 411.
77 Ibid., 411.
78 Ibid., 372.

Chapter 5 Carnivalised Time: Martin Margiela

1 Mikhail Bakhtin, *Rabelais and His World*, trans. Hélène Iswolsky (Bloomington, IN: Indiana University Press, 1984), 10.
2 Ibid., 213.
3 On these debates within art history, see, for instance, the responses in relation to the substantial and somewhat radical updating of the canonical survey text from 1962 by H. W. Janson, *History of Art*, which was revised in 2006 and republished by Penelope J. E. Davies, Ann M. Roberts and Walter B. Denny under the title *Janson's History of Art: The Western Tradition* (Upper Saddle River, NJ: Prentice Hall, 2006). (For a range of responses to the substantial revision, see Randy Kennedy, 'Revising Art History's Big Book: Who's In and Who Comes Out', *New York Times*, 7 March 2006).
4 Linda Sandino, 'Here Today, Gone Tomorrow: Transient Materiality in Contemporary Cultural Artefacts', *Journal of Design History* 17, no. 3: 283–93; Caroline Evans, *Fashion at the Edge: Spectacle, Modernity, and Deathliness* (New Haven, CT: Yale University Press, 2003), 36–9, 249–60.
5 Julia Kristeva, 'Women's Time', in *Feminism: Critical Concepts in Literary Cultural Studies* vol. II, ed. Mary Evans (London: Routledge, 2001), 30.

6 Barbara Burman Baines, *Fashion Revivals: From the Elizabethan Age to the Present Day* (London: B.T. Batsford, 1981).
7 For visual and written documentation of the exhibition and the dialogues between Caroline Evans and Judith Clark, see Judith Clark, *Spectres: When Fashion Turns Back* (London and Antwerp: Victoria and Albert Publications and ModeMuseum, 2004).
8 The expression 'carnivalised time' is surprisingly seldom used within Bakhtinian literature. The few times it surfaces, it is generally synonymous with carnival time: it retains the more expansive meaning of the cyclical and renewable time of carnival festivities. Bakhtin uses the term to refer to time in Dostoyevsky's novels, as pointed out by Richard Peace in 'On Rereading Bakhtin', *Modern Language Review* 88, no. 1 (January 1993): 137–46. The only other ocurrence of the term in the literature (at least, as far as I was able to discover) can be found in an article on Seneca's *Apocolocyntosis* to refer to the monstrous body of Claudius: see Susanna Morton Braund and Paula James, 'Quasi Homo: Distortion and Contortion in Seneca's *Apocolocyntosis*', *Arethusa* 31, no. 3 (1998): 285–311.
9 La Maison Martin Margiela, *Martin Margiela (9/4/1615)* (Rotterdam: Museum Boijmans Van Beuningen, 1997).
10 The literature on new history and historiography and the ways theories is, of course, vast, but for an exhaustive summery of these debates, see Keith Jenkins, ed., *The Postmodern History Reader* (London: Routledge, 1997). For a nuanced discussion, see also Peter Burke, ed., *New Perspectives on Historical Writing*, 2nd edn. (University Park, PA: Pennsylvania State University Press, 2001).
11 Burke, 'Overture: The New History: Its Past and its Future', in *New Perspectives*, 3, 6.
12 Alison Gill, 'Deconstruction Fashion: The Making of Unfinished, Decomposing and Re-assembled Clothes'. *Fashion Theory* 2, no. 1 (1998): 35.
13 Richard Martin and Harold Koda, 'Unpublished Checklist for the Exhibition Infra-Apparel', in *Infra-Apparel* (New York: Metropolitan Museum of Art, Costume Institute, in association with Harry N. Abrams, 1993), 28. I am also grateful to the staff at the Metropolitan Museum of Art, Costume Institute for their stimulating discussions of theatre costumes.
14 Alexandra Palmer, 'Looking is Research' (paper presented at the conference *Locating Fashion Studies*, Parsons School of Design – the New School, 12 November 2010).
15 La Maison Martin Margiela, Martin Margiela (9/4/1615) (Rotterdam: Museum Boijmans Van Beuningen, 1997).
16 Ibid.
17 On Margiela and surrealism, see Thimo te Duits, 'Shocking: Surrealism and Fashion Now', in *Surreal Things: Surrealism and Design*, ed. Ghislaine Wood (London: V&A, 2007): 139–60.
18 Arjun Appadurai, 'Consumption, Duration and History', in *Modernity at Large: Cultural Dimensions of Globalization* (Minneapolis, MN: University of Minnesota Press, 2005), 75–9.
19 Ibid., 77.
20 Ibid., 78.
21 Both Barbara Vinken and Alison Gill strengthen this argument, as they point to Margiela's tendency of leaving production processes readable, which translates into his fashion's lack of seamlessness. See Gill, 'Deconstruction Fashion' and Barbara Vinken, 'Martin Margiela: Signs of Time', in *Fashion Zeitgeist: Trends and Cycles in the Fashion System*, trans. Mark Hewson (Oxford: Berg, 2005), 140–51.

22 Linda Hutcheon, 'Irony, Nostalgia and the Postmodern', University of Toronto English Language (UTEL) Library, Main Collection, 1998, accessed 1 June, 2010, http://www.library.utoronto.ca/utel/criticism/hutchinp.html.
23 Fredric Jameson, 'Nostalgia for the Present', in *Postmodernism, or, The Cultural Logic of Late Capitalism* (Durham, NC: Duke University Press, 1991), 286.
24 Linda Hutcheon, *A Poetics of Postmodernism: History, Theory, Fiction* (New York, NY: Routledge, 1988).
25 Hutcheon, 'Irony'.
26 Susannah Radstone, 'Cinema/memory/history', *Screen* 36, no. 1 (Spring 1995): 37.
27 Marco Pecorari, 'Contemporary Fashion History in Museum' in *Fashion and Museums: Theory and Practice*, ed. Marie Riegels Melchior and Birgitta Svensson (London: Bloomsbury, 2014), 51–4.
28 Sandino, 'Here Today, Gone Tomorrow', 283.
29 Ibid., 289.
30 On the symbolic capital of patina, see ibid., 284; also Appadurai, 'Consumption', 75–6. Both refer to Grant McCracken, *Culture and Consumption: New Approaches to the Symbolic Character of Consumer Goods and Activities* (Bloomington, IN: Indiana University Press, 1988).
31 Evans, 'Patina', in *Fashion at the Edge*, 253–56.
32 Appadurai, 'Consumption', 75–6.
33 Vinken, 'Martin Margiela', 142.
34 Evans, 'The Golden Dustman', 85.
35 See, in particular, Jean Epstein, 'Bonjour Cinema and Other Writings [1921–1930]', trans. Tom Milne, *Afterimage* 10 (1981): 9–38.
36 As quoted in Elliott H. King, *Dalí, Surrealism and Cinema* (London: Kamera Books, 2007), 170.
37 For an English translation of the film's voiceover narration, see *Impressions of Upper Mongolia*, translated by Colombina Zamponi (2008). Ubu website: http://ubu.com.
38 Evans, 'The Golden Dustman', 92.
39 Karen de Perthuis, 'The Synthetic Ideal: The Fashion Model and Photographic Manipulation', *Fashion Theory* 9, no. 4 (December 2005): 416, 422.
40 Evans, 'The Golden Dustman', 91.
41 Clark dedicated a chapter of *The Nude* to what he describes as the alternative canon – one that closely resembles the grotesque canon and stands in opposition to classical beauty. Kenneth Clark, 'The Alternative Convention', in *The Nude: A Study of Ideal Art*. (London: John Murray, 1956), 308.

Chapter 6 Carnival Iconography: Bernhard Willhelm

1 Sigmund Freud, 'Repression', in *The Standard Edition of the Complete Psychological Works of Sigmund Freud*, vol. XIV, trans. and ed. by James Strachey (London: Hogarth Press, 1958), 149. See also 'Unconscious' (1915) in the same volume.
2 For a discussion of repression and the maternal, see Chapter 2.
3 Kaat Debo, interview with the author, Antwerp, September 2007.
4 On enterprising culture, see Paul Heels and Paul Morris, eds, *The Values of the Enterprise Culture: The Moral Debate* (London: Routledge, 1992).

5 On the enterprising self and self-help literature in the twenty-first century, see Janice Peck, 'The Anxieties of the Enterprising Self and the Limits of the Mind Cure', in *The Age of Oprah: Cultural Icon for the Neoliberal Era* (Boulder, CO: Paradigm Publishers, 2008); on neoliberalism, see David Harvey, *A Brief History of Neoliberalism* (London: Oxford University Press, 2005).
6 Daryoush Haj-Najafi, 'Bernhard Willhelm: Maverick with a Mission', *Hint Magazine*, 2005, accessed 7 November 2008, http://www.hintmag.com.
7 Ruth Mellinkoff, *Outcasts: Signs of Otherness in Northern European Art* (Berkeley, CA: University of California Press, 1993), 89–94.
8 Ibid., 69, 89.
9 Peter Stallybrass and Allon White, *The Politics and Poetics of Transgression* (Ithaca, NY: Cornell University Press, 1986), 53.
10 Mikhail Bakhtin, *Rabelais and His World*, trans. Hélène Iswolsky (Bloomington, IN: Indiana University Press, 1984), 81–2.
11 Ibid., 20.
12 Ibid., 20, 22.
13 Ingeborg Harms, 'Keep It Unreal', in *Bernhard Willhelm: Het Totaal Rappel*, ed. Kaat Debo (Antwerp: ModeMuseum, 2007), 121–27.
14 As quoted ibid., 121–22.
15 Bakhtin, *Rabelais*, 259; Harms, 121. In her discussion of Willhelm's use of the trope of the diamond pattern, Harms also traces Harlequin's lineage back to the underworld.
16 Bakhtin, *Rabelais*, 266–67, 374.
17 Francesca Zimei, ed., *The Comic Mask in the Commedia dell'Arte* (Arscomica: Reggio Emilia, 2004).
18 Mellinkoff, 'Patterns', in *Outcasts*, 5–31. Mellinkoff also suggests that the patterned attires of fools, jesters and minstrels prefigures Harlequin's costume (ibid., 17).
19 Bakhtin, *Rabelais*, 375.
20 As Kaat Debo points out in the text accompanying Bernhard Willhelm's exhibition at the ModeMuseum in Antwerp, the news programme recorded was the 'ARD Tagesschau'. My description of the show is based on a video recording available at the ModeMuseum library.
21 Robert Stam, *Subversive Pleasures: Bakhtin, Cultural Criticism, and Film* (Baltimore, MD: Johns Hopkins University Press, 1989), 116.
22 Ibid.
23 Stallybrass and White, *Politics and Poetics*, 53.
24 Davide Revere McFadden, ed. *Pricked: Extreme Embroidery* (New York, NY: Museum of Art and Design, 2007).
25 *Oxford English Dictionary*, online edition.
26 Bakhtin, *Rabelais*, 422–23.
27 RoseLee Goldberg, *Performance Art: From Futurism to the Present* (New York: Thames and Hudson, 2001), 66–72. On Dada and Surrealism performance in the first quarter of the twentieth century, see Annabelle Henking Melzer, *Dada and Surrealist Performance* (Baltimore, MD: John Hopkins University Press, 1994).
28 Stam, *Subversive Pleasures*, 98. Here, Stam is referring to Allon White's theories, later further developed in White and Stallybrass, *The Politics and Poetics of Transgression* (see in particular pages 189–90).
29 Goldberg, *Performance Art*.

30 Jon McKenzie, 'The Liminal Norm', in *The Performance Studies Reader*, ed. Henry Bial (New York, NY: Routledge, 2004), 27. On the relation between performance and borders, see also Marvin Carlson, *Performance: A Critical Introduction* (London: Routledge, 1996) and Richard Schechner, 'What is Performance Studies Anyway?' in *The Ends of Performance*, ed. Peggy Phelan and Jill Lane (New York: New York University, 1998), 357–63.
31 Arnold Van Gennep as quoted in Victor Turner, 'Liminality and Communitas', *The Ritual Process: Structure and Anti-Structure* (Chicago, IL: Aldine, 1969), 94.
32 Ibid., 95.
33 McKenzie, 'The Liminal Norm', 28–9.
34 Turner, *The Ritual Process*, 110.
35 Ginger Gregg Duggan, 'The Greatest Show on Earth: A Look at Contemporary Fashion Shows and Their Relation to Performance Art', *Fashion Theory* 5, no. 3 (September 2001): 243–70.
36 Susan Sontag, 'Notes on "Camp"' in *Against Interpretation and Other Essays*. (New York: Anchor Books Doubleday, 1986), 282.
37 Caryl Flinn, 'The Deaths of Camp', in *Camp: Queer Aesthetics and the Performing Subject*, ed. Fabio Cleto (Ann Arbor, MI: University of Michigan Press, 1999), 435.
38 Sontag, 'Notes on "Camp"', 287.
39 Ibid., 288.
40 Pierre Bourdieu, *Distinction: A Social Critique of the Judgment of Taste* (Cambridge, MA: Harvard University Press, 1992).
41 Chuck Kleinhans, 'Taking out the Trash: Camp and the Politics of Parody', in *The Politics and Poetics of Camp*, ed. Moe Meyer (London: Routledge, 1994), 189. The subversive potential of camp, particularly in its relation to gay culture, is also discussed in Richard Dyer, 'It's Being So Camp that Keeps Us Going', in Cleto, *Camp*, 110–16.
42 Bakhtin, *Rabelais*, 19.
43 Ibid., 373.
44 On table manners and the civilizing process, see Norbert Elias, *The Civilising Process*, trans. Edmund Jephcott (New York, NY: Urizen Books, 1978).
45 Stallybrass and White, *Politics and Poetics*, 143–48.
46 Ibid, 145.
47 The text was reprinted in the exhibition catalogue *Bernhard Willhelm: Modern Mode*, ed. Nicolaus Schafausen and Vanessa Joan Müller (Mühlweg: Ursula Blickle Stiftung, 2003). It was also reprinted in the exhibition copy accompanying Willhelm's solo exhibition at MoMu.
48 Bakhtin, *Rabelais*, 151.
49 Susan Signe Morrison, *Excrement in the Late Middle Ages* (New York, NY: Palgrave Macmillan, 2008).
50 Julia Kristeva, *Powers of Horror: An Essay on Abjection*, trans. Leon S. Roudiez (New York, NY: Columbia University Press, 1981), 3.
51 Peter de Potter, 'Interview with Bernhard Willhelm', Butt 1 (May 2001): 14–18.

Chapter 7 The Proliferation of the Grotesque: Lady Gaga

1 See, for instance, Horacio Silvia, 'The World According to Gaga', T, (3 March 2010).

2 Pascale Renaux, 'Artifice – An Interview with Orlan and Walter Van Beirendonck', in Walter Van Beirendonck & Wild and Lethal Trash, *Believe* (Rotterdam: Museum Boijmans Van Beunigen, 1998).
3 On the collaboration among Mullins, McQueen and Knight, see Vivian Sobchack, 'A Leg to Stand On: Prosthetics Metaphor and Materiality', 17–41, and Marquard Smith, 'The Vulnerable Articulate: Hames Gillingham, Aimee Mullins, and Matthew Barney', 43–56, in *The Prosthetic Impulse: From a Posthuman Present to a Biocultural Future*, edited by Marquard Smith and Joanne Morra (Cambridge, MA: MIT Press, 2006).
4 J. Jack Halberstam, *Gaga Feminism: Sex, Gender, and the End of Normal* (Boston, MA: Beacon Press, 2012).
5 Mikhail Bakhtin, *Rabelais and His World*, trans. Hélène Iswolsky (Bloomington, IN: Indiana University Press, 1984), 225
6 Julia Kristeva, *The Powers of Horror*, trans. Leon S. Roudiez (New York: Columbia University Press, 1981), 96.
7 For an example of such criticism, see 'Looking Meatier! Lady Gaga Shows Off her New Fuller Figure after "Gaining 30lbs" in her Favourite Carnivorous Creation', *The Daily Mail*, 19 September 2010.
8 Lynda Nead, *The Female Nude: Art, Obscenity and Sexuality* (London: Routledge, 1992), 10.
9 Susannah Frankel, 'Ready To Wear: Editors Take Note … This Look is Flat Rather than Fat', *Independent*, 15 October 2012.
10 Kathleen LeBesco, 'Situating Fat Suits: Blackface, Drag, and the Politics of Performance', *Women and Performance: A Journal of Feminist Theory* 15, no. 2 (2005): 231–42.
11 Caroline Evans, *Fashion at the Edge: Spectacle, Modernity, and Deathliness* (New Haven, CT: Yale University Press, 2003), 4.
12 On performativity and gender, see Judith Butler, *Gender Trouble: Feminism and the Subversion of Identity* (New York, NY: Routledge, 2006) *Bodies that Matter: On the Discursive Limits of 'Sex'* (New York, NY: Routledge, 1993).
13 Richard Schechner, *Performance Studies: An Introduction* (New York, NY: Routledge, 2006), 19.
14 Judith Butler, 'Performative Acts and Gender Constitution' in *The Performance Studies Reader*, ed. Henry Bial (London: Routledge, 2004), 164.
15 Jon McKenzie, 'Genre Trouble: (The) Butler Did It' in *The Ends of Performance*, 220.
16 Butler, *Bodies that Matter* (New York, NY: Routledge, 1993), XIII.
17 Peter Stallybrass and Allon White, *The Politics and Poetics of Transgression* (Ithaca, NY: Cornell University Press, 1986), 105.
18 Ibid.
19 Frances Connelly, ed., *Modern Art and the Grotesque* (Cambridge: Cambridge University Press, 2003).
20 Karen de Perthuis, 'The Synthetic Ideal: The Fashion Model and Photographic Manipulation', *Fashion Theory* 9, no. 4 (December 2005): 416, 422.

BIBLIOGRAPHY

BOOKS AND ARTICLES

Adlam, Carol, ed. *Face to Face: Bakhtin in Russia and the West*. (Sheffield: Sheffield Academic Press, 1997).
Alford, Lucinda. 'Fashion: Holed Out'. *Observer*, 26 September 1993.
Allen, Robert Clyde. *Horrible Prettiness: Burlesque and American Culture*. Chapel Hill, NC: University of North Carolina Press, 1991.
Allen, Virginia M. *The Femme Fatale: Erotic Icon*. Troy, NY: Whitston, 1983.
Als, Hilton. 'Bump and Mind'. *Artforum* 35 (December 1996): 21–2.
___ 'Life as a Look'. *New Yorker*, 30 March 1998: 82–6.
Appadurai, Arjun. *Modernity at Large: Cultural Dimensions of Globalization*. Minneapolis, MN: University of Minnesota Press, 2005.
Apter, Emily. 'Reflections on Gynophobia'. In *Coming Out of Feminism?*, edited by Mandy Merck, Naomi Segal and Elizabeth Wright, 102–21. Oxford: Blackwell Publishing, 1998.
Arnold, Rebecca. 'Heroin Chic'. *Fashion Theory* 3, no. 3 (August 1999): 279–296.
___. 'The Brutalised Body'. *Fashion Theory* 3, no. 4 (November 1999): 487–501.
___ *Fashion, Desire, and Anxiety: Image and Morality in the Twentieth Century*. New Brunswick, NJ: Rutgers University Press, 2001.
___ 'Vivienne Westwood's Anglomania'. In *The Englishness of English Dress*, edited by Christopher Breward, Caroline Cox, and Becky Conekin, 161–73. Oxford: Berg, 2002.
Arthur, Elissa. 'The Decorative Abstraction, and the Hierarchy of Art and Craft in the Art Criticism of Clement Greenberg'. *Oxford Art Journal* 27, no. 3 (2004): 339–64.
Athanassoglou-Kallymer, Nina. 'Ugliness'. In *Critical Terms of Art History*, edited by Robert S. Nelson and Richard Shiff, 281–296. Chicago, IL: University of Chicago Press, 2003.
Babcock, Barbara A., ed. *The Reversible World: Symbolic Inversion in Art and Society*. Ithaca, NY: Cornell University Press, 1978.
Bachmann, Ingrid C. 'Intimate Textiles'. *Textile Journal of Cloth and Culture* 3, no. 1 (January 2005): 88–99.
Baines, Barbara Burman. *Fashion Revivals: From the Elizabethan Age to the Present Day*. London: Batsford, 1981.
Bakhtin, Mikhail. *The Dialogical Imagination*. Translated by Caryl Emerson and Michael Holquist. Austin, TX: University of Texas Press, 1981.
___ *Problems of Dostoevsky's Poetics*. Translated by Caryl Emerson. Minneapolis, MN: University of Minnesota Press, 1984.

___ *Rabelais and His World*. Translated by Hélène Iswolsky. Bloomington, IN: Indiana University Press, 1984.
Bal, Mieke. 'Visual Essentialism and the Object of Visual Culture'. *Journal of Visual Culture* 2, no. 1 (2003): 5–32.
Barnard, Malcolm, ed. *Fashion Theory: A Reader*. London: Routledge, 2007.
Barta, Peter I., Paul Allen Miller, Charles Platter and David Shepherd, eds. *Carnivalizing Difference: Bakhtin and the Other*. Routledge: London, 2001.
Baudrillard, Jean. *Simulacra and Simulation*. Translated by Sheila Faria Glaser. Ann Arbor, MI: University of Michigan Press, 1994.
Beard, Steve, and Jim McClellan. 'Cerebral Couture'. *i-D* 1, no. 57 (Special issue: 'The Surreal Issue'; April 1988): 72–6.
Beigbeder, Frédéric. *Barbie*. Paris: Éditions Assouline, 1998.
Bergson, Henri. 'Laughter'. In *Comedy*, edited by Wylie Sypher, 61–190. New York, NY: Doubleday Anchor Books, 1966.
Berman, Marshall. *All That Is Solid Melts into Air: The Experience of Modernity*. New York, NY: Viking Penguin, 1988.
Berrong, Richard M. 'Finding Anti-Feminism in Rabelais or, A Response to Wayne Booth's Call for an Ethical Criticism'. *Critical Inquiry* 11, no. 4 (June 1985): 687–96.
Bial, Henry, ed. *The Performance Studies Reader*. New York, NY: Routledge, 2004.
Blanchard, Tamsin. 'Fashion's Bumpy Night of Lumps and Humps'. *Independent*, 10 October 1996.
Blum, Dyls, 'Fashion and Surrealism'. In *Surreal Things: Surrealism and Design*, edited by Ghislaine Wood, 139–59. London: V&A, 2007.
Bolton, Andrew. *Wild: Fashion Untamed*. New York: Metropolitan Museum of Art, 2004.
Bonami, Francesco. *La Syndrome di Pantagruel: Catalogue to First Turin Triennial*. Milan: Skira, 2005.
Booth, Wayne. 'Freedom of Interpretation: Bakhtin and the Challenge of Feminist Criticism'. *Critical Inquiry*, no. 9 (September 1982): 45–76.
Bordwell, David, and Kristen Thompson. *Film Art: An Introduction*. Boston, IL: McGraw Hill, 2004.
Bourdieu, Pierre. *Language and Symbolic Power*. Edited with an introduction by John B. Thompson. Translated by Gino Raymond and Matthew Adamson. Cambridge, MA: Harvard University Press, 1991.
___ *Distinction: A Social Critique of the Judgment of Taste*. Cambridge, MA: Harvard University Press, 1992.
Brampton, Sally. 'The Cut: High Chic Gets the Boot in Paris'. *Guardian*, 14 October 1993.
Braund, Susanna Morton and Paula James. 'Quasi Homo: Distortion and Contortion in Seneca's *Apocolocyntosis*'. *Arethusa* 31, no. 3 (1998): 285–311.
Bremmer, Jan, and Herman Rodenburg, eds. *A Cultural History of Humour*. Cambridge: Polity Press, 1997.
Breward, Christopher. *The Culture of Fashion: A New History of Fashionable Dress*. Manchester: Manchester University Press, 1995.
___ 'Cultures, Identities, Histories: Fashioning a Cultural Approach to Dress'. *Fashion Theory* 2, no. 4 (1998): 301–314.
___ *Fashion* Oxford: Oxford University Press, 2003.
Brewster, Maureen. '*Bump Watch: Fashioning Celebrity Pregnancy as Performance and Product*'. MA thesis, The New School, New York, 2014.
Britton, Andrew, ed. *The American Nightmare: Essays on the Horror Film*. Toronto: Festival of Festivals, 1979.

Buchloh, Benjamin H.D. *Neo-Avantgarde and Culture Industry: Essays on European and American Art from 1955 to 1975*. Cambridge, MA: MIT Press, 2001.

Buckett, Debbie. 'Raw Talent Design with a Conscience or King of Destroy Couture?'. *Guardian* (29 October 1992).

Buckley, Richard and Anne Bogart, 'London: That Brit Wit's Missing', *WWD* 153 (16 March 1987): 1, 12.

Burke, Peter. *Varieties of Cultural History*. Ithaca, NY: Cornell University Press, 1997.

___ ed. *New Perspectives on Historical Writing*. 2nd edn. University Park, PA: Pennsylvania State University Press, 2001.

___ ed. *What is Cultural History?* Cambridge: Polity Press, 2004.

Butler, Judith. *Bodies that Matter: On the Discursive Limits of 'Sex'*. New York, NY: Routledge, 1993.

___ 'Performative Acts and Gender Constitution'. In *The Performance Studies Reader*, edited by Henry Bial, 154–66. London: Routledge, 2004. Previously published in *Theatre Journal* 40, no. 4 (1988).

___ *Gender Trouble: Feminism and the Subversion of Identity*. New York, NY: Routledge, 2007.

Calefato, Patrizia. *The Clothed Body*. Translated by Lisa Adams. Oxford: Berg, 2004.

Callaghan, Helen. 'Birth Dirt'. In *Exploring the Dirty Side of Women's Health*, edited by Mavis Kirkham, 8–25. London: Routledge, 2007.

Carlson, Marvin. *Performance: A Critical Introduction*. London: Routledge, 1996.

Carroll, Noël. 'The Specificity of Media in the Arts'. *Journal of Aesthetic Education* 19, no. 4 (Winter 1985): 5–20.

Carter, Angela. *Shaking a Leg: Journalism and Writings*. London: Chatto and Windus, 1997.

Cavallaro, Dani, and Alexandra Warwick. *Fashioning the Frame: Boundaries, Dress and Body*. Oxford: Berg, 1998.

Carter-David, Siobhan. 'Fashioning Essence Women and Ebony Men: Sartorial Instruction and the New Politics of Racial Uplift in Print, 1970–1993'. PhD diss., Indiana University, 2011.

Chang, Ivy I-Chu. *Queer Performativity and Performance*. Taipei: Booksmann Books, 2003.

Chenoune, Farid. *Jean Paul Gaultier*. New York, NY: Assouline Publishing, 2005.

Chivaratanond, Sylvia, ed. *Skin Tight: The Sensibility of the Flesh*. San Francisco, CA: Museum of Contemporary Art, 2004.

Cixous, Hélène. 'The Laugh of the Medusa'. In *The Signs Reader: Women, Gender, and Scholarship*, edited by Elizabeth Abel and Emily K. Abel, 279–97. Chicago, IL: University of Chicago Press, 1990.

Clark, James M. *The Dance of Death in the Middle Ages and the Renaissance*. Glasgow: Jackson Son and Company, 1950.

Clark, Judith. *Spectres: When Fashion Turns Back*. London: Victoria and Albert Publications/Antwerp: ModeMuseum, 2004.

Clark, Kenneth. *The Nude: A Study of Ideal Art*. London: John Murray, 1956.

___ *Feminine Beauty*. New York: Rizzoli, 1980.

Cleto, Fabio, ed. *Camp: Queer Aesthetics and the Performing Subject: A Reader*. Ann Arbor, MI: University of Michigan Press, 1999.

Clover, Carol J. 'Her Body, Himself: Gender in the Slasher Film'. In *The Dread of Difference*, edited by Barry Keith Grant, 66–113. Austin, TX: University of Texas Press, 1996.

Coles, Alex, and Alexia Defert, eds. *The Anxiety of Interdisciplinarity*. London: BACKless Books in association with Black Dog, 1998

Condra, Jill, ed. *Greenwood Encyclopaedia of Clothing through World History*. 3 vols. Westport, CT: Greenwood Press, 2008.

Connelly, Frances, ed. *Modern Art and the Grotesque*. Cambridge: Cambridge University Press, 2003.
Creed, Barbara. 'Horror and the Monstrous-Feminine: An Imaginary Abjections'. In *The Dread of Difference*, edited by Barry Keith Grant. Austin, TX: University of Texas Press, 1996.
Cunningham, Bill. 'The Collections'. *Details*. September 1989.
___ 'Fashion du Siècle'. *Details*. March 1990.
Daly, Mary. *Gyn/Ecology: The Metaethics of Radical Feminism*. Boston, MA: Beacon, 1978.
Davies, Penelope J.E., Ann M. Roberts and Walter B. Denny. *Janson's History of Art: The Western Tradition*. Upper Saddle River, NJ: Prentice Hall, 2006.
Davis, Lennard J. *Enforcing Normalcy: Disability, Deafness and the Body*. New York, NY: Verso, 1995.
de Perthuis, Karen. 'The Synthetic Ideal: The Fashion Model and Photographic Manipulation'. *Fashion Theory* 9, no. 4 (December 2005): 407–24.
de Potter, Peter. 'Interview with Bernhard Willhelm'. Butt 1 (2001): 14–18.
Debo, Kaat, ed. *6+Antwerp Fashion at the Flemish Parliament*. Ghent: Ludion, 2007.
Debord, Guy. *The Society of the Spectacle*. Translated by Donald Nicholson-Smith. New York, NY: Zone Books, 1995.
Derrida, Jacques. *Dissemination*. Translated by Barbara Johnson. Chicago, IL: University of Chicago Press, 1981.
___ *Deconstruction in a Nutshell*, edited by John D. Caputo. New York, NY: Fordham University Press, 1997.
Derycke, Luc, and Sandra Van de Veire, eds. *Belgian Fashion Design*. Ghent: Ludion, 1999.
Deutscher, Penelope. *How to Read Derrida*. London: Granta Books, 2005.
Dilys, Blum. *Shocking! The Art and Fashion of Elsa Schiaparelli*. Philadelphia, PA: Philadelphia Museum of Art, 2003.
Doswald, Cristoph, ed. *Olaf Breuning: Ugly*. Ostfildern, Germany: Hatje Cantz Publishers, 2002.
Douglas, Mary. *Purity and Danger: An Analysis of Concepts of Pollution and Taboo*. London: Routledge, 2002.
Du Gay, Paul, Stuart Hall, Linda Janes, Hugh Mackay and Keith Negus. *Doing Cultural Study: The Story of the Sony Walkman*. London: Sage Publications and the Open University, 2013.
Duggan, Ginger Gregg. 'The Greatest Show on Earth: A Look at Contemporary Fashion Shows and Their Relationship to Performance Art'. *Fashion Theory* 5, no. 3 (September 2001): 243–70.
Dyer, Richard. *The Matter of Images: Essays on Representation*. London: Routledge, 1993.
___ 'It's Being So Camp that Keeps Us Going'. In *Camp: Queer Aesthetics and the Performing Subject*, edited by Fabio Cleto, 110–16. Ann Arbor, MI: The University of Michigan Press, 1999.
Eagleton, Terry. *Criticism and Ideology: A Study in Marxist Literary Theory*. London: New Left Books, 1981.
Eco, Umberto, V.V. Ivanov and Monica Rector. *Carnival*, edited by Thomas A. Sebeok with Marcia E. Erickson. New York, NY: Mouton Publishers, 1984.
Elias, Norbert. *The Civilizing Process*. Translated by Edmund Jephcott. New York: Urizen Books, 1978.
Entwistle, Joanne. '"Power Dressing" and the Construction of the Career Woman'. In *Buy this Book: Studies in Advertising and Consumption*, edited by Mica Nava, Andrew Blake, Iain MacRury, and Barry Richards, 311–23. London: Routledge, 1997.
Epstein, Jean. 'Bonjour Cinema and Other Writings [1921–1930]'. Translated by Tom Milne. *Afterimage* 10 (1981): 9–38.

Evans, Caroline. 'The Golden Dustman: A Critical Evaluation of the Work of Martin Margiela and a Review of Martin Margiela Exhibition (9/4/1615)', *Fashion Theory* 2, no. 1 (March 1998): 73–93.

___ 'Masks, Mirrors and Mannequins: Elsa Schiaparelli and the Decentred Subject'. *Fashion Theory* 3, no. 1 (March 1999): 3–31.

___ 'John Galliano: Modernity and Spectacle'. In *The Fashion Business: Theory, Practice, Image*, edited by Nicola White and Ian Griffiths, 143–66. Oxford: Berg, 2000.

___ 'Yesterday's Emblems and Tomorrow's Commodities: The Return of the Repressed in Fashion Imagery Today'. In *Fashion Cultures: Theories, Exploration and Analysis*, edited by Stella Bruzzi and Pamela Church Gibson, 93–113. London: Routledge, 2000.

___ 'Enchanted Spectacle'. *Fashion Theory* 5, no. 3 (September 2001): 271–310.

___ '"Dress Becomes Body Becomes Dress": Are You an Object or a Subject? Comme des Garçons and Self-Fashioning'. *032c Magazine* (Special edition 'Embrace Instability'), no. 4 October 2001): 82–7.

___ *Fashion at the Edge: Spectacle, Modernity, and Deathliness*. New Haven, CT: Yale University Press, 2003.

___ 'No Man's Land'. In *Hussein Chalayan*, edited by Barbera van Kooij, and Sue-an van der Zijpp. Groningen: NAi Publishers, 2005.

___ and Minna Thornton. *Women and Fashion: A New Look*. London: Quartet Books, 1989.

Evans, Jessica and Stuart Hall, eds. *Visual Culture: The Reader*. London: Sage Publications, 1999.

The Face Magazine. 'Trojan's Story', January 1987.

Fiske, John. *Understanding Popular Culture*. London: Routledge, 1991.

Flinn, Caryl. 'The Deaths of Camp'. In *Camp: Queer Aesthetics and the Performing Subject: A Reader*, edited by Fabio Cleto, 433–57. Ann Arbor, MI: University of Michigan Press, 1999.

Foster, Hal. *The Return of the Real: The Avant-garde at the End of the Century*. Cambridge, MA: MIT Press, 1996.

___ 'Trauma Studies and the Interdisciplinary: An Interview'. In *The Anxiety of Interdisciplinarity*, edited by Alex Coles and Alexia Defert, 157–68. London: BACKless Books in association with Black Dog, 1998.

Foucault, Michel. *Madness and Civilization: A History of Insanity in the Age of Reason*. New York, NY: Vintage Books, 1973.

___ *The History of Sexuality*, Vol. 1: *An Introduction*. New York, NY: Random House, 1978.

___ *Power Knowledge: Selected Interviews and Other Writings 1972–1977*. New York:, NYHarvester Press, 1980.

___ 'Technologies of the Self'. In *Technologies of the Self: A Seminar with Michel Foucault*, edited by Luther H. Martin, Huck Gutman and Patrick H. Hutton, 16–49. Amherst, MA: University of Massachusetts Press, 1988.

Frankel, Susannah. 'Like it or Lump it'. *Guardian*, 1 May 1997.

___ 'Ready To Wear: Editors Take Note … this Look is Flat rather than Fat'. *Independent*, 15 October 2012.

Freise, Matthias. 'After the Expulsion of the Author: Bakhtin as an Answer to Poststructuralism'. In *Face to Face: Bakhtin in Russia and the West*, edited by Carol Adlam, 131–41. Sheffield: Sheffield Academic Press, 1997.

Freud, Sigmund. *The Standard Edition of the Complete Psychological Works of Sigmund Freud*, translated and edited by James Strachey. 24 vols. London: The Hogarth Press, 1953–74.

Frisa, Maria Luisa and Stefano Tonchi, eds. *Excess: Fashion and the Underground in the 80s*. Milano: Charta, 2004.

Gamman, Lorraine. 'Visual Seduction and Perverse Compliance: Reviewing Food Fantasies, Large Appetites and "Grotesque" Bodies'. In *Fashion Cultures: Theories, Explorations and Analysis*, edited by Stella Bruzzi and Pamela Church Gibson, 61–78. London: Routledge, 2000.

Gardiner, Michael, 'Ecology and Carnival: Traces of a 'Green' Social Theory in the Writings of M.M. Bakhtin'. *Theory and Society* 22, no. 6 (December 1993): 765–812.

___ ed. *Mikhail Bakhtin*. London: Sage, 2003.

___ and Michael Mayerfeld Bell, eds. *Bakhtin and the Human Sciences*. London: Sage, 1998.

Gehring, Wes D. *Parody as a Film Genre: Never Give a Saga an Even Break*. Westport, CT: Greenwood Press, 1999.

Giddens, Anthony. *Runaway World: How Globalisation is Reshaping our Lives*. New York: Routledge, 2000.

Gill, Alison. 'Deconstruction Fashion: The Making of Unfinished, Decomposing and Re-assembled Clothes'. *Fashion Theory* 2, no. 1 (1998): 25–49.

Godzich, Wlad. 'Correcting Kant: Bakhtin and Intercultural Interactions'. *Boundary 2 Magazine* 18, no. 1 (Spring 1991): 5–17.

Goldberg, RoseLee. *Performance Art: From Futurism to the Present*. New York: Thames and Hudson, 2001.

Granata, Francesca. 'Fashioning the Grotesque'. In *Bernhard Willhelm and Jutta Kraus*, edited by Ingeborg Hams and Sue-an Van der Zijpp, 450–57. Amsterdam: The Groninger Museum of Modern and Contemporary Art and NAi Publishers, 2010.

___ 'Deconstruction Fashion: Carnival and the Grotesque'. *Journal of Design History* 26, no. 2 (2012): 182–98.

Grant, Keith Barry, ed. *The Dread of Difference*. Austin, TX: University of Texas Press, 1996.

Greenberg, Clement. 'Milton Avery'. In *The Collected Essays and Criticism*. Vol. 4, *Modernism with a Vengeance*, edited by John O'Brian, 39–43. Chicago, IL: University of Chicago Press, 1993.

___ 'Modernist Painting'. In *The Collected Essays and Criticism*. Vol. 4, *Modernism with a Vengeance*, edited by John O'Brian, 85–93. Chicago, IL: University of Chicago Press, 1993.

Greer, Fergus. *Leigh Bowery Looks*. London: Violette Editions, 2002.

Halberstam, J. Jack. *Gaga Feminism: Sex, Gender, and the End of Normal*. Boston, MA: Beacon Press, 2012.

Haj-Najafi, Daryoush. 'Bernhard Willhelm: Maverick with a Mission'. *Hint Magazine*, 2005. Accessed 7 November 2008. http://www.hintmag.com.

Harden, Victoria A. *AIDS at 30*. (Dulles, VA: Potomac Books, 2012).

Harms, Ingeborg. 'Keep It Unreal'. In *Bernhard Willhelm: Het Totaal Rappel*, edited by Kaat Debo, 121–7. Antwerp: ModeMuseum, 2007.

Harrison, Charles. 'Modernism'. In *Critical Terms for Art History*, edited by Robert S. Nelson and Richard Shiff, 142–49. Chicago, IL: University of Chicago Press, 1996.

Harvey, David. *A Brief History of Neoliberalism*. London: Oxford University Press, 2005.

Haynes, Deborah. *Bakhtin and the Visual Arts*. Cambridge: Cambridge University Press, 1995.

Healy, Robin. 'Where the Sun Shines: Leigh Bowery the Super-Fashion Heavyweight'. In *Take a Bowery: The Art and (Larger than) Life of Leigh Bowery*, edited by Vivienne Webb, 78–85. Melbourne: Museum of Contemporary Art, 2003.

Heels, Paul and Paul Morris, eds. *The Values of the Enterprise Culture: The Moral Debate*. London: Routledge, 1992.

Hollander, Anna. *Seeing through Clothes*. New York, NY: Viking Press, 1978.

Holquist, Michael. 'The Surd Heard: Bakhtin and Derrida'. In *Literature and History: Theoretical Problems and Russian Case Studies*, edited by Gary Saul Morson, 137–56. Stanford, CA: Stanford University Press, 1986.

Houser, Craig, Leslie C. Jones, and Simon Taylor, eds. *Abject Art: Repulsion and Desire in American Art, Selections from the Permanent Collection.* New York, NY: Whitney Museum of American Art, 1993.

Hoving, Kirsten A. 'Convulsive Bodies: The Grotesque Anatomies of Surrealist Photography'. In *Modern Art and the Grotesque*, edited by Frances Connelly, 220–40. Cambridge: Cambridge University Press, 2003.

Hutcheon, Linda. 'The Politics of Postmodernism: Parody and History'. *Cultural Critique*, no. 5 (Winter 1986–87): 179–207.

___ *A Poetics of Postmodernism: History, Theory, Fiction.* New York: Routledge, 1988.

___ 'Modern Parody and Bakhtin'. In *Rethinking Bakhtin: Extensions and Challenges*, edited by Gary Saul Morson and Caryl Emerson, 87–103. Evanston, IL: Northwestern University Press, 1989.

___ '*Irony, Nostalgia and the Postmodern*'. University of Toronto English Language (UTEL) Library, Main Collection, 1998. Accessed 1 June, 2010 http://www.library.utoronto.ca/utel/criticism/hutchinp.html.

Hyman, Timothy and Roger Malbert, eds. *Carnivalesque.* London: The Hayward Gallery, 2000.

i-D 1, no. 57 (Special issue: 'The Surreal Issue'; April 1988).

Irigaray, Luce. *This Sex Which Is Not One.* Translated by Catherine Porter with Carolyn Burke. Ithaca, NY: Cornell University Press, 1985.

Isaak, Jo Anna. *Feminism and Contemporary Art: The Revolutionary Power of Women's Laughter.* London: Routledge, 1996.

Jackson, Shannon. 'Performing Show and Tell: Disciplines of Visual Culture and Performance Studies'. *Journal of Visual Culture* 4, no. 3 (2005): 163–77.

Jameson, Fredric. *Postmodernism, or, The Cultural Logic of Late Capitalism.* London: Verso, 1991.

Jenkins, Keith, ed. *The Postmodern History Reader.* London: Routledge, 1997.

Jetzer, Gianni. 'Olaf Breuning: In Search of Lost Purpose'. *Parkett*, no. 71 (2004): 49–53.

Jobey, Liz, 'Designing Women'. *Vogue UK*, July 1987: 111.

Jobling, Paul. 'Who's That Girl? 'Alex Eats', A Case Study in Abjection and Identity in Contemporary Fashion Photography'. *Face Magazine* 2, no. 3 (September 1998): 209–24.

Johnson, Robert. 'The Bulges: Merce Cunningham's "Scenario"'. *Ballet International*, no. 12 (December 1997): 48–53.

Johnston, Ruth D. 'The Staging of the Bourgeois Imaginary in *The Cook, the Thief, His Wife, and Her Lover* (1990)'. *Cinema Journal* 41, no. 2 (Winter 2002): 19–40.

Jones, Amelia, ed. *The Feminism and Visual Culture Reader.* London: Routledge, 2003.

Kaplan, Louis. *Gumby.* New York, NY: Harmony Books, 1986.

Kawamura, Yuniya. *Fashion-ology: An Introduction to Fashion Studies.* Oxford: Berg, 2005.

Kayser, Wolfgang. *The Grotesque in Art and Literature.* Translated by Ulrich Weisstein. Bloomington, IN: Indiana University Press, 1963.

Kennedy, Randy. 'Revising Art History's Big Book: Who's In and Who Comes Out'. *New York Times.* 7 March 2006.

King, Elliott H. *Dalí, Surrealism and Cinema.* London: Kamera Books, 2007.

Kirkham, Mavis, ed. *Exploring the Dirty Side of Women's Health.* London: Routledge, 2007.

Kismaric, Susan and Eva Respini. *Fashioning Fiction in Photography since 1990.* New York, NY: Museum of Modern Art, 2004.

Kleinhans, Chuck. 'Taking out the Trash: Camp and the Politics of Parody'. In *The Politics and Poetics of Camp*, edited by Moe Meyer, 182–201. London: Routledge, 1994.

Koda, Harold. 'Rei Kawakubo and the Aesthetic of Poverty'. *Dress: The Journal of the Costume Society of America* 11, no. 1 (1985): 5–10.

___ *Extreme Beauty: The Body Transformed*. New York, NY: The Metropolitan Museum of Art, 2001.

Kotz, Liz. 'The Body You Want: Liz Kotz Interviews Judith Butler'. *Artforum* 31, no. 3 (November 1992): 82–5.

Kourlas, Gia. 'Comme Dancing'. *Time Out New York*, 9–16 October 1997: 21–3.

Kristeva, Julia. *Powers of Horror: An Essay on Abjection*. Translated by Leon S. Roudiez. New York, NY: Columbia University Press, 1981.

___ *Revolution in Poetic Language*. Translated by Margaret Waller. New York, NY: Columbia University Press, 1984.

___ *Tales of Love*. Translated by Leon S. Roudiez. New York, NY: Columbia University Press, 1987.

___ *Black Sun*. Translated by Leon S. Roudiez. New York, NY: Columbia University Press, 1989.

___ *Strangers to Ourselves*. Translated by Leon S. Roudiez. New York, NY: Columbia University Press, 1991.

___ 'Institutional Interdisciplinarity in Theory and Practice: An Interview'. *The Anxiety of Interdisciplinarity*, edited by Alex Coles and Alexia Defert, 3–21. London: BACKless Books in association with Black Dog, 1998.

___ 'Women's Time'. In *Feminism: Critical Concepts in Literary Cultural Studies*. Vol. II, edited by Mary Evans, 27–47. London: Routledge, 2001.

Kujundzic, Dragan. 'Laughter as Otherness in Bakhtin and Derrida'. In *Mikhail Bakhtin*. Vol. IV, edited by Michael E. Gardiner, 39–60. London: Sage, 2003.

Kunzle, David. *Fashion and Fetishism: A Social History of the Corset, Tight-Lacing, and Other Forms of Body Sculpture in the West*. Totowa NJ: Rowman and Littlefield, 1982.

La Maison Martin Margiela. See Margiela, Martin.

Lambert, Christopher, Honolulu and Richard Torry. 'Interview with Leigh Bowery'. Richard Torry's Old Compton Street Studio, Soho, London, 1989. Duration 1 hour, 12 minutes. Posted as an audiostream on SHOWstudio. http://www.showstudio.com/projects/bowery/interview.html (accessed 1 February 2010).

Laqueur, Thomas W. *Making Sex: Body and Gender from the Greeks to Freud*. Cambridge, MA: Harvard University Press, 1990.

LeBesco, Kathleen. 'Situating Fat Suits: Blackface, Drag, and the Politics of Performance'. *Women and Performance: A Journal of Feminist Theory* 15, no. 2 (2005): 231–42.

___ *Revolting Bodies?: The Struggle to Redefine Fat Identity*, Amherst, MA: University of Massachusetts Press, 2006.

Le Corbusier [Charles-Édouard Jeanneret-Gris]. 'Spirit of Truth'. In *French Film Theory and Criticism 1907–1939*, edited by Richard Abel. Princeton, NJ: Princeton University Press, 1988.

Lechte, John and Mary Zournazi, eds. *The Kristeva Critical Reader*. Edinburgh: Edinburgh University Press, 2003.

Leventon, Melissa. *Artwear: Fashion and Anti-fashion*. New York, NY: Thames & Hudson/Fine Arts Museums of San Francisco, 2005.

Lipovetsky, Gilles. *The Empire of Fashion: Dressing Modern Democracy*. Translated by Catherine Porter. Princeton, NJ: Princeton University Press, 1994.

'Looking Meatier! Lady Gaga Shows Off her New Fuller Figure after "Gaining 30 lbs" in her Favourite Carnivorous Creation'. *The Daily Mail*, 19 September 2010.
Lunn, Felicity and Heike Munder. *When Humour Becomes Painful*. Zurick: Migros Museum für Genegenwartskunst, 2005.
Malbert, Roger. 'Exaggeration and Degradation: Grotesque Humour in Contemporary Art'. In *Carnivalesque*, edited by Timothy Hyman and Roger Malbert, 74–97. London: The Hayward Gallery, 2000.
Margiela, Martin [La Maison Martin Margiela]. *Martin Margiela (9/4/1615)*. Rotterdam: Museum Boijmans Van Beuningen, 1997.
Martin, Emily. *Flexible Bodies: Tracking Immunity in America from the Days of Polio to the Age of AIDS*. Boston, MA: Beacon Press, 1994.
Martin, Emily. 'The Fetus as Intruder: Mother's Bodies and Medical Metaphors'. In *Cyborg Babies: From Techno-sex to Techno-tots*, edited by Robbie Davis-Floyd and Joseph Dumit, 125–42. New York, NY: Routledge, 1998.
Martin, Richard. *Fashion and Surrealism*. New York: Rizzoli, 1987.
___ and Harold Koda. 'Analytical Apparel'. In *Infra-Apparel*, edited by Richard Martin and Harold Koda, 94–105. New York, NY: Metropolitan Museum of Art, in association with Harry N. Abrams, 1993. Published in conjunction with the exhibition 'Infra-Apparel', shown at the New York Metropolitan Museum of Art, 1993.
McCracken, Grant. *Culture and Consumption: New Approaches to the Symbolic Character of Consumer Goods and Activities*. Bloomington, IN: Indiana University Press, 1988.
McDonough, Yona Zeldis, ed. *The Barbie Chronicles*. New York, NY: Touchstone Books, 1999.
McFadden, Davide Revere, ed. *Pricked: Extreme Embroidery*. New York, NY: Museum of Art and Design, 2007.
McKenzie, Jon, 'Genre Trouble: (The) Butler Did It'. In *The Ends of Performance*, edited by Peggy Phelan and Jill Lane, 217–35. New York, NY: New York University Press, 1998.
___ 'The Liminal Norm'. In *The Performance Studies Reader*, edited by Henry Bial, 26–31. New York, NY: Routledge, 2004.
McRobbie, Angela. *British Fashion Design: Rag Trade or Image Industry?* London: Routledge, 1998.
Mears, Patricia. 'Fraying the Edges: Fashion and Deconstruction'. In *Skin + Bones: Parallel Practices in Fashion and Architecture*, edited by Brooke Hodge, 30–37. Los Angeles, CA: Museum of Contemporary Art, 2007.
Mellinkoff, Ruth. *Outcasts: Signs of Otherness in Northern European Art*. Berkeley, CA: University of California Press, 1993.
Melzer, Annabelle Henking. *Dada and Surrealist Performance*. Baltimore, MD: Johns Hopkins University Press, 1994.
Mendoza, Katherina R., 'Seeing Through the Layers: Fat Suits and Thin Bodies in *The Nutty Professor* and *Shallow Hal*'. In *The Fat Studies Reader*, edited by Esther D. Rothblum and Sondra Solovay, 280–88. New York: NYU Press, 2009.
Menkes, Suzy, 'Margiela Quits the Fashion House He Built'. Finance Section, *The International Herald Tribune*, 9 December 2009.
Miller, Amy. *Dressed to Kill: British Naval Uniform, Masculinity and Contemporary Fashions 1748–1857*. London: National Maritime Museum, 2007.
Mirzoeff, Nicholas, ed. *The Visual Culture Reader*. New York, NY: Routledge, 2002.
Mitchell, W. J. T., 'Interdisciplinarity and Visual Culture'. *Art Bulletin* 7, no. 4 (December, 1995): 540–44.
___ Showing and Seeing: A Critique of Visual Culture'. *Journal of Visual Culture* 1, no. 2 (2002): 165–81.

___ 'There Are No Visual Media'. *Journal of Visual Culture* 4, no. 2 (2005): 257–66.
Molloy, John T. *Women: Dress for Success*. New York, NY: Peter H. Wyden, 1980.
Morris, Bernadine. 'Paris is Glowing, Kindled by Lagerfeld'. *New York Times* (16 March 1991).
Morris, Catherine and Dara Meyers-Kingsley. 'Off the Wall: The Development of Robert Kushner's Fashion and Performance Art, 1970–1976'. *Fashion Theory* 5, no. 3 (2001): 311–30.
Morrison, Susan Signe. *Excrement in the Late Middle Ages*. New York: Palgrave Macmillan, 2008.
Morson, Gary Saul, ed. *Literature and History: Theoretical Problems and Russian Case Studies*. Stanford, CA: Stanford University Press, 1986.
Motherwell, Robert, ed. *The Dada Painters and Poets: An Anthology*. Cambridge, MA: The Belknap Press of Harvard University Press, 1981.
Meyer, Moe, ed. *The Politics and Poetics of Camp*. London: Routledge, 1994.
Mulvey, Laura. 'Visual Pleasures in Narrative Cinema', *Screen* 16, no. 3 (Autumn 1975): 6–18.
Nead, Lynda. *The Female Nude: Art, Obscenity and Sexuality*. London: Routledge, 1992.
Ockman, Caro. 'Barbie Meets Bouguereau: Constructing an Ideal Body for the Late Twentieth Century'. In *The Barbie Chronicles*, edited by Yona Zeldis McDonough, 75–90. New York: Touchstone Books, 1999.
Oliver, Kelly. *Reading Kristeva: Unraveling the Double-bind*. Bloomington, IN: Indiana University Press, 1993.
___ *Knock Me Up, Knock Me Down: Images of Pregnancy in Hollywood Films*. New York: Columbia University Press, 2012
O'Neill, Alistair. *London – After a Fashion*. London: Reaktion Books, 2007.
Palmer, Alexandra. 'Looking is Research'. Paper presented at the conference *Locating Fashion Studies*. Parsons School of Design – the New School, 12 November 2010.
Paul, William. *Laughing and Screaming: Modern Hollywood Horror and Comedy*. New York: Columbia University Press, 1994.
Peace, Richard. 'On Rereading Bakhtin'. *Modern Language Review* 88, no. 1 (January 1993): 137–46.
Peck, Janice. *The Age of Oprah: Cultural Icon for the Neoliberal Era*. Boulder, CO: Paradigm Publishers, 2008.
Pecorari, Marco. 'Contemporary Fashion History in Museum'. In *Fashion and Museums: Theory and Practice*. Edited by Marie Riegels Melchior and Birgitta Svensson, 51–4. London: Bloomsbury, 2014
Peers, Juliette. *The Fashion Doll: From Bébé Jumeau to Barbie*. Oxford: Berg, 2004.
Proctor, Robert. 'The Architect's Intention: Interpreting Post-War Modernism through the Architect Interview'. *Journal of Design History* 19, no. 4 (2006): 295–307.
Prown, Jules David. 'The Truth of Material Culture: History or Fiction'. In *American Artifacts: Essays in Material Culture*, edited by Jules David Prown and Kenneth Halthman, 11–27. East Lensing, MI: Michigan University Press, 2000.
___ *Art as Evidence: Writings on Art and Material Culture*. New Haven, CT: Yale University Press, 2001.
Purdy, Daniel Leonhard, ed. *The Rise of Fashion*. Minneapolis, MN: University of Minnesota Press, 2004.
Quinn, Bradley. *The Fashion of Architecture*. Oxford: Berg, 2003.
Rabelais, François. *Gargantua*. Translated by Andrew Brown. London: Hesperus Press, 2003.
___ *Pantagruel*. Translated by Andrew Brown. London: Hesperus Press, 2003.

Radstone, Susannah. 'Cinema/memory/history'. *Screen* 36, no. 1 (Spring 1995): 33–47.
Rand, Erica. *Barbie's Queer Accessories*. Durham, NC: Duke University Press, 1995.
Rechowicz, Hannah. 'Exploring the Connection Between Artistic "Creativity" and Childhood Play through the Examination of the Work of Four Diverse Artists'. BA diss., Central Saint Martins, London, 1996.
Renaux, Pascale. 'Artifice – An Interview with Orlan and Walter Van Beirendonck'. In *Believe*, edited by Walter Van Beirendonck & Wild and Lethal Trash. Rotterdam: Museum Boijmans Van Beuningen, 1998.
Respini, Eva. *Cindy Sherman*. New York: Museum of Modern Art, 2012.
Rich, Adrienne. *Of Women Born: Motherhood as Institution and Experience*. New York, NY, Bantam: 1976.
Roach, Joseph. 'History, Memory, Necrophilia'. In *The Ends of Performance*, edited by Peggy Phelan and Jill Lane, 26–31. New York: New York University Press, 1998.
Rodriguez, Carissa. 'Olaf Breuning: Technician of the Sacred'. *Parkett*, no. 71 (2004): 32–6.
Rogers, Mary F. *Barbie Culture*. Thousand Oaks, CA: Sage Publications, 1999.
Rose, Nikolas. 'Governing the Enterprising Self' in *The Values of the Enterprise Culture: The Moral Debate*, edited by Paul Heels and Paul Morris, 141–64. London: Routledge, 1992.
___ *The Politics of Life Itself: Biomedicine, Power, and Subjectivity in the Twenty-First Century*. Princeton: Princeton University Press, 2007.
Ross, Andrew. 'Uses of Camp'. In *Camp: Queer Aesthetics and the Performing Subject*, edited by Fabio Cleto, 308–29. Ann Arbor, MI: University of Michigan Press, 1999.
Russo, Mary J. *The Female Grotesque: Risk, Excess, and Modernity*. New York: Routledge, 1995.
Sandino, Linda. 'Here Today, Gone Tomorrow: Transient Materiality in Contemporary Cultural Artifacts'. *Journal of Design History* 17, no. 3 (September 2004): 283–93.
___ 'Oral Histories and Design: Objects and Subjects'. *Journal of Design History* 19, no. 4 (2006): 275–282.
Schafausen, Nicolaus, and Vanessa Joan Müller, eds. *Bernhard Willhelm: Modern Mode*. Mühlweg: Ursula Blickle Stiftung, 2003.
Schechner, Richard. *Performance Theory*. New York: Routledge, 1988.
___ 'What is Performance Studies Anyway?' In *The Ends of Performance*, edited by Peggy Phelan and Jill Lane, 357–63. New York: New York University Press, 1998.
___ *Performance Studies: An Introduction*. New York, NY: Routledge, 2006.
Schor, Naomi. *Reading in the Detail: Aesthetics and the Feminine*. New York: Methuen, 1987.
___ 'The Essentialism Which is Not One'. In *The Essential Difference*, edited by Naomi Schor and Elizabeth Weed, 40–62. Bloomington, IN: Indiana University Press, 1994.
Scriviner, Leslie. 'Nude and Pregnant: Is it Pretty or Porn?', *The Toronto Star*, 4 August 1991: A1
Sheumaker, Helen. 'This Look You See: Nineteenth-Century Hair Work as the Commodified Self'. *Fashion Theory* 1, no. 4 (December 1997): 421–45.
Shillingford, Katie. 'Outer Limits'. *Dazed and Confused* 2, no. 54 (October 2007): 122–31.
Silvia, Horacio. 'The World According to Gaga'. *T* (3 March 2010).
Smith, Marquard. 'The Vulnerable Articulate: Hames Gillingham, Aimee Mullins, and Matthew Barney'. In *The Prosthetic Impulse: From a Posthuman Present to a Biocultural Future*, ed. Marquard Smith and Joanne Morra, 43–56. Cambridge, MA: MIT Press, 2006.
___ and Joanne Morra, eds. *The Prosthetic Impulse: From a Posthuman Present to a Biocultural Future*. Cambridge, MA: MIT Press, 2006.
Sobchack, Vivian. 'A Leg to Stand On: Prosthetics Metaphor and Materiality'. In *The Prosthetic Impulse: From a Posthuman Present to a Biocultural Future*, ed. Marquard Smith and Joanne Morra, 17–41. Cambridge, MA: MIT Press, 2006.

Sontag, Susan. *Against Interpretation and Other Essays*. New York, NY: Anchor Books Doubleday, 1986.
___ *Aids and its Metaphors*, New York, NY: Picador, 1988.
Spelman, Elizabeth. *Inessential Woman: Problems of Exclusion in Feminist Thought*. London: The Women's Press, 1988.
Spindler, Amy. 'Coming Apart'. *New York Times*, 25 July 1993.
Stafford, Barbara Maria. 'Conceiving'. In *Modern Art and the Grotesque*, edited by Frances S. Connelly, 63–97. Cambridge: Cambridge University Press, 2003.
Stallybrass, Peter. 'From Carnival to Transgression'. In *The Subcultures Reader*, edited by Ken Gelder and Sarah Thornton, 293–301. London: Routledge, 1997.
___ 'The Grotesque Satiric Body'. In *Jonathan Swift*, edited by Nigel Wood, 158–70. New York: Longman, 1999.
Stallybrass, Peter. 'Worn Worlds: Clothes, Mourning, and the Life of Things'. In *Cultural Memory and the Construction of Identity*, edited by Dan Ben-Amos and Liliane Weissberg, 27–44. Detroit, MI: Wayne State University Press, 1999.
___ and Allon White. *The Politics and Poetics of Transgression*. Ithaca, NY: Cornell University Press, 1986.
Stam, Robert. *Subversive Pleasures: Bakhtin, Cultural Criticism, and Film*. Baltimore, MD: Johns Hopkins University Press, 1989.
___ and Toby Miller, eds. *Film and Theory: An Anthology*. Oxford: Blackwell Publishers, 2000.
Steele, Valerie. *Fetish, Fashion, Sex and Power*. Oxford: Oxford University Press, 1996.
___ 'A Museum of Fashion is More than a Clothes-Bag'. *Fashion Theory* 2, no. 4 (November 1998): 327–35.
___ *The Corset: A Cultural History*. New Haven, CT: Yale University Press, 2001.
Stewart, Susan. *On Longing, Narratives of the Miniature, the Gigantic, the Souvenir, the Collection*. Durham, NC: Duke University Press, 1993.
Stone, Alison. 'Essentialism and Anti-Essentialism in Feminist Philosophy'. *Journal of Moral Philosophy* 1, no. 2 (2004): 135–53.
Sudjic, Deyan. *Rei Kawakubo and Comme des Garçons*. New York: Rizzoli, 1990.
Taylor, Lou. *The Study of Dress History*. Manchester: Manchester University Press, 2002.
___ *Establishing Dress History*. Manchester: Manchester University Press, 2004.
Te Duits, Thimo. *Believe: Walter Van Beirendonck and Wild and Lethal Trash*. Rotterdam: Van Beuningen Museum, 1998.
___ 'Shocking: Surrealism and Fashion Now'. In *Surreal Things: Surrealism and Design*, edited by Ghislaine Wood, 139–60. London: V&A, 2007.
Thomas, Jeannie Banks. *Naked Barbies, Warrior Joes and Other Forms of Visible Gender*. Urbana, IL: University of Illinois Press, 2003.
Thompson, Paul. *The Voice of the Past: Oral History*. Oxford: Oxford University Press, 1988.
Thornton, Sarah. *Club Cultures: Music, Media and Subcultural Capital*. London: Polity Press, 1995.
Tilley, Sue. *Leigh Bowery: The Life and Times of an Icon*. London: Hodder & Stoughton, 1997.
Townsend, Chris. *Rapture: Art's Seduction by Fashion*. London: Thames and Hudson, 2002.
Treichler, Paula A., *How to Have Theory in an Epidemic: Cultural Chronicles of AIDS*. Durham, NC: Duke University Press, 1999
Turner, Victor. *The Ritual Process: Structure and Anti-Structure*. Chicago, IL: Aldine, 1969.
Vaughan, David. *Merce Cunningham: Fifty Years*. New York, NY: Aperture, 1997.
——— *Merce Cunningham: Fifty Forward*. New York, NY: Cunningham Dance Foundation, 2005.
Vinken, Barbara. *Fashion Zeitgeist: Trends and Cycles in the Fashion System*. Translated by Mark Hewson. Oxford: Berg, 2005.

Violette, Robert, ed. *Leigh Bowery*. New York: D.A.P., 1998.
Wahler, Marc-Oliver. 'Olaf Breuning: See? It Is Always the Same Story'. *Parkett*, no. 71 (2004): 28–31.
___ 'Olaf Breuning: Whatever'. *Art Press*, no. 308 (January 2005).
Wark, Jayne. *Radical Gestures: Feminism and Performance Art in North America*. Montreal: McGill-Queen's University Press, 2006.
Webb, Vivienne, ed. *Take a Bowery: The Art and, Larger than, Life of Leigh Bowery*. Sydney: Museum of Contemporary Art, 2004.
Welters Linda, and Abby Lillethun, eds. *Fashion Reader*. Oxford: Berg, 2007.
White, Allon. 'The Struggle Over Bakhtin: Fraternal Reply to Robert Young'. *Cultural Critique*, no. 8 (Winter 1987–88): 217–41.
Wigley, Mark. *White Walls, Designer Dresses: The Fashioning of Modern Architecture*. Cambridge, MA: MIT Press, 1995.
Wilcox, Claire. *Radical Fashion*. London: V&A, 2001.
___ *Vivienne Westwood*. London: V&A, 2004.
Wilson, Elizabeth. *Adorned in Dreams, Fashion & Modernity*. London: Virago, 1987.
___ 'These New Components of the Spectacle: Fashion and Postmodernism'. In *Postmodernism and Society*, edited by Roy Boyne and Ali Rattansi, 209–36. Basingstoke: Macmillan, 1990.
___ 'Fashion and the Postmodern Body'. In *Chic Thrills: A Fashion Reader*, edited by Juliet Ash and Elizabeth Wilson, 3–16. Berkeley, CA: University of California Press, 1992.
___ 'Magic Fashion'. *Fashion Theory* 8, no. 4 (December 2004): 375–85.
___ Review of *Understanding Fashion History*, by Valerie Cumming. *Fashion Theory* 10, no. 3 (2006): 409–12.
___ 'A Note on Glamour'. *Fashion Theory* 11, no. 1 (March 2007): 95–108.
Windels, Veerle. *Young Belgian Fashion Design*. Ghent: Ludion, 2001.
Winwood, Lou. 'Fashion: Shredded Bliss'. *Guardian*, 11 April 1998.
Witchel, Leigh. 'Merce In and Outside Time'. *Ballet Review* 35 (Winter 1997): 35–41.
Wollen, Peter, ed. *Addressing the Century: 100 Years of Art & Fashion*. London: Hayward Gallery Publishing, 1998.
Wood, Ghislaine. *Surreal Things: Surrealism and Design*, London: V&A Publications, 2008.
Wood, Robin. 'Return of the Repressed'. *Film Comment* (July/August 1978): 24–32.
Yaeger, Lynn. 'Material World'. *Village Voice*, 1 April 1997.
Zangrillo, Frances Leto. *Fashion Design for the Plus-Size*. New York, NY: Fairchild Publications, 1990.
Zimei, Francesca, ed. *The Comic Mask in the Commedia dell'Arte*. Arscomica: Reggio Emilia, 2004.

FILMOGRAPHY

Atlas, Charles. *Merce Cunningham: A Lifetime of Dance*. (New York: Fox Lerber Center Stage, 2001).
___ *The Legend of Leigh Bowery*. (New York: Atlas Film & Palm Pictures, 2004).
Breuning, Olaf. *Home*. 2004. Available at http://olafbreuning.com/ (accessed 1 February 2010).
Stallybrass, Peter. and Berhnard Willhelm. *Ghost*. 2003. Available at http://olafbreuning.com/ (accessed 1 February 2010).
Cunningham, Merce [Merce Cunningham Dance Company]. *Rune Garnier event I, Garnier Event II [and] Scenario*. Present. (Paris: Merce Cunningham Foundation, 1998).
Dalí, Salvador and José Montes-Baquer. *Impressions of Upper Mongolia – Homage to Raymond Roussel*. (Germany: Westdeutscher Rundfunk (WDR), and Polyphon Hamburg, 1975).
Margiela, Martin. *Seven Women*. 1983. La Maison Martin Margiela.
Scott, Ridley. *Alien*. (Los Angeles: Brandywine Productions, 1979).
Shils, Barry. *Wigstock: The Movie*. (New York: The Wigstock Venture & Samuel Goldwyn Company, 1995).
Zemeckis, Robert. *Back to the Future*. (Los Angeles: Universal Pictures, 1985).

INDEX

absurd, the 130, 133, 134–8
absurdist 49, 78
absurdity 72, 79
aesthetics 9, 20, 80, 87, 140, 159
AIDS 2–3, 9, 24, 43, 60, 70, 71, 114, 155, 159
Alaïa, Azzedine 25, 26, 28, 170, 171
Alighiero e Boetti 133
Als, Hilton 38, 39, 63, 72
Appadurai, Arjun 111, 115
Arnold, Rebecca 5, 7, 36, 45, 60
  Fashion, Desire and Anxiety 5, 7
artifice 65, 82, 83, 139
asymmetry 32, 42
Atlas, Charles 56, 59, 165
Auburn, Rachel 23, 54, 55, 176, 177

Babcock, Barbara 81
  The Reversible World: Symbolic Inversion on Art and Society 81
Baines, Barbara Burman 104
  Fashion Revivals from the Elizabethan Age to the Present Day 104
Bakhtin, Mikhail M. 1, 5, 7, 8, 9, 10, 14, 19, 20, 21, 46, 48, 54, 59, 67, 73, 79, 80, 81, 83, 93, 97, 101, 103, 104, 111, 120, 126, 127, 128, 134, 138, 140, 145, 151, 152, 158
  Rabelais and His World 1, 21, 79, 134, 152
  The Dialogical Imagination 46
  The Problems of Dostoevsky's Poetics 46
Bartsch, Susanne 55
beauty 2, 3, 9, 40, 41, 42, 60, 64, 80, 87, 100, 150, 153, 159, 173, 174

Benjamin, Lee 162, 164, 166
biological essentialism 31
Björk 120, 150
bodily fluids 9, 71
body, the
  augmented/surgically enhanced 24, 150
  classical 36, 93, 117
  dancers' 48
  disabled/differently-abled 47, 100
  female 7, 9, 15, 17, 18, 20, 21, 24, 25, 30, 32, 36, 38, 47, 60, 63, 71, 101, 153
  feminine/women's 36, 153, 171
  healthy' 71
  ideal 22, 83, 92, 93, 94
  male 16, 21, 59–60
  masculine/men's 38, 60
  maternal 7, 8, 9, 11, 14, 17, 18–22, 28, 29, 30, 31, 36–53, 59, 63, 68, 69, 71, 72–3, 74, 104, 117, 119, 158
  'natural' 7, 18, 30, 32, 61, 67, 82, 83, 88, 93, 171
  normative 2, 82, 88, 120, 159
  perfect' 2, 17, 24, 26, 36, 87, 94, 171
  pregnant 3, 7, 8, 9, 17, 18, 19, 20, 39, 41, 47, 48, 59, 62, 63, 69, 83, 156, 159
  queer/gay men 72, 146, 148, 159
body-/muscle-building 36, 38, 71, 120
body-out-of-bounds 2, 30, 88, 153, 157, 159
border crossings 4, 135, 150

borders 1, 11, 19, 95, 135, 146, 159
    bodily 1, 2, 3, 7, 9, 10, 19, 43, 46, 63, 71, 114, 120, 151, 152, 155, 159
Bordwell, David 12
    Film Art: An Introduction 12
Bourdieu, Pierre 139
Bowery, Leigh 7, 8, 9, 10, 12, 17, 22–3, 24, 54–73, 74, 80, 83, 95, 96, 114, 118, 127, 139, 140, 146, 149, 151, 155, 156, 159, 161–8, 176, 177
    birth performances 8, 9, 63–71, 164
    Look 10 62, 72–3
    Look 32/33, 62, 162
    Look 9 62, 162
    Minty 9, 57, 63, 161
Bowery, Nicola 11, 56, 59, 60, 63, 69, 71, 161–8
Brampton, Sally 77, 78
Breton, André 100
Breuning, Olaf 120, 131, 138–40
Breward, Christopher 14
Brooklyn Academy of Music (BAM) 8, 48
Brüno 146
Butler, Judith 5, 6, 31, 67, 68, 69, 70, 154, 156, 157
    Bodies That Matter 5, 6
    Gender Trouble 5, 6

Cage, John 51
Cahun, Claude 43, 101
camp 65–8, 95, 96–7, 139–40, 155
capitalism 5, 32, 34, 94, 95, 112
Carter, Angela 77
Cartesian model/subject, the 18, 46, 47, 95
Casadio, Mariuccia 22
Cézanne, Paul 20
Chalayan, Hussein 150, 175
Clark, Judith 104
    'Malign Muses: When Fashion Turns Back' 104
Clark, Kenneth 10, 20, 29–30, 118–20
Clark, Michael 55, 165, 166
clowns 59, 84, 128
    see also fools
Cohen, Sacha Baron 146
Comme des Garçons 3, 8, 11, 12, 17, 36, 40, 41, 43, 149, 153, 155
    Six 12, 41

commedia dell'arte 10, 49, 64, 121, 128–30, 132
    Doctor Balanzone 128
    Harlequin 49, 65, 128, 130
    Pierrot 128, 130, 177
Connelly, Frances 4, 21, 98, 158
Conran, Sebastian 178
conservatism 2, 3, 112
containment 30, 37, 61, 94
Crawford, Cindy 41
Crolla, Scott 23, 24, 55, 169, 170, 172, 173, 177
cultural anthropology 14, 81, 135
Cunningham, Bill 9, 13, 75–7, 79
Cunningham, Merce 8, 36, 48–51
    Scenario 8, 36, 48–51

d'Offay, Anthony 55, 154, 168
Dada 134–5
Dalí, Salvador 110, 116–7
    Impressions of Upper Mongolia – Homage to Raymond Roussel 116
dance, general 1, 3
de Perthuis, Karen 117, 158
debasement 21, 140–8
decay 76, 86, 87
deconstruction/deconstructivist fashion 9, 10, 74–102, 115
degradation 21, 59, 128, 140
Derrida, Jacques 79–80, 89, 90–1
deviation 22, 80, 88, 94, 160
dialogism 46
disease 2, 5, 18, 60, 113–4
Divine 63, 64, 65, 68, 162, 163
Dixon, Tom 23, 176
doll clothes 10, 88, 89, 91, 92
dolls
    Barbie 10, 27–9, 82, 88–9, 91–5, 96, 97, 171, 173
    GI Joe 88, 92, 95
    Ken 10
Don Quixote 111
Douglas, Mary 19
drag 11, 60, 63–4, 67–8, 70, 71, 162, 163, 165
    see also Lady Gaga, fat drag
Duggan, Ginger Gregg 138

Elias, Norbert 5, 73, 87
  The Civilizing Process 5
Enlightenment, the 18, 19
enterprising self, the 7, 15, 32–3, 37
Entwistle, Joanne 32, 34
Evans, Caroline 5, 7, 36, 86, 94, 98, 104, 115, 116, 138
  Fashion at the Edge 5, 138
exaggeration 15, 25, 54, 59, 63, 65, 68, 72, 83, 121, 139, 172
Excess: Fashion and the Underground in the 80s 38
exhibitions
  'London Goes to Tokyo' 23, 177
  'Pricked: Extreme Embroidery' 133
  see also individual designers
Exploring the Dirty Side of Women's Health 19

fashion practitioners 2, 4
femininity 16, 18, 25, 27–9, 31, 34, 35, 64, 68, 71, 93, 94, 152, 173, 176, 177, 178
feminism 2, 3, 4, 7, 14, 22–3, 27–8, 31, 36, 43, 72, 155, 159, 169
feminist art 20, 150, 152
feminist theory 4, 14, 30, 159
fertility dolls/imagery 27, 29, 30, 31, 171, 173
film/film studies 3, 4, 5, 12, 14, 92, 112
films
  Alien 51, 52
  Back to the Future 16
  Bonnie and Clyde 106
  Female Trouble 63, 68, 162
  Ghost 138–9
  Paris Is Burning 68, 152
  The Legend of Leigh Bowery 56, 59
  Working Girl 8, 15, 16
Fiske, John 68, 87
Flinn, Caryl 67, 97
fools 59, 125, 128, 130
  see also clowns
Formichetti, Nicola 149, 150
Foucault, Michel 2, 34, 71, 82
Freud, Lucian 55, 60, 70, 161, 165, 166
Freud, Sigmund 10, 14, 52, 119, 120, 157
functionality 9, 10, 97, 98, 100, 101, 130, 151

Gaultier, Jean Paul 41, 76, 166
gender 2, 4, 5–8, 11, 14, 18, 21, 23, 24, 32, 34, 48, 53, 62, 67–9, 70, 92, 127, 128, 135, 138, 152, 155, 156, 158, 159
  construction 5–6, 48, 70, 152, 155
  equality 34
  see also identity, gender; norms, gender
Gill, Alison 79–80, 89, 108
Godley, Georgina 7, 8, 9, 10, 12, 13, 15–35, 36, 54, 59, 61, 72, 73, 74, 80, 83, 86, 95, 100, 101, 114, 118, 121, 150, 156, 159, 169–78
  'Corporate Coding' 7, 32–5, 121, 177
  'Body and Soul' 25, 170, 172
  'Bump and Lump' 8, 22, 25, 54, 169, 170, 171, 172, 173, 178
  'Dolly's Date' 178
  'Earthly Mater' 178
  'Recent Decent' 174, 175, 177
  'School Colours' 33, 175
Greer, Fergus 62, 168
Grosz, George 134
grotesque imagery 2
grotesque realism 1, 20, 140
gynophobia 8, 17–8, 20, 21, 39, 68, 71, 118, 119

Halberstam, Jack 151–2
  Gaga Feminism: Sex, Gender and the End of Normal 151
Harms, Ingeborg 128
Harvey, David 3
Hayward Gallery 22, 170, 178
Head, Tim 34, 177
Hermès 92, 121
Hintnaus, Tom 60
HIV 71
horror 10, 43, 51, 120, 130, 131, 138–40
Hoving, Kirsten A. 100–1
humour 4, 8, 9, 10, 49, 65, 68, 74, 78, 80, 81, 101, 103, 120, 128, 130, 134, 138, 140, 153
humour, carnivalesque 4, 80, 81
Hutcheon, Linda 111–2

iconography 10, 63, 119–48
identity 6, 11, 46, 48, 67, 152, 154, 155
   construction of 6, 46, 48, 156, 158, 159
   gender 5–6, 11, 67–8, 69, 155, 156, 158
   sexual 5
   social 5, 6
in-betweenness 4, 11, 135
incongruity 84, 130–1, 134
inversion 9, 10, 14, 80–1, 84, 94, 101, 102, 114, 116, 117, 121, 125, 127, 128, 130, 146

Jackson, Michael 133
Jacobs, Marc 92
Jameson, Fredric 112
jesters 125, 128, 130, 138
Jewel, Dick 163

Kant, Immanuel 140
Kawakubo, Rei 3, 4, 7, 8, 9, 11, 12, 13, 17, 20, 22, 36–53, 54, 57, 59, 61, 63, 72–3, 74, 77, 80, 83, 86, 95, 99, 100, 101, 118, 149, 150, 151, 153, 156, 159, 178
   'Body Meets Dress' 8, 22, 36, 43, 44, 54, 153
   'Dress Becomes Body' 46, 178
   'Transcending Gender' 43
Kinky Gerlinky 63, 162, 163
Klein, Calvin 59, 60, 92
Kleinhans, Chuck 139–40
Knight, Nick 149, 151
Koda, Harold 89, 108
Kosugi, Takehisa 48
Kraus, Jutta 120
Kristeva, Julia 7, 46–7, 52–3, 68, 104, 145, 152, 158
   Powers of Horror 145
   Revolution in Poetic Language 46
   Strangers to Ourselves 52
   subject-in-process 46, 47, 95, 104, 118

Lacan, Jacques 46
Lacroix, Christian 166
Lady Gaga 11, 149–160

Calderone, Jo 151
fat drag 11, 152–5
Haus of Gaga 151
Laib, Conrad 125, 126
   Crucifixion 125
liminality 4, 11, 135–6, 156
linearity 9, 97, 103, 104, 108, 158
Livingston, Jennie 68
London Fashion Week 55
Lycra 62, 72, 162, 164, 174
Lyon, Lisa 36, 37, 60

Madonna 150
magazines
   Artforum 38
   Butt 13, 148
   Dazed and Confused 13, 149, 150
   Details 13, 75
   Elle 40
   Fashion Theory 12, 79, 138
   Flash Art 165
   Gap 13
   Hint 13, 125
   i-D 12, 25, 55
   Lovely Jobly 165
   New Yorker 63
   Officiel 13
   Purple 12
   The Face 12
   Vanity Fair 41, 152
   Visionaire 12
   Vogue 26, 40
Malbert, Roger 64
mannequins 43, 82, 114, 167, 171, 177
Mapplethorpe, Robert 36
Margiela, Martin 9, 10, 11, 12, 13, 74–102, 103–118, 121, 130, 138, 153, 157, 159
Martin, Emily 47, 71
Martin, Richard 22, 89, 108
masculinity 3, 23, 159, 177
maternity 47, 48, 68, 71
McCracken, Grant 115
McInerney, Niall 13
McKenzie, Jon 135, 156
McLaren, Malcolm 24
McQueen, Alexander 151

Mellinkoff, Ruth 125
Metropolitan Museum of Art, New York 11, 113
  Costume Institute 11, 89, 92
Middle Ages 5, 10, 80, 87, 117, 120, 125, 130, 133, 134, 145
minstrels 130
misogyny 17, 21
ModeMuseum, Antwerp (MoMu) 11, 13, 84, 88, 92, 100, 113, 125, 128
Molloy, John T. 8, 15
  The Woman's Dress for Success Book 8, 15
Montana, Claude 92
Montes-Baquer, José 116
Morrison, Susan Signe 145
Mugler, Thierry 24, 150, 166
Museum Boijmans Van Beuningen, Rotterdam 113

Nead, Linda 21, 28, 36–7, 153
  The Female Nude 28–30, 153
neoliberalism 2, 3, 7, 8, 11, 15, 33, 122, 153, 159
New Right 33
Newton, Helmut 36
norms
  bodily 2, 3, 5, 22, 60–1, 68, 71, 82, 88, 94, 100, 101, 152, 153, 155, 157, 160
  gender 2, 6, 23, 43, 63, 138, 156
  social 71, 135, 138, 155, 156, 157
nostalgia 96–7, 111–2, 113, 115

Ockman, Carol 93
Oliver, Kelly 47, 68
Orlan 150, 151, 152

Painlevé, Jean, *Impressions* 116
parody 26, 53, 70, 72, 79, 132, 138, 140
performance art 4, 113, 134, 135, 138, 150, 152, 159
performativity 5, 6, 155–7
photography 3, 14, 101, 117, 158
plastic surgery 38, 46, 150, 151
pornography 10, 41, 120, 146, 148
post-Fordism 33

power dressing/power suit 7, 8, 15–35, 125, 157, 177
Prada 92
pregnancy
  as boundary transgression 32, 39, 42, 47, 48, 54–73, 170, 173, 174
  as celebrity accessory 19, 157
proportionality 9, 10, 120, 159
prosthesis 150–1
Prown, Jules 12
psychoanalysis 14, 47, 52

queer theory 4, 67, 152

Rabelais, François 1, 84, 101, 145
  Gargantua and Pantagruel 1, 84
Radstone, Susannah 112
Reagan, Ronald 2, 3, 15, 33
Renaissance 1, 20, 43, 80, 105, 108
  Italian 10, 120
Respini, Eva 43
Ritts, Herb 59–60
Rose, Nikolas 34
Ross, Andrew 96
Rouault, Georges 20
Russo, Mary 18, 21, 153
  The Female Grotesque 18, 153

Sagat, François 146
Saint Laurent, Yves 113
Sandino, Linda 36, 87, 113, 115
Scene from the Life of Young Tobias 125
Schechner, Richard 155, 156
Schiaparelli, Elsa 25, 101, 110, 129
Scott, Ridley 51
sexual orientation 18
sexuality 23, 41, 71, 146, 148, 169, 177
Sherman, Cindy 3, 36, 42, 43
silhouette
  distorted 38, 54
  female 22, 36, 41, 54
  ideal 24, 38
  masculine 8, 17, 25, 26, 174, 178
  masculinised female 7, 45
  oversized 121
  pregnant 7, 17, 25, 31, 36, 41

social constructionism 31
Sontag, Susan 2, 65, 139
Spindler, Amy 77, 78
Stallybrass, Peter 5, 14, 21, 54, 81, 126, 133, 135, 142, 143, 157
  The Politics and Poetics of Transgression (with Allon White) 54
Stam, Robert 4, 53, 132
Steele, Valerie 12
Sterbak, Jana 152
  'Vanitas: Flesh Dress for an Albino Anorectic' 152
Stewart, Susan 61, 84, 88, 94–5
Stone, Alison 31
Sudjic, Deyan 41
Surrealism 10, 22, 25, 100, 101, 110, 116, 134, 135
symmetry 9, 10, 20, 61, 74, 80, 87, 94, 120, 121, 159

temporality 9, 70, 95, 97, 103–5, 108, 109, 115, 135, 137, 158
Thatcher, Margaret 2, 3, 15, 33, 34, 176, 177
The Marvellous Malady of Harlequin 65
The Oprah Winfrey Show 122
Thompson, Kristen 12
  Film Art: An Introduction 12
Tillmans, Wolfgang 148
Torry, Richard 61, 164
Totentanz 133
transience 87, 104, 113, 115

Trojan 55, 177
Turner, Victor 135, 138

UK 2, 3, 32
Urquhart, Donald 61
US 3, 15, 32, 40, 120, 122, 133

Van Beirendonck, Walter 120, 154
van Gennep, Arnold 135
Van Noten, Dries 77
Victoria and Albert Museum, London (V&A) 11, 33, 170, 175, 176
Vinken, Barbara 82, 115
visual arts 3, 4, 14
Vreeland, Diana 113

Waters, John 63
Weaver, Sigourney 52
Weber, Bruce 59–60
Westwood, Vivienne 17, 24, 42, 166
White, Allon 5, 14, 21, 54, 81, 126, 133, 135, 142, 143, 157
  The Politics and Poetics of Transgression (with Peter Stallybrass) 54
Wigstock 63, 164, 165
Willhelm, Bernhard 10, 13, 96, 101, 118, 119–48, 150, 159
Wilson, Elizabeth 70
World War I 134
World War II 130

Yamamoto, Yohji 77, 169